Intuition and Construction

T. K. SEUNG

Intuition and Construction
The Foundation of Normative Theory

Yale University Press

New Haven and London

Designed by Sonia L. Scanlon.
Set in Times Roman type by Tseng Information Systems.
Printed in the United States of America by Edwards
Brothers, Ann Arbor, Michigan.

Library of Congress Cataloging-in-Publication Data
Seung, T. K., 1930–
Intuition and construction : the foundation of normative
theory / T. K. Seung.
p.   cm.
Includes index.
ISBN 0-300-05740-7
1. Intuition.   2. Constructivism (Philosophy)
3. Rationalism.   I. Title.
BD181.S485   1993
149–dc20   92-516
CIP

A catalogue record for this book is available from the
British Library.

The paper in this book meets the guidelines for permanence
and durability of the Committee on Production Guidelines
for Book Longevity of the Council on Library Resources.

10 9 8 7 6 5 4 3 2 1

For William M. Morse, Jr.,
my friend and champion of the ideals
of excellence and perfection
in this imperfect world

Contents

Preface

The publication of John Rawls's *Theory of Justice* in 1971 was probably the most memorable event in normative philosophy in the second half of this century. It gave new life to political philosophy, which had been pronounced dead by many. It appeared to sweep away all the cobwebs of normative skepticism and to lay down solid rules of decision procedure for normative questions. Before the arrival of Rawls's theory, all normative talk appeared to be no more than ideological assertions or emotive expressions, involving no questions of objective truth. With his theory of pure procedural justice, Rawls seemed to carve out a solid domain of normative truths and to bring new respectability to normative philosophy as a whole. No wonder his proceduralism, or Kantian constructivism, became a new movement and a big industry during the ensuing two decades. For some time, nobody could even consider saying anything important in moral and political philosophy without invoking the authority of his formal procedure or questioning its touted efficacy.

Lately, the reign of Rawlsian proceduralism has been showing clear signs of decline. There is an increasing tendency in normative discourse to make a direct appeal to normative intuitions and to forget or ignore the complicated machinery of procedural arguments. In practice, a new vogue of normative intuitionism has begun to replace the old vogue of formal proceduralism, although nobody has yet proposed a new theory of normative intuition. This recent trend poses two interrelated dangers. On one hand, we may wind up discarding Rawls's proceduralism on the dumping ground of obsolete fads and fashions, without clearly recognizing its real contributions to normative philosophy. On the other hand, direct appeal to intuitions may return and reduce our normative discourse to the lowly level of emotive exhortations or ideological manipulations.

This book is addressed to these two dangers. I am undertaking a systematic assessment of proceduralism and intuitionism. I devote the first three chapters to Rawls's Kantian constructivism and the next two to the procedural programs of formal and instrumental rationality. So I recognize three different types of formal procedure, and these three are the best known forms of constructivism. By *constructivism* I refer to the thesis that normative propositions and standards are constructed by human beings. This thesis is opposed to intuitionism, the thesis that normative propositions and standards are discovered by rational intuition.

Though the three forms of constructivism are different from each other, they are motivated by a common concern, namely, normative skepticism. There are many ways of expressing normative skepticism: one may deny the existence of moral reality, claim the relativity of moral truth, or stress the noncognitive function of moral assertions. But all these forms of normative skepticism stem from one common source, the distrust of normative intuitions, or rather the normative ideas delivered by our intuitive understanding.

Kant's categorical imperative is the fountainhead of the constructivism of purely formal rationality, which has been revived by R. M. Hare and Alan Gewirth. It may be called formal constructivism; its method is to derive normative rules and standards from the formal principle of rationality without appealing to substantive ideas, which are given by normative intuition. The idea of formal rationality need not be restricted to the idea of logical consistency, which is governed by the formal rules of logic. Jürgen Habermas and Bruce Ackerman have proposed using such formal conditions of speech as freedom of expression and equality of participation in a dialogue for the constitution of normative decision procedures. Whether formal constructivism is implemented in terms of the formal rules of thought or the formal conditions of dialogue, its ultimate concern is to circumvent normative skepticism by refusing to rely on normative intuitions.

The constructivism of instrumental rationality may be called instrumental constructivism. Its tradition is even older than that of formal constructivism. It began with Hobbes's theory of social contract, and his conception of instrumental rationality was reaffirmed in Hume's thesis that reason can be only the slave of the passions. To be a slave is to be an instrument. Reason can perform only the instrumental function of devising a system of rules and standards for the fulfillment of our passions because it is incapable of having its own norms and values. This is the heart of instrumental constructivism, which has recently been elaborated in David Gauthier's version of social contractarianism. Instrumental constructivism is also meant to circumvent normative skepticism by avoiding the use of intuitive normative ideas.

In one important respect, Rawls's version of constructivism differs from these two versions. He does not believe that normative constructivism can get anywhere by totally rejecting normative intuitions. Though he does not derive his two principles of justice directly from intuitive ideas, he acknowledges his use of intuitions in setting up the constructivist procedure in the original position. He says that the social ideals of liberty and equality are the ultimate source for the constitutive constraints on the original position. Hence his procedure should be called ideal constructivism. Unlike formal and instrumental constructivism, ideal constructivism is meant not to avoid, but only to tame and control our intuitive ideas and normative skepticism.

In my examination of these three forms of constructivism, I try to clarify their relations to normative intuitionism. These relations are not always what they are claimed to be by their advocates. Some of them surreptitiously introduce substantive intuitive ideas in their constructivist projects under the guise of formal requirements. In this volume, I demonstrate the impossibility of constructing a normative system without using some normative intuitions. One way or another, we have to rely on our normative intuition in any constructivist project, though our reliance may be covert. To that extent, I vindicate Rawls's contention that programs of construction can get nowhere without relying on some normative intuitions. What then is the nature of normative intuition? This question is addressed in the last four chapters of this book.

Though there are many forms of normative intuitionism, I am chiefly concerned with two of them: transcendent and immanent. Immanent intuition is the intuition of positive or prevailing normative standards in any given society; transcendent intuition is the intuition of normative standards that transcend all particular societies. Immanent intuition is a part of our daily life; every day we recognize the positive norms of our society and govern our life in accordance with them except for the rare occasions on which their authority appears to be suspect. These positive norms constitute not only the order of our society, but the selfhood of its members. Hence our intuition of those positive norms belongs to our nature as social beings; immanent intuition is "natural" intuition. It appears to be as natural as our perception of colors and sounds or as our natural language. Our linguistic and moral intuitions belong to what is generally known as commonsense intuition, and our common sense should be regarded as an essential feature of our nature.

As long as we do not question positive social norms, we rely on our natural intuition. And those social norms appear to be as solid as any natural objects. The school of moral realism has traditionally derived its plausibility from this solid sense of natural intuition by maintaining that moral properties and relations are as real as the physical properties and relations of natural objects. But this commonsense feeling is the naive moral consciousness which cannot withstand the challenge of critical consciousness. Our critical view of positive norms can develop under the impetus of either scientific materialism or normative relativism. If the ultimate reality is purely physical, it can allow no room for the existence of norms and values. Our normative intuitions may very well be no more than subjective feelings or figments of imagination. The cultural relativity of normative standards can have the same deadly impact on the naive normative consciousness. If different societies can have different normative standards, they may be no more than the encoding of provincial prejudices.

Thus the scientific consciousness and the consciousness of cultural relativity can, jointly or singly, shatter the naive consciousness of natural or uncritical intuition.

Loss of confidence in natural intuition leads to normative subjectivism and skepticism. Such a loss can take place on an individual or a collective level and at any time in history. It has induced massive cultural upheaval on two occasions in the West: in Renaissance Europe and in Sophistic Athens. On both occasions, distrust of natural or positive intuition created a normative crisis for the whole culture. Under those circumstances, there are only two ways to overcome the normative chaos. One of them is the positivistic appeal to the power that can sustain a social order. The other is the idealistic appeal to transcendental norms, which requires transcendental intuition. In ancient Athens, Socrates and Plato proposed transcendental intuitionism against the positivism of Thrasymachus and Callicles. In Renaissance Europe, the positivism of Machiavelli and his heirs was countered by rational intuitionism. Both versions of intuitionism presuppose transcendental norms or ideals.

The critical thinkers of modern Europe distrusted both positivism and idealism. They could not endorse positivism on normative grounds (Might is right); they could not accept idealism on epistemic grounds (How can we know there are transcendental ideals?). Since they could embrace neither, they had to devise their own procedures for constructing normative standards. Thus began the modern tradition of normative constructivism. My examination of this tradition is meant to show that ideal constructivism is the only viable form of constructivism. Since ideal constructivism is still based on some normative ideals, we cannot avoid the question: Where do those ideals come from? They can come from only one of two sources: the transcendental norms or the positive norms of our culture. If ideal constructivism stands on transcendental ideas, it is an extension of transcendental idealism. On the other hand, if it derives its normative ideals from the positive norms of our culture, it is a special form of normative positivism. Either way, ideal constructivism cannot avoid choosing between idealism and positivism for its ontological foundation.

Transcendental normative idealism is none other than Platonism. There are two ways of understanding normative Platonism, and these may be designated as the skyscraper and the bedrock versions. The skyscraper version paints a lavish picture of Platonic Heaven: it is adorned with a complete system of normative rules and standards. The bedrock version does not paint such a lavish picture; its modest claim is that Platonic Heaven gives only the basic normative ideals. The difference between these two versions can perhaps be better understood in terms of mathematical Platonism. The skyscraper version claims that Platonic Heaven contains the complete edifice of mathematics from arithmetic and geometry to calculus and topology. On the other hand, the bedrock version holds that it contains only the most basic mathematical ideas, and that mathematical systems have to be constructed from those basic ideas. Constructivism is essential for completing the bedrock version of Platonism.

In Rawls's description, normative constructivism is presented as a competing alternative to normative intuitionism. This is true only if normative intuitionism is taken as the skyscraper version of Platonism. Though this version of Platonism has usually been taken as the standard teaching of Plato himself, I show that the mature Plato came to reject this view of transcendental normative standards and to advocate the bedrock version. The distinction between the bedrock and the skyscraper versions also obtains for the classical and the medieval theories of natural law, another label for the doctrine of transcendental normative standards. In the skyscraper version, natural law is understood as a complete system of eternal rules and standards for the government of human behavior, "a brooding omnipresence in the sky" in Oliver Wendell Holmes's inimitable depiction. In its bedrock version, natural law is supposed to contain only the basic precepts for constructing a normative system. Aquinas appears to subscribe to this view of natural law in his distinction between its primary and secondary precepts. He says that primary precepts are self-evident and ungenerated and that secondary precepts are derived from primary ones by practical reason. In that case, primary precepts belong to the bedrock foundation of natural law and secondary precepts to its superstructure, the skyscraper. The former are objects of intuition; the latter are products of construction.

The idea of transcendental normative standards has long been an object not only of distrust but of ridicule (Felix Cohen called it "transcendental nonsense") because it has usually been taken in its skyscraper version. It is indeed quixotic lunacy even to hope to discover a complete system of moral rules or mathematical propositions by scanning Platonic Heaven. But the bedrock view of transcendental ideals is a different story because its rejection is incompatible with the basic features of our normative experience. As we have already noted, it is impossible to dispense with basic intuitive ideas in any sensible program of construction. Those basic ideas are equally indispensable for the constitution of any positive morality. It has often been said that positive morality is produced by cultural indoctrination. But no cultural indoctrination can inculcate positive norms in cows and donkeys; moral inculcation is possible only in those who are already equipped with some basic ideas of right and wrong. Moreover, positive morality is not always revered; it can be criticized, repudiated, or reformed. This critical task cannot be performed without appealing to some basic normative ideas that transcend positive morality. The bedrock version of transcendental normative standards is thus indispensable not only for the inculcation of positive norms, but for their critical evaluation.

Though the bedrock version is much more plausible than the skyscraper version, it has one serious drawback. On this view of Platonic Forms, normative intuition can deliver only the basic ideas, which are too general and too indeterminate to be a direct guide for human conduct. To remedy this drawback, intuitionism has to turn to constructivism. The art of construction can hone the basic normative ideas to a sharpness that allows them to cut straight through practical problems. For practical efficacy, intuitionism must depend on constructivism. On the other hand, as we noted, constructivism must depend on intuitionism for its ontological foundation. This mutual dependence between intuition and construction is my central thesis. To substantiate this thesis, I take my readers through the complicated dialectical interplay of many normative theories, starting with Rawls's original position and finally ascending to Platonic Heaven.

This journey of ideas is meant to continue and extend the journey that John Rawls initiated in his theory of justice. He has tried to take his normative theory back to Kant. But his journey of retrieval cannot stop with the sage of Königsberg because the sage's own normative theory is suspended in a noetic vacuum. It is desperately in need of a fixed point. But Kant cannot find it without either descending to the world of positive facts or ascending to the world of transcendental norms. In his later writing, Kant realized this point and sought the Archimedean point in Plato's theory of Forms. Thus I have tried to complete Rawls's journey of retrieval by renewing the Kantian flight to Platonic Heaven.

In the course of writing this book, I have received generous help from numerous friends and colleagues. I am grateful to James Fishkin for our frequent discussions on many of the topics included in this volume, and to J. M. Balkin for arguing out almost every major point of contention with me in the spring of 1991. I have received continuous help in formal semantics from Herbert Hochberg and Aloysius Martinich, and in decision and game theories from Daniel Bonevac and Rob Koons. Alexander Mourelatos, Jim Hankinson, and Steven Long have improved my understanding of Greek philosophy, and Paul Woodruff has been my indispensable partner in constructing a highly unconventional reading of Plato. I am especially grateful to him for our continuous dialogue on Plato and a few other topics.

My special gratitude also goes to my splendid teacher Robert S. Brumbaugh, who initiated me into the mystery of Platonism thirty-five years ago. He went over the entire manuscript with loving care, corrected many errors, and graciously endorsed my normative version of Platonism. My gratitude also goes to Christopher Morris and Joo Sung Kim for their perceptive readings of my manuscript and constructive suggestions for improving it. I would like to thank Robert King for his generous support of my work throughout his long tenure as dean of our college. Finally, I am deeply appreciative of the ceaseless encouragement I have received from the great Korean poet Chul Bum Lee.

I would also like to mention that a substantial portion of chapter 6 comes from my article "Virtues and Values: A Platonic Account," which appeared in *Social Theory and Practice* (Summer 1991). This is the special issue that printed the proceedings of a conference held in Austin, Texas, on March 2 and 3, 1990, in honor of my late friend and colleague Edmund Pincoffs. I am grateful for the journal's permission to use a part of that article in this book.

Intuition and Construction

CHAPTER ONE

Formal Procedure

There are two stages in John Rawls's theory of justice, the intuitive stage and the procedural stage. In the intuitive stage, Rawls relies on intuitive ideas for formulating, articulating, and justifying the two principles of justice. But he encounters one serious drawback with this intuitive approach: it seldom delivers determinate results because our intuitions are usually indeterminate. As a way of overcoming the problem of indeterminacy, he introduces a decision procedure known as the original position. He asks us to imagine what sort of principles of justice will be chosen by rational people behind a veil of ignorance. This is his formal procedure, which constitutes the procedural stage.

No doubt much of the excitement over Rawls's theory of justice has been due to his formal procedure. The idea of the original position was indeed ingenious and inventive; it appeared to offer a totally new method for resolving all the intractable normative disputes. The excitement over the procedural stage has tended to push the intuitive stage beyond the sphere of our attention. But the intuitive stage has its own importance for Rawls's theory, and we cannot properly understand the role of the procedural stage without relating it to the intuitive stage. So I propose to consider the nature of the intuitive stage and its relation to the procedural stage.

The Intuitive Stage

The two principles of justice are formulated and articulated in three successive stages. Because their formulation takes place outside the original position, Rawls has to appeal to his intuitive ideas. This is the intuitive stage of his constructivism, which precedes the procedural stage. I propose to consider three questions. What sort of intuitive ideas does Rawls use for formulating the two principles of justice? What sort of indeterminacy results from this intuitive approach? How effective is his formal procedure for resolving this problem of indeterminacy?

In the first formulation, the two principles of justice are stated as follows (*TJ* 60):[1]

First: Each person is to have an equal right to the most extensive basic liberty compatible with a similar liberty for others.

Second: Social and economic inequalities are to be arranged so that they are both (a) reasonably expected to be to everyone's advantage, and (b) attached to positions and offices open to all.

These two principles are too general and indeterminate; they are open to differing interpretations. Rawls wants to give them the best possible interpretation, and this interpretive work belongs to the intuitive stage.

The interpretation of the first principle is relatively easy. Rawls specifies the domain of basic liberties as political liberty together with freedom of speech and assembly; liberty of conscience and freedom of thought; freedom of the person along with the right to hold (personal) property; and freedom from arbitrary arrest and seizure (*TJ* 61). This enumeration of basic liberties involves one of the most difficult questions for his theory of justice: What is the criterion for the demarcation of basic from nonbasic liberties?[2] There are two ways of handling the question of demarcation: procedural and intuitive. The procedural method is to ask the parties in the original position to agree upon a list of basic liberties. The intuitive method is to consult our intuition. Since Rawls has not yet taken us to the original position, he takes the intuitive approach for the enumeration of basic liberties.

The intuitive approach cannot easily deliver the list of basic liberties Rawls would like to have for his first principle of justice. On the scope of basic liberties, our intuitions can be as indeterminate or as controversial as our intuitions on what rights and liberties should be protected by our Constitution. Reasonable people can have reasonable disagreements on this issue. Surprisingly, however, Rawls does not seem to notice this problem. Later we shall see whether the procedural method can be used for resolving the indeterminacy of our intuitions on this question.

The second principle concerns the distribution of income and wealth and of power and authority in the design of social institutions. Rawls points out that the second principle contains two ambiguous phrases: "to everyone's advantage"

1. *TJ* refers to *A Theory of Justice* (Cambridge, Mass.), 1971.
2. These liberties are often associated with the constitutionally guaranteed liberties, but they are not interchangeable. Rawls's list of basic liberties does not include some of the constitutionally protected liberties, for example, the right to bear arms and the rights against self-incrimination and cruel and unusual punishment. On Rawls's theory, moreover, the constitutionally protected rights should be enumerated not in the original position, but in a constitutional convention.

and "open to all." He compares three ways of interpreting these problematic phrases: natural liberty, liberal equality, and democratic equality (*TJ* 65–90). The system of natural liberty is a laissez-faire capitalism with a free market (*TJ* 66). Positions and careers are only formally or legally open to talents. The system of natural liberty guarantees a formal equality of opportunity; all have the same legal rights of access to advantaged social positions. It can satisfy the "open to all" clause. The distribution of income and wealth under such a system can be distributively efficient; it can satisfy the "to everyone's advantage" clause.

In a system of natural liberty, Rawls points out, the distribution of income and wealth is largely determined by the initial distribution of assets, which is in turn the cumulative effect of prior distributions (*TJ* 72). Those who are born into poor families or low classes do not have the chance to develop their talents and abilities and cannot take advantage of the positions and careers supposedly open to all. It is obviously, in Rawls's view, a case of injustice that such social contingencies favor some people over others. He writes, "Intuitively, the most obvious injustice of the system of natural liberty is that it permits distributive shares to be improperly influenced by these factors so arbitrary from a moral point of view" (*TJ* 72). He appeals to his intuition. But his intuition is negative; it only says what is unjust.

The next interpretation of the second principle is called the liberal interpretation, and it replaces formal equality with fair equality of opportunity (*TJ* 73). The principle of fair equality is much stronger than the principle of formal equality. Although the latter provides a legal equality, it leaves intact the social barriers for entry that accrue from lack of training and education. The fair equality of opportunity eliminates these social barriers by maintaining equal opportunities of education and other cultural benefits for all. In a system of liberal equality, people born with similar native talents and abilities should have the same prospects of success, regardless of their social positions (*TJ* 73).[3]

"While the liberal conception seems clearly preferable to the system of natural liberty," Rawls notes, "intuitively it still appears defective" (*TJ* 73). He identifies two defects in the system of liberal equality. Even if the fair equality of opportunity works to perfection in eliminating social barriers, it still permits the distribution of income and wealth to be determined by the natural distribution of talents and abilities. Such a system of distribution remains arbitrary from a moral perspective; the outcome of a natural lottery is not any more justifiable than the outcome of a social lottery. Moreover, the fair equality of opportunity can never be fully implemented; the existence of the family is a

---

3. The fair equality of opportunity itself is open to different interpretations. For a good discussion of this point, see Thomas Pogge, *Realizing Rawls* (Ithaca, 1989), 161–81.

formidable obstacle to its realization. Even if equality of education is secured, different people cannot equally develop themselves because they are born into different families and social circumstances.

Natural liberty and liberal equality are alike in permitting social and natural contingencies to determine the distributive shares. Both of them can lead to callous meritocracies, which can produce glaring differences between the advantaged and the disadvantaged. This assertion reflects Rawls's basic idea that everyone should have an equal life prospect, without being influenced by the arbitrariness of fortune. This is the positive intuition that underlies his negative intuition of distributive justice. This positive idea of distributive justice, Rawls says, can be fulfilled by the democratic interpretation of the second principle, which combines the fair equality of opportunity with the difference principle. With the addition of the difference principle, the second principle is reformulated as follows (*TJ* 83):

> Social and economic inequalities are to be arranged so that they are both (a) to the greatest benefit of the least advantaged and (b) attached to offices and positions open to all under conditions of fair equality of opportunity.

The difference principle prescribes the maximization of the distributive shares for the most disadvantaged class. Although Rawls anticipates no objection to the fair equality of opportunity, he feels the need to justify the difference principle. What reasons can be offered for maximizing the distributive shares of the least advantaged? Here again he appeals to his intuition, the intuitive idea of reciprocity in social cooperation (*TJ* 15). He says that the difference principle can be justified in the name of social cooperation, because it alone can call forth the willing cooperation of the disadvantaged. He writes (*TJ* 103),

> To begin with, it is clear that the well-being of each depends on a scheme of social cooperation without which no one could have a satisfactory life. Secondly, we can ask for the willing cooperation of everyone only if the terms of the scheme are reasonable. The difference principle, then, seems to be a fair basis on which those better endowed, or more fortunate in their social circumstances, could expect others to collaborate with them when some workable arrangement is a necessary condition of the good of all.

This argument does not prove but presupposes the fairness of the difference principle. Rawls appears to confuse two assertions:

1. The difference principle is fair because it can call forth the willing cooperation of the least advantaged.
2. The difference principle can call forth the willing cooperation of the least disadvantaged because it is fair.

The second assertion presupposes the fairness of the difference principle. Perhaps he wants to make the first assertion. It is this reading of his argument that provokes Robert Nozick's counterargument:

> No doubt, the difference principle presents terms on the basis of which those less well endowed would be willing to cooperate. (What *better* terms could they propose for themselves?) But is this a fair agreement on the basis of which those *worse* endowed could expect the *willing* cooperation of others? With regard to the existence of gains from social cooperation, the situation is symmetrical. The better endowed gain by cooperating with the worse endowed, *and* the worse endowed gain by cooperating with the better endowed. Yet the difference principle is not neutral between the better and the worse endowed. Whence the asymmetry?[4]

If the symmetry argument is correct, the difference principle cannot be fair because it is not neutral between the better and the worse endowed. Rawls now appeals to the spirit of fraternity (*TJ* 105): "The difference principle, however, does seem to correspond to a natural meaning of fraternity: namely, to the idea of not wanting to have greater advantages unless this is to the benefit of others who are less well off." He points out that the spirit of fraternity is contrary to the spirit of individual maximization. The members of a family, if properly imbued with a sense of fraternity, do not simply look after their own individual interests, without concern for the well-being of others.

Intuition and Indeterminacy

The introduction of the spirit of fraternity raises some difficult questions. Up to this point, Rawls has used the idea of equality for the vindication of the difference principle. He has presented the three systems—natural liberty, liberal equality, and democratic equality—as three ways of implementing the idea of social equality. Now he appears to claim that democratic equality and its difference principle should be understood as an elaboration of the idea of fraternity. What is the intuitive basis of the difference principle? Is it the idea of equality or of fraternity? Can either of these two ideas be a sufficient basis for the difference principle? Or can they be a sufficient basis only when they are used together? All these questions can be restated for the concept of justice: Which of these two ideas is the intuitive basis for the concept of justice?

Because Rawls has never raised these questions, we have no way of knowing how he might have answered them. But we can be certain that reasonable people can disagree on these questions. Some may say that the idea of equal life

4. Robert Nozick, *Anarchy, State, and Utopia* (New York, 1974), 192–93.

prospect is a sufficient intuitive basis for a theory of justice; others may say that ideas of equality and fraternity are equally important for constructing a theory of justice. Still others may say that the idea of fraternity alone is essential for it. Then there are those who may say that neither of these two ideas is relevant to the question of justice, and that the idea of justice should be based on some other intuitive ideas such as the concepts of desert, effort, and contribution.

What intuitive ideas should be the basis for constructing the principles of justice? This is the question of relevance, and there is no determinate answer to it. This may be called the indeterminacy of relevance. It is a most difficult problem for any theory of justice. There is one further problem of indeterminacy in Rawls's intuitive approach: the indeterminacy of realization. Even if we all accept the idea of equality in life prospects as the basic idea of justice, there are many ways of realizing and articulating this idea. This is true of all general ideas.

The relation of a general idea to its realization is the relation of a universal to its particulars. It is the relation of one to many. The systems of natural liberty, liberal equality, and democratic equality are three different ways of realizing the idea of equality. The indeterminacy of realization means that it is sometimes difficult to tell which is the best way of realizing a given ideal. Rawls has no difficulty in ranking the three systems of equality, but there are other ways of realizing the idea of equality that are difficult to rank. Let us consider a few other proposals for realizing the idea of equality.

One obvious alternative to Rawls's proposal is the idea of equality in welfare.[5] The welfarists have argued that equality limited to the distribution of primary goods does not do justice to the severely handicapped. The handicapped cannot achieve equality of well-being or life prospect with normal people if they receive the same amount of primary goods as others. In their view, what is important is the equality of well-being rather than that of primary goods, because primary goods are mere means for achieving well-being. What should be sought is the equality of end-states rather than of means. This is a highly outcome-oriented view of equality.

Welfare egalitarianism can take many forms. First, there are various competing concepts of well-being.[6] Some people identify well-being with the subjective state of happiness; others identify it with the satisfaction of objective needs; still others identify it with objective achievements. These different concepts of well-being produce different versions of welfare egalitarianism. Second, wel-

5. Amartya Sen, "Utilitarianism and Welfarism," *The Journal of Philosophy* 76 (1979): 463–88; and Ronald Dworkin, "What Is Equality? Part I: Equality of Welfare," *Philosophy and Public Affairs* 10 (1981): 185–246.
6. For a good discussion of the concept of well-being, see James Griffin, *Well-Being* (Oxford, 1986), 7–72.

fare egalitarianism need not be tied to a strict egalitarianism; it can introduce inequalities if they can improve the welfare of all or of the least advantaged. The many ways of accommodating considerations of efficiency can lead to different forms of welfare egalitarianism.

Some Marxists have maintained that the most important object of equalization is not primary goods or well-being or even resources. All these are objects of distribution. In the Marxist perspective, production is far more important than distribution. The principle of equality should be realized in the world of production. In this Marxist vein, Robert Paul Wolff laments "Rawls' failure to focus squarely on the structure of *production* in the economy rather than on alternative patterns of *distribution*."[7] Some Marxists hold that equality in production can be achieved only by giving workers control over production. The workers should have equal rights to participate in making critical decisions in all phases of production, from hiring and firing people and setting production goals to managing the plants and deciding the pay scale.[8]

Then there is the libertarian interpretation of equality, as advocated by Robert Nozick.[9] For the libertarians, the only equality that really counts is the equality of liberty. As long as we have the same liberties, we are all socially equal. If Rawls's first principle of justice can secure the equality of all basic liberties, there is no need for having his second principle. And the distribution of income and wealth will be determined by the exercise of basic liberties. To handle the problem of distribution in any other way in the name of justice requires the redistribution of income and wealth, which disregards the inviolability of basic liberties. Any other idea of equality besides the equality of basic liberties is an illegitimate extension of the social ideal.

These are but a few examples of the articulation of the social ideals of liberty and equality. Rawls can dismiss Nozick's proposal as an apology for the system of natural liberty. But he cannot easily demonstrate the superiority of the difference principle to the proposals of the welfare and the resource egalitarians. Some of them may be better than others by some criterion, but the latter may be better than the former by some other criterion. There appear to be no secure criteria for ranking these competing proposals, all things considered. They are truly indeterminate.

These are the problems of indeterminacy in the realization and articulation of social ideals, and they are as intractable as the problems of indeterminacy in relevance. These two types of indeterminacy—relevance and realization—are

---

7. Wolff, *Understanding Rawls* (Princeton, 1977), 207.

8. Karl Ove Moene makes such a proposal in his article "Strong Unions or Worker Control," in Jon Elster and Karl Ove Moeve, eds., *Alternatives to Capitalism* (Cambridge, Mass., 1989), 83–97.

9. Nozick, *Anarchy, State, and Utopia*.

inherent and inevitable in any intuitive procedure. Although Rawls does not discuss these two types of indeterminacy, he is much concerned with another form of indeterminacy. He states that we often appeal to our intuitions when we try to find a right balance of two or more competing principles. For example, consider the problem of balancing the two principles of efficiency and equity in a distributive scheme. Their conflict is the familiar aggregative-distributive dichotomy. Rawls explains, "It has two principles: the basic structure of society is to be designed first to produce the most good in the sense of the greatest net balance of satisfaction, and second to distribute satisfactions equally" (*TJ* 36).

Two scales are needed for balancing these two principles. We need one scale for measuring total satisfaction and another for measuring the degree of equal distribution. But we cannot devise any reliable scales for measuring these nebulous quantities. Even if we had such scales, we would still have the problem of determining their relative weight. How much efficiency should be sacrificed for how much equity and vice versa? Rawls concedes that there is no other way of settling this question than that of appealing to our intuitions. But our intuitions are indeterminate; they can give different answers (*TJ* 37).

The Original Position

Rawls's foremost methodological problem is how to cope with the indeterminacy of intuitions. The best way to deal with the problem of their indeterminacy is to eliminate them altogether. But that is impossible. He writes, "No doubt any conception of justice will have to rely on intuition to some degree. Nevertheless, we should do what we can to reduce the direct appeal to our considered judgments" (*TJ* 41). The second best solution is to minimize the direct appeal to intuitive ideas, and this goal of minimization is meant to be achieved by the use of the original position as a formal procedure.

The constitution of the original position involves three critical concepts: the basic structure of society, the rationality of the parties, and the veil of ignorance. The basic structure of society means the social structure for the distribution of primary goods. This basic structure will be determined by the principles chosen by the parties in the original position. They are assumed to be rational in making this choice. They do not suffer from envy; they want only to maximize their respective shares of primary goods. They make their choice behind the veil of ignorance; they do not know what social positions they occupy or what natural and social assets they command. The veil of ignorance makes it impossible for them to tailor their choice to their unfair advantage. Under these conditions, Rawls maintains, his two principles of justice will be chosen in the original position. If the parties do choose the two principles, the original position will be shown to be an effective formal procedure for overcoming the indeterminacy of the intuitive stage.

Rawls says that the parties in the original position will start with a general principle of equality: equal liberty for all, equality of opportunity, and equal distribution of income and wealth (*TJ* 151). But there is no need for them to stick to this benchmark of initial equality. They can introduce inequalities, if by so doing they make everyone better off. The introduction of inequalities, however, produces a complicated problem of social choice. Given different configurations of social inequality, what sort of criteria can be used for ranking them?

Rawls recognizes three criteria: the Paretean, the utilitarian, and the maximin rule. For illustration, let us consider the following distributive schemes for five representative positions A, B, C, D, and E:

Figure 1

	A	B	C	D	E	Total	Average
S_0	5	5	5	5	5	25	5
S_1	10	34	45	73	88	250	50
S_2	15	21	27	38	99	200	40
S_3	20	36	37	43	44	180	36
S_4	25	26	27	28	29	135	27

S_0 is a society of strict equality; S_1 through S_4 allow various degrees of inequality in the distribution of primary goods. The numbers in the columns A, B, C, D, and E indicate the shares of primary goods for each social arrangement. The numbers in the Total column stand for the total primary goods summed over the five different positions in each social arrangement; the numbers in the Average column stand for the average shares.

The parties in the original position can agree to move from S_0 to any one of four other social arrangements because to do so would make everyone better off. S_1 through S_4 are all Pareto-optimal; by the Paretean criterion, none of them is any better than the others. However, the principle of utility is a well-known measure for ranking those four social arrangements. J. C. Harsanyi has maintained that the social arrangement with the highest average utility will be chosen behind a veil of ignorance (1955).[10] By this criterion of expected

10. Harsanyi does not use the expression "the veil of ignorance" but uses the same device in his claim that the maximization of the average utility is not only a rational but a fair criterion for social choice. For details, see "Cardinal Utility in Welfare Economics and the Theory of Risk Taking," *Journal of Political Economy* 61 (1953), and "Cardinal Welfare, Individualistic Ethics, and Interpersonal Comparisons of Utility," *Journal of Political Economy* 63 (1955). Harsanyi defends his utilitarian solution against Rawls's maximin solution in his critical review of *A Theory of Justice:* "Can the Maximin Principle Serve as a Basis for Morality? A Critique of John Rawls' Theory," *American Political Science Review* 69 (1975): 594–606.

utility, S_1 would be chosen in the original position. It commands the highest average, 50. But the maximin rule dictates a different choice, S_4; it aims at the highest payoff (25) for the lowest position.

Rawls admits that the most natural rule of choice is that of maximizing the expected return on the basis of probability computation, as Harsanyi maintains (*TJ* 154). But he argues against this standard method of maximization for three special conditions that obtain in the original position. First, there is insufficient information for making reliable probability calculations because it is blocked out by the veil of ignorance. Second, what can be gained by taking a chance above the maximin level is not worth the risk. Third, conversely, what can be lost by not taking the maximin solution is intolerable. Under these three conditions, he says, the maximin rule is the best or the most rational decision procedure in the original position (*TJ* 153–56). This is his celebrated maximin argument.

Has Rawls proven his case against Harsanyi? There is no simple answer to this question because it really involves two questions: first, the question of relevant information and then the question of decision procedures under uncertainty. The decision theorists distinguish between two types of circumstances for making decisions: the decision under risk and the decision under uncertainty (or ignorance). The decisions are made under risk if the circumstances provide enough information for computing the probabilities of expected utilities. They are made under uncertainty if the circumstances provide no such information. They have to be made without the benefit of probability calculation.

These two types of decision situations represent two different kinds of veil of ignorance. Information required for probability computation is blocked out by Rawls's veil of ignorance, while it is admitted by Harsanyi's. Rawls's veil is much thicker than Harsanyi's, and the difference between these two veils constitutes the difference between the decision under uncertainty and the decision under risk. The method of maximizing expected utility is for making decisions under risk; the maximin rule is for making decisions under uncertainty. Rawls concedes that the method of maximizing expected utilities is the best method for making decisions behind a thin veil, but he claims that the maximin rule is better suited for making decisions behind a thick veil. He further claims that the parties in the original position should adopt the maximin solution because they deliberate behind a thick veil. But why should the original position be equipped with a thick rather than a thin veil? This is the question of veils.

The question of veils concerns the question of relevant information: What sorts of information are truly relevant to making decisions in the original position? This is the first of the two questions concerning Rawls's claim for the maximin rule. Setting aside this question for a while, let us take up the other question: whether the maximin rule is the best for making decisions behind the thick veil of ignorance. The adoption of a thick veil does not automatically endorse the maximin rule as the best method for making decisions under uncertainty. It is only one of many rules that have been proposed and are still debated by the decision theorists. Let us consider some of them: the maximax rule, the optimism-pessimism rule, the minimax regret rule, and the principle of insufficient reason.[11]

The maximax rule is the opposite of the maximin rule. The latter is concerned solely with the worst outcomes; it maximizes the lowest payoffs. The maximax rule is concerned solely with the best outcomes; it maximizes the highest payoffs. It is the policy of "Caesar or nothing." In figure 1, this solution will pick S_2, which has the highest distributive share, 99. The optimism-pessimism index rule combines the maximin and the maximax rules into one; it considers both the highest and the lowest shares. We can compute the optimism-pessimism indices for figure 1 by adding the highest and the lowest shares in each row (for the sake of simplicity, the ratio of optimism and pessimism is assumed to be one): 10 for S_0, 98 for S_1, 114 for S_2, 64 for S_3, and 54 for S_4. By this rule, S_2 is the favored solution.

The minimax regret rule is to pick the option whose maximum regret is minimal.[12] From figure 1, we can construct a regret table, as in figure 2:

Figure 2

	A	B	C	D	E
S_1	15*	2	0	0	11
S_2	10	15	18	35*	0
S_3	5	0	8	30	55*
S_4	0	10	18	45	70*

For example, the regret numbers for column A are determined by subtracting each distributive share in that column from the highest share (25). Then we pick out the highest regret number for each row, which is starred. Regret can be minimized by selecting S_1, which contains the lowest of the highest regret factors.

In one regard, the rule of insufficient reason is different from all these methods. Each of the latter makes a selective use of available information in figure 1. For example, the maximin rule considers the returns only for the lowest position, while the maximax rule is concerned solely with the returns for the highest position. The principle of insufficient reason makes an equal use of all available information. In figure 1, it adds up all the distributive shares for each row and

11. For a good discussion of these proposed solutions, see Michael D. Resnik, *Choices: An Introduction to Decision Theory* (Minneapolis, 1987), 21–44.
12. The minimax regret rule is called the minimax risk criterion by R. Duncan Luce and Howard Raiffa, *Games and Decisions* (New York, 1957), 280.

selects the row with the highest number, S_1. This is the solution favored by Harsanyi.

These are five well-known ways of making decisions under uncertainty, and there may be a few others. The problem of making decisions under uncertainty is so difficult that it has called forth many more proposals than the problem of making decisions under risk. There is no objective method of ranking these proposed methods. Each of them is designed to meet some special requirements or circumstances. For example, the maximin rule is concerned with the security level; it guards against disasters. The maximax rule is meant for those who are intent on seeking the highest return at any cost. The optimism-pessimism index rule is meant to combine both concerns. The minimax regret rule is designed for those seriously concerned with regret factors. The principle of insufficient reason is for using all available information with equanimity.

Rawls believes that the parties in the original position should adopt the maximin rule because they should be concerned with their security level. He has given two reasons for adopting the maximin rule. First, what can be gained by taking a chance above the maximin level is not worth the risk. Second, what can be lost by not taking the maximin solution is intolerable. These two reasons make sense only on the condition that the maximin level is the same as the disaster level. In figure 1, let us assume, the disaster level coincides with the maximin of 25. Under that stipulation, any distributive shares lower than this figure can be regarded as intolerable, and to gain anything above that level may not be worth the risk involved.

But there is no reason to assume that the maximin level should coincide with the disaster level. In the constitution of the original position, Rawls says nothing about the disaster level. Neither does he say whether or not information concerning the disaster level is permitted by the veil of ignorance. To be sure, the parties in the original position should be concerned with the security level, if they are rational. As James Fishkin and many others have pointed out, Rawls's maximin argument may not be claiming anything more than the guaranteed social minimum.[13] Rawls himself says that the two principles of justice "guarantee a social minimum" (*TJ* 156, 87). In that case, he is advancing only an argument for security. As R. M. Hare says, he may be confusing the maximin rule with the insurance strategy.[14]

The requirement for a social minimum is much weaker than the maximin requirement. Perhaps I should distinguish the argument for security from the argument from security. The argument for security directly aims at establish-

13. James Fishkin, *Tyranny and Legitimacy* (Baltimore, 1979), 108.
14. R. M. Hare, "Rawls' Theory of Justice," in Norman Daniels, ed., *Reading Rawls* (New York, 1975), 104. Originally published in *Philosophical Quarterly* 23 (1973): 144–55, 241–51.

ing a social minimum, and the parties in the original position should be told where the disaster level lies. They can set the lowest payoff above the disaster level; they do not even have to consider the maximin rule. The argument from security does not aim at securing a social minimum; it only uses the sense of security as a tactic for installing the maximin rule. For this purpose, it refuses to tell the parties in the original position where the disaster level lies, and the only thing they can do to protect themselves against disasters is to set the lowest payoff level as high as possible. It can lead to the adoption of the maximin rule.

The argument from security is a scare tactic; it scares the parties with the problem of security level so that they cannot use any other decision rules under uncertainty than the maximin rule. This scare tactic works only insofar as it keeps the parties in the dark about the security level. But Rawls has not yet explained why such vital information as the one concerning the disaster level should not be permitted behind the veil of ignorance. If the veil of ignorance cannot exclude disaster level information, it cannot invalidate the use of the other decision rules in the original position. Let us assume that the disaster level is set at 12 for figure 1. In that case, S_2, S_3, and S_4 are viable options. Their lowest payoffs are higher than the disaster level.

Even the exclusion of disaster level information does not deliver a conclusive victory for the maximin rule. It is one thing to assume that the parties in the original position are concerned with the security level. But it is another thing to assume that they are concerned with it and nothing else. Only under the condition of exclusive concern with the security level can the maximin rule beat out the other decision rules. But such an exclusive concern may be incompatible with the rationality requirement for the parties in the original position. It appears to be highly irrational for them to be so concerned with the security level as to disregard all other considerations for the basic structure of their society.

If there is no conclusive argument for adopting the maximin rule, Rawls's justification of the difference principle remains incomplete. The same problem arises in his justification of the priority rule, which asserts the priority of liberty over economic prosperity; the parties in the original position will not sacrifice their basic liberties for the sake of improving their economic well-being (*TJ* 151–52). Such a high ideal, Rawls admits, cannot be accepted for all societies. Hence it is excluded from the general conception of justice and accepted only for the special conception. Whereas the general conception of justice applies to all societies, the special conception applies only to those societies in which the basic wants of people are fulfilled, and their fundamental rights are effectively established (*TJ* 152, 542–43).

The priority rule concerns the question of trade-off between liberty and prosperity. Under what circumstances is it rational to sacrifice liberty for economic prosperity? Rawls recognizes the rationality of such a trade-off under economic hardships, which make it impossible to fulfill the basic needs. As the conditions of civilization improve, he maintains, the marginal value of social and economic advantages decreases relative to the value of liberty. At that point, it becomes irrational to sacrifice the interests of liberty for economic improvements (*TJ* 542). The priority rule is dictated by the principle of rational maximization, and the parties in the original position are rational enough to accept the priority rule.

This is roughly Rawls's argument for the priority rule. It assumes a cutoff point at which the decreasing marginal value of economic gains cannot justify the sacrifice of basic liberties. It may be called the liberty–prosperity exchange cutoff point. This point varies considerably from society to society, from class to class, and from individual to individual. For any given society, the lower class may not have reached the cutoff point, although the higher class may have already passed it. The higher class would not sacrifice their liberties for greater prosperity, but the lower class would love to. The situation may be reversed. In some societies, the lower class would not sacrifice their basic liberties for greater prosperity, but some members of the higher class would give up their civil liberties for a better prospect for their economic adventures. Even in the same social class of the same society, individuals may have different liberty–prosperity exchange cutoff points.

Rawls's argument for the priority rule is valid only for the society whose members have all passed the liberty–prosperity exchange cutoff point. But such a society requires no prohibitory rule on the exchange of liberty for prosperity because none of its members even considers such an exchange. It is hard to tell when human civilization will reach such an ideal state, but it is obvious that not all societies have reached it. In that case, the priority principle cannot be dictated by the principle of rational maximization. As H. L. A. Hart says, it is obviously irrational for the parties in the original position to impose such a restriction as the priority rule on their future society.[15]

The priority rule becomes even more difficult to justify when it involves the conflict between liberty and equality. The fair equality of opportunity is not exactly a question of prosperity, although it is protected under the second principle. The conflict of liberty and equality can be illustrated by a Supreme Court case, *Wisconsin v. Yoder*. In the name of religious freedom, Amish parents demanded the right to keep their children out of secular schools. If those children were excluded from secular schools, they would never have the fair equality of opportunity. Religious freedom is one of the basic liberties falling under Rawls's first principle of justice, and the fair equality of opportunity is guar-

---

15. H. L. A. Hart, "Rawls on Liberty and Priority," *University of Chicago Law Review* 40 (1973): 534–55. Reprinted in Daniels, *Reading Rawls*, 230–53.

anteed by his second principle. The Amish parents' demand created a conflict between these two values.[16]

The Supreme Court ruled in favor of religious freedom on the ground that the Amish alternative to formal state education can fulfill "the social and political responsibilities of citizenship without compelling attendance beyond the eighth grade." [17] The requirement of fulfilling social and political responsibilities is much weaker than the requirement of fair equality of opportunity. In an industrial state such as that of the United States, eight years of elementary education can never give young people a fair chance to compete with those who have had twelve or sixteen years of education. The Court decision is in accord with Rawls's priority rule, and he would concur with it.[18] He says that religious freedom should be respected as long as the children's education includes an adequate knowledge of their basic rights and prepares them to be fully cooperating members of society.[19]

To be fully cooperating members of society, however, is far from enjoying the fair equality of opportunity. Some of us may believe that the fair equality of opportunity is more important than the freedom of conscience. On that ground, we may question the rationality and legitimacy of the Supreme Court decision and of Rawls's priority rule. These points can be dramatized by comparing *Wisconsin v. Yoder* with *Brown v. Board of Education of Topeka*.[20] The Supreme Court ruled against segregated schools by repudiating the separate but equal doctrine. If a system of segregated schools cannot give the students equal opportunities, the principle of fair equality ought to be protected by banning segregation. But the desegregation order infringes upon freedom of association, as Herbert Wechsler maintains.[21] There are many white and some black students who do not want to attend desegregated schools. Freedom of association is one of the basic liberties, and the Supreme Court has sacrificed it for the sake of equality. The *Brown* case goes against Rawls's priority rule.

What position would Rawls take on the *Brown* case if he wanted to retain the priority rule? There are two alternatives available to him. He can say that the *Brown* case is incompatible with the priority rule because freedom of asso-

16. This case involves more than the conflict of religious freedom and equality of opportunity. It also involves the conflict between the right of children and the right of their parents, and the conflict between these rights and the right of the state.
17. *Wisconsin v. Yoder,* 406 U.S. 205 (1972).
18. A good discussion of this topic is Joo Sung Kim, "The Problem of Value for Liberalism" (Ph.D. diss., The University of Texas at Austin, 1990).
19. Rawls, "The Priority of Right and Ideals of the Good," *Philosophy and Public Affairs* 17 (1988): 267.
20. *Brown v. Board of Education,* 347 U.S. 483 (1954).
21. Wechsler, "Toward Neutral Principles of Constitutional Law," *Harvard Law Review* 73 (1959): 1–34.

ciation is a basic liberty that has priority over the fair equality of opportunity. Desegregated schools do not violate the two principles of justice as long as they teach students their basic rights and duties and prepare them to be fully cooperating members of society. He can also say that the *Brown* case is compatible with the priority rule. Freedom of association is never meant to be protected by his first principle of justice because it is not a basic liberty.

Whichever position Rawls might take, he has to rule on the question whether freedom of association is one of the basic liberties. This brings back our earlier question: How do we demarcate basic from nonbasic liberties? I have noted that our intuitions can give no determinate solution to this difficult problem. Now we must admit that rational deliberation in the original position cannot do any better in resolving this question.

Procedural Indeterminacy

The priority rule and the difference principle are two special issues that Rawls has tried to settle conclusively by using the original position as a formal procedure. On these two issues, unfortunately, the deliberation in the original position has turned out to be as indeterminate as our intuitions. The indeterminacy arising from the original position may be called procedural indeterminacy. There are two dimensions of procedural indeterminacy: internal and external. The internal indeterminacy takes place within the original position. It is internally indeterminate whether or not the priority rule will be adopted in the original position. The adoption of the maximin rule also belongs to its internal indeterminacy. External indeterminacy takes place outside the original position; it concerns its constitution. It is externally indeterminate whether the original position be equipped with a thick or thin veil of ignorance. There is no conclusive way of determining what sort of veil is best suited for the original position.

To be sure, Rawls gives his reasons in support of the thick veil. It is about time for us to take a close look at those reasons. The first of them is his generality requirement: the veil of ignorance should admit only general information and block out all particular information. Rawls's demarcation between general and particular information corresponds to his distinction between general and particular facts. But the idea of generality is ambiguous. Some facts are absolutely general; they obtain in all societies at any stage of human history. But some facts have only relative generality; they are general only in some societies. Rawls says that only absolutely general information can be admitted behind the veil of ignorance. For illustration, let us consider the information concerning the security level. We may entertain two conceptions of security level. It is plausible to say that there is one absolutely general security level for all societies. If we know what that is, it is admissible behind the veil of ignorance. On the other hand, it is also plausible to say that the security level varies from one culture to another. In that case, the security level information is not absolutely, but relatively general. Hence it will be excluded by the veil of ignorance.

The function of the veil is to block out not only personal information, but also relatively general information (*TJ* 137). The exclusion of personal information is obviously for the sake of impartiality. But what is the purpose of excluding relatively general information? Rawls tries to justify the exclusion by listing three formal constraints of generality, simplicity, and unanimity. If relatively general information is not excluded, Rawls says, the problem of deliberation will be "hopelessly complicated" (*TJ* 140). The simplified information can make it easy for anybody to simulate the deliberation behind the veil of ignorance, at whatever stage of history he or she may be situated. Moreover, Rawls says, the same policy of simplification makes possible a unanimous choice of principles. Thus these three formal constraints can explain the exclusion of relatively general information from the original position.

Rawls is mistaken about what is required for unanimity. The unanimity of the original position is obtained not by the simplicity of information, but by the singularity of the deliberator. As Rawls says, the principles are chosen from the position of one person (*TJ* 139). If unanimity has nothing to do with the extent of information, we are left with only two formal constraints, generality and simplicity. By admitting only absolutely general information behind the veil of ignorance, the original position can produce principles of justice that can be valid in all societies. Rawls says that the generality requirement also satisfies the simplicity requirement. If the principles of justice were to be based on special circumstances that obtain only in some societies, we would need many different sets of principles. This is the sort of complication Rawls wants to avoid by the formal constraint of simplicity (*TJ* 125).

Although Rawls admits the possibility that even general information may be too complex to meet the constraint of simplicity (*TJ* 142), he decides to stay with the generality requirement. But he complicates the problem of information restriction by violating his own rule and admitting certain relatively general facts behind the veil. First, he allows the parties behind the veil to know that their society is subject to such circumstances of justice as the condition of moderate scarcity and the possibility of mutually beneficial cooperation (*TJ* 137). He also allows the parties to know that they will be living under a set of circumstances favorable enough to accept the priority of the first over the second principle of justice. Those circumstances include a high enough living standard to appreciate the value of liberty more than that of greater prosperity, and a stable enough political condition to allow an effective establishment of basic liberties (*TJ* 542–43). Information concerning such special circumstances should be excluded by the requirement of absolute generality.

In fact, Rawls has demarcated the special from the general conception of justice. The two principles of justice belong to the special conception, and the general conception is stated in much more general terms:

All social values—liberty and opportunity, income and wealth, and the bases of self-respect—are to be distributed equally unless an unequal distribution of any, or all, of these values is to everyone's advantage. (*TJ* 62)

Whereas the general conception of justice applies to all societies at any stage of human history, the special conception applies only to those societies under a set of special conditions. The two principles of justice are not absolutely general principles, and the requirement of absolute generality is incompatible with Rawls's two principles of justice. Hence the requirements of generality and simplicity cannot endorse the thick veil of ignorance. Probably for this reason, Rawls offers in his John Dewey Lectures a completely different argument for the thick veil. After distinguishing the thick from the thin veil, he says that the thin veil is required by the Humean rationale of impartiality, and the thick veil by the Kantian rationale of liberty and equality. What is really required by the Kantian rationale that is not required by the Humean rationale? This is the mystery question about the Kantian rationale. He explains, "It does not suffice that they [the parties in the original position] are impartial in the sense of being unable to take advantage of their superior position (if such they have). The parties are not to be influenced by any particular information that is not part of their representation as free and equal moral persons with a determinate (but unknown) conception of the good, unless this information is necessary for a rational agreement to be reached."(*KC* 549)[22]

While the Humean veil is good enough for securing the impartiality of contract negotiation, Rawls seems to say, the Kantian veil is meant to accomplish more than impartiality. Its function is to show perspicuously the intimate connection between the principles and the conception of the person as being free and equal. Rawls believes that this connection will be obscured by permitting information concerning general institutional facts. What sort of information, then, can be admitted behind the veil of ignorance, without obscuring the link between the principles to be adopted and the conception of moral persons? The only information that can be so admitted appears to be the information that moral persons are free and equal. Any other information should be blocked out as extraneous and irrelevant. Such a veil of ignorance will be as thick as it can be. Rawls says that the Kantian outlook demands the thickest possible veil (*KC* 549).

Why should the thickest possible veil be regarded as Kantian? Does Kantian

---

22. *KC* refers to John Rawls, "Kantian Constructivism in Moral Theory: The John Dewey Lectures 1980," *The Journal of Philosophy* 77 (1980): 512–72.

ethics really demand such a thick veil of ignorance? Kant himself never talks about the veil of ignorance. We can perhaps locate the Kantian counterpart to the veil of ignorance by equating the level of abstraction to the thickness of a veil. In Kant's ethics the level of abstraction is an important issue in the selection of moral maxims. Though it can be done on many different levels of abstraction, Kant never says which is the right level. But many things he says about the selection of maxims tend to indicate that the highest level of abstraction is the right one.

In the notorious essay "On a Supposed Right to Lie from Altruistic Motives," he faces the following question: What sort of contingent circumstances should be allowed to override the moral maxim of veracity? He firmly states that the maxim must hold absolutely. It cannot be overridden even by altruistic motives. Suppose, Kant says, you have just hidden in your house a helpless girl running away from a pursuing assailant. He knocks on your door and asks you whether you have seen the girl. Kant thinks you have a duty to tell him the truth because the maxim of veracity should hold without exception under any and all circumstances. This is Kant's well-known rigorism.

Because Kantian moral maxims cannot allow any exceptions that may arise from contingent circumstances, they are adopted on the highest possible level of abstraction. Such a high level of abstraction, which disregards all contingent facts, plays the same role as that of the thickest veil of ignorance. As there is a continuum from the highest to the lowest level of abstraction, so there is a continuum from the thickest to the thinnest veil of ignorance. Rawls's thick veil of ignorance allows only the information that the parties in the original position are free and equal. The Kantian equivalent is to select moral maxims on the highest level of abstraction, which recognizes only the liberty and equality of all human beings.

Let us reconsider the maxim of veracity. Should I tell the truth to this determined assailant at my door, looking for his victim? Because this maxim is adopted on the highest level of abstraction, which takes into account only the conception of all humans as being free and equal, Kant would say, I should disregard the fact that I am talking to an assailant because it is a contingent fact. The only thing I should know is the fact that we are talking as free and equal persons. Any other information is irrelevant on this high level of abstraction. Such a high level of abstraction may establish a direct connection between the maxim and the conception of human beings as being free and equal; but it can give no rational direction to our action. The rationality of action requires much more information than the recognition of our liberty and equality.

Information that is permitted by the veil of ignorance may be of two kinds: information concerning the parties in the original position and information concerning the objects of their projected choice. The knowledge that the parties are free and equal persons belongs to the first kind. If such knowledge were to be the only information permitted by the veil of ignorance, the parties could make no meaningful choice because they would be totally in the dark about the objects of their purported choice. They have to know something about the objects; they need some information of the second kind. If the Kantian veil excludes all information of the second kind, it eliminates the information base for all rational choices.

So far we have assumed that a high level of abstraction can effectively generate moral maxims. But that assumption is doubtful. Should we really accept the maxim of never telling lies regardless of contingent circumstances? It is very hard to give an affirmative answer to this question. What sort of maxims should be accepted on such a high level of abstraction as the one that recognizes only freedom and equality? It is impossible to give any determinate answer to this question. The higher the levels of abstraction, the more indeterminate their maxims will be. Likewise, to increase the thickness of the veil is to expand the range of its indeterminacy. The Kantian veil delivers much more indeterminate results than the Humean veil. Here lies the irony of the Kantian veil. In adopting the procedural device of the original position, Rawls's motive was to reduce the indeterminacy of his intuitive approach. But his installment of the Kantian veil has expanded it.

The Constitution of the Original Position

What considerations have led Rawls to adopt the thick veil of ignorance? He says that the original position has been constructed by improving upon the idea of an impartial observer. Let us see wherein this improvement lies. When the idea of an impartial observer was proposed and developed by Francis Hutcheson, Adam Smith, and David Hume, it was intended to be a device for impartially regarding the competing claims of different people. For example, let us examine the role of an impartial observer in considering the claims of three individuals, A, B, and C, in the following possible configurations of distribution:

Figure 3

	A	B	C	Total
d_1	10	30	55	95
d_2	15	35	40	90
d_3	20	25	30	75

Which one of these three distributive schemes, d_1 d_2 or d_3, will be chosen by the impartial observer? Since the impartial observer identifies herself with all three members of this society, she imagines that she will take up all three positions. Hence she adds up all three distributive shares and treats their sum as her own. From her perspective, d_1 is better than d_2 or d_3 because it gives the highest sum. Let us now regard A, B, and C not as individuals, but as three social classes. The total population is allocated to these three classes as follows: 30 percent for A, 60 percent for B, and 10 percent for C. Let us assume that the numbers in the three columns A, B, and C indicate the individual shares for each of the three classes. The impartial observer cannot simply add up the shares in each row in order to make her decision; she has to factor in the size of each class.

Figure 4

	A	B	C	Total
d_1	10×30	30×60	55×10	2650
d_2	15×30	35×60	40×10	2950
d_3	20×30	25×60	30×10	2400

The impartial observer has to choose d_2, which gives the highest total.

The Humean (thin) veil of ignorance is different from the impartial observer in one regard. A person who has to choose one of the three distributive schemes in figure 3 from behind such a veil need not assume that he will be all three persons at once. He knows that he will be one of them, although he does not know which one. He will assign equal probabilities for his being one of them, and pick d_1 because it gives the highest total. If he is asked to select from figure 4, he will treat the population ratios of the three classes as his probabilities of being assigned to those three classes. He will pick d_2, which gives the highest expected share. In both decisions, the selection made behind the Humean veil of ignorance coincides with the selection of the impartial observer.

Although a person behind the Humean veil of ignorance does not identify himself with all three people or positions in figures 3 and 4, as the impartial observer does, he has to treat them with equal concern because he has a chance of being in any one of those positions. This approach of equal concern produces the same outcome as the selection procedure of an impartial observer. The approach of equal concern justifies the probability computations that amount to treating the individual shares of different people as though they were to belong to one person. In substance, the Humean veil disregards the separateness of individuals just as the impartial observer does. Both of them are devices of aggregation and not distribution. As such, they are suitable only for the individual decisions of rational prudence. They are not equipped with normative resources for making social choices; they cannot take into account the relative standing of distributive shares for different individuals.

This is the gist of Rawls's critique of the impartial observer and of the Humean veil. He has tried to reconstitute an impartial observer in such a way that she may be sensitive to the separateness of individuals (*TJ* 190–91). With this new sensitivity, the impartial observer can split herself into all members of society and refuses to amalgamate their distributive shares into one lump sum. She is an impartial observer with a social perspective, which is not available to the impartial observer of utilitarianism. The impartial observer with a social perspective would not accept the probability computations of the utilitarian impartial observer because such computations disregard the distinctness of individuals. She is as sensitive to the question of distribution as to that of aggregation. Let us call such an impartial observer the Rawlsian adjudicator.

If the utilitarian impartial observer is not equipped with the normative resources necessary for making social choices, he should be replaced by the Rawlsian adjudicator. This substitution produces a different initial situation. The utilitarian impartial observer dictates one kind of contract situation, and the Rawlsian adjudicator dictates another kind. At this point, Rawls faces a critical choice: What is the right way to translate the Rawlsian adjudicator into the constraints on the original position? There appear to be two ways to handle this problem. One way is to retain the Humean veil and replace the rational maximizer with the Rawlsian adjudicator. The other way is to retain the rational maximizer and alter the Humean veil.

Because the Rawlsian adjudicator behind the Humean veil is sensitive to the question of distribution, she cannot make social choices without appealing to her intuitions. Instead of aggregating the interests of different people, she has to weigh them against one another. She has to rely on her intuitions. Since her intuitive approach is indeterminate, installing her in the original position does not provide the supposed advantage of a formal procedure. In that case, Rawls has to retain the rational maximizer and alter the Humean veil. If the veil of ignorance is thick enough to deny the rational maximizer the information required for making probability calculations, then the rational maximizer cannot compute the total or average distributive shares. Such a thick veil will force the rational maximizer to adopt a social perspective, to respect the distinction of individuals, and to reject the utilitarian solution. These appear to be the considerations that have led Rawls to adopt the Kantian veil of ignorance.

This is only a conjecture regarding Rawls's motivation and deliberation. If it is correct, it proves the primacy of intuitive ideas over formal procedures. Rawls can detect the deficiency in the theory of an impartial observer as a device of social choice only by appealing to an intuitive idea of justice. He can make an effort to improve upon it only by consulting the same intuitive idea. He can test the adequacy of the improved version by comparing it with the original version, but this comparison cannot be made without appealing to the same intuitive idea. In fact, the two veils of ignorance are two different ways of implementing the intuitive idea of impartiality, and their comparison can be made only by appealing to the same intuitive idea. The construction of a veil of ignorance begins and ends with our intuitions.

Unfortunately, the Kantian veil does not deliver any better result than the Humean veil. As we have seen, the rational maximizer behind the Kantian veil has no special reason to be solely concerned with the worst outcome. She may adopt the maximin rule, the principle of insufficient reason, or some other decision rule in the original position. Whichever decision rule she may adopt, she does so from the perspective of individual choice. The thickness of her veil cannot change the character of her perspective. She is as much a rational maximizer as anyone behind the Humean veil of ignorance. The only difference between them lies in the extent of available information. The Kantian rational maximizer has to operate with much less information than the Humean rational maximizer. The Kantian rational maximizer is thrown into a far greater domain of indeterminacy than the Humean rational maximizer because the thickness of the veil only increases the indeterminacy of rational choice.

CHAPTER TWO

Procedural Reflection

John Rawls wants to prove not only that his two principles of justice will be adopted in the original position, but also that they are better principles than any other. For that purpose, he has drawn up a list of alternative conceptions of justice to be given to the parties in the original position (*TJ* 124):[1]

    A. The Two Principles of Justice
        1. the principle of greatest equal liberty
        2. (a) the fair equality of opportunity
           (b) the difference principle
    B. Classical Teleological Conceptions
        1. the classical principle of utility
        2. the principle of average utility
        3. the principle of perfection
    C. Mixed Conceptions (various mixtures of A and B)
        1. A1 and B2
        2. A1 and B2 plus the constraint of a social minimum
        3. A1 and B2 plus the constraint of a social minimum
           and the fair equality of opportunity
    D. Intuitionistic Conceptions
        1. to balance total utility against the principle of equal distribution
        2. to balance average utility against the principle of redress
        3. to balance a list of prima facie principles
    E. Egoistic Conceptions

This list contains eleven conceptions of justice, and Rawls wants to prove that his two principles will be chosen over the others in the original position. He adopts the method of comparative justification; it is to compare all the competing theories and pick the best. He recognizes two ways of comparing competing theories:

---

1. The list given here does not exactly duplicate Rawls's own list. I have changed the positions of B and C for the convenience of exposition. Because "C. Mixed Conceptions" are combinations of A and B, it should naturally come after A and B.

intuitive and procedural. In the intuitive method we use our intuition of justice for selecting the best theory. Because this method is inevitably indeterminate and disputable, Rawls favors the procedural method, also called the contract method. It is much more complicated than the intuitive method.

Competing Conceptions of Justice

The procedural method of comparison can take one of two forms: a monistic or a pluralistic scheme. A monistic scheme singles out the best interpretation of the initial situation and compares all competing conceptions of justice from this single perspective. A pluralistic scheme recognizes many different interpretations of the initial situation, and not one of them can provide a universal perspective for comparing all the different theories of justice. The pluralistic scheme presupposes a one-to-one correspondence between theories of justice and the contract situations that produce those theories. For example, Rawls recognizes an isomorphism between the impartial observer and the principle of utility. The impartial observer obliterates the distinction between persons by impersonally adding up all the different distributive shares of different people to a single sum (*TJ* 186–87). Likewise, the principle of utility does not recognize the separateness of individuals. Hence the adoption of an impartial observer necessarily endorses the principle of utility. The isomorphism between the impartial observer and the principle of utility leads Rawls to the general thesis that every conception of justice is uniquely connected with a particular interpretation of the initial situation (*TJ* 121): "We may conjecture that for each traditional conception of justice there exists an interpretation of the initial situation in which its principles are the preferred solution. Thus, for example, there are interpretations that lead to the classical as well as the average principle of utility."

This general thesis may be called the parallel postulate of contract situations and theories of justice. Rawls does not limit the scope of this parallel postulate to the competing theories of justice but extends it to all moral theories. He writes, "Different moral theories arise from different interpretations of this point of view, of what I have called the initial situation" (*TJ* 264). Different interpretations of the initial situation represent different moral points of view. Given the one-to-one matching relation between competing theories of justice and their corresponding contract situations, we can compare different contract situations and accept as the best theory of justice whichever theory is produced by the best contract situation. This is the pluralistic scheme.

In the two schemes of procedural comparison, the original position plays different roles. In a monistic scheme, the original position is the most favored contract situation; it offers a universal perspective for comparing all the competing conceptions of justice and selecting the best. In a pluralistic scheme, the original position is only one of many possible contract situations, and each of them favors a particular conception of justice. The pluralistic scheme has no common vantage point.

Figure 1. A Monistic Scheme of Comparison

Original Position
- Justice as Fairness
- Utilitarianism
- Mixed Conceptions of Justice
- Perfectionist Conceptions
- Egoistic Conceptions

Figure 2. A Pluralistic Scheme of Comparison

Original Position	Justice as Fairness
Impartial Observer	Utilitarianism
Mixed Position	Mixed Conception of Justice
Perfectionist Position	Perfectionist Conceptions
Egoist Position	Egoistic Conceptions

These two schemes of procedural comparison can be restated in terms of moral points of view. As we have seen, Rawls believes that different interpretations of the initial situation represent different moral points of view (*TJ* 264). In the monistic procedure, the original position is taken to represent the only moral point of view from which to survey and compare all the competing conceptions of justice. In the pluralistic procedure, the original position is taken to represent one among many possible moral points of view. Rawls often says that the original position represents the Kantian moral point of view. He suggests "that we think of the original position as the point of view from which the noumenal selves see the world" (*TJ* 255). No doubt a utilitarian self would not see the world from a Kantian moral point of view.

Which of the two schemes of procedural comparison does Rawls really use? He uses both of them, and even the intuitive method of comparison in some cases. This point is important for understanding the relation of the two stages in his justification of the two principles. In the first stage, Rawls wants to demonstrate that the two principles will be chosen in the original position. In the second stage, he wants to show that the two principles are superior to all other conceptions of justice. Since both of these stages belong to the problem of justification, many commentators have mistakenly assumed that both of them take place in the original position. Though the monistic scheme of comparison is compatible with this assumption, Rawls does not stick to it all the times.

Rawls does use the original position as the common vantage point for comparing his conception of justice with the perfectionist conceptions. He argues that the parties in the original position would reject the principles of perfection (*TJ* 325–32). He is chiefly concerned with cultural perfectionism: the ideals of excellence in arts, sciences, and culture should be the supreme political goals. He recognizes two variants of cultural perfectionism (*TJ* 325). The stringent version recognizes cultural perfection as the only political principle, as advocated by Nietzsche. The moderate version accepts cultural perfection along with such other social ideals as liberty and equality.

Rawls has no trouble in showing that the stringent version of cultural perfectionism will be rejected by the parties in the original position. It does not allow them the basic liberties and equalities. But the moderate version is not subject to this criticism because it can guarantee basic liberties and even the social minimum for basic needs. At this point, Rawls changes the direction of his argument. Now he says that the parties in the original position would have no reason to choose the principle of perfection because of their motivational structure (*TJ* 328). They cannot even consider the principle of perfection as an alternative. Their value structure is shaped by Rawls's thin theory of the good, too thin to include any ideals of personal or cultural perfection.

The thin theory of the good is exclusively limited to social primary goods of rights and liberties, income and wealth.[2] So the parties in the original position neither know what the ideals of perfection really mean nor have any concern for those ideals. The perfectionist theories of justice cannot be meaningful alternatives for the parties in the original position. Their adoption is precluded by the original position, but that does not prove the superiority of his two principles to the perfectionist theories. It may only indicate the inadequacy of the original position. If the original position has to reject such a reputable theory as perfectionism not on its own merit but by a device of preclusion, it appears to be operating under an unduly narrow perspective. In that case, it is grossly unfair to use the original position for assessing the other theories of justice.

Rawls appears to be aware of this point in his critique of the mixed conceptions of justice and refrains from using the original position as the common vantage point (*TJ* 315–25). When he compares the difference principle with the social minimum principle, he does not say that the parties in the original position would choose the difference principle over the social minimum principle. The concept of a decent social minimum is not one of the available options in the original position. So he makes the comparison of the social minimum principle with the difference principle outside the original position. He abandons the procedural method of comparison for the intuitive one.

For the superiority of the difference principle to the social minimum principle,

2. For critiques of Rawls's thin theory of the good, see Brian Barry, *The Liberal Theory of Justice* (Oxford, 1973), 1933; Thomas Nagel, "Rawls on Justice," *Philosophical Review* 82 (1973): 220–34; Adina Schwartz, "Moral Neutrality and Primary Goods," *Ethics* 83 (1973): 294–307; Michael Sandel, *Liberalism and the Limits of Justice* (Cambridge, 1982), 165–68.

Rawls offers two arguments. First, the problem of fixing the social minimum involves all the difficulties and uncertainties of intuitionism. Since the social minimum has to be adjusted to the changing circumstances, there is no easy formula for determining it (*TJ* 316). This is the argument from indeterminacy. Second, the concept of an appropriate social minimum is so indeterminate that in practice it comes out to be the same as the maximin solution of the difference principle (*TJ* 317). This is the argument from equivalence.

These two arguments are incompatible. If the concept of an appropriate social minimum is indeterminate, it cannot yield an outcome equivalent to what is dictated by the difference principle. Whereas a determinate principle dictates one clearly defined outcome, an indeterminate principle prescribes many loosely defined outcomes. One clearly defined outcome cannot be equivalent to many loosely defined outcomes. At most, one of the loosely defined outcomes may match up with the clearly defined one. Even that coincidence can happen by chance. One accidental matchup cannot prove the equivalence of the two principles any more than one stray swallow can prove the arrival of spring. The argument from equivalence cannot be true if the argument from indeterminacy is true, and vice versa.

There is another way of interpreting Rawls's claim. The concept of a decent social minimum is so indeterminate that the only way to implement it is to use the difference principle in its place. This may be called the substitution thesis. Rawls appears to be thinking along this line when he writes, "How do we know, then, that a person who adopts the mixed view [with the constraint of an appropriate social minimum] does not in fact rely on the difference principle?" (*TJ* 317). This is not to say that the person is conscious of substituting the difference principle for the social minimum principle. Rawls says that the person may even repudiate the difference principle. If the substitution takes place, it is an unconscious occurrence.

The substitution thesis would be valid on two conditions. First, the concept of a decent social minimum is so indeterminate that it is impossible to have any meaningful agreement on it. Second, the difference principle is determinate. Neither of these conditions may obtain. For the first condition, we had better recognize the distinction between total and partial indeterminacy. Total indeterminacy means total arbitrariness. If the concept of a decent social minimum is totally indeterminate, it can be set at any totally arbitrary level. Then it can never be used as a practical guide. But its indeterminacy may be only partial; it can be set at many different levels within certain limits. It can be used as a practical guide, although it is bound to generate many disputes.

Although the difference principle is theoretically determinate, it is practically indeterminate. Which level of distribution brings about the greatest shares for the least advantaged? The answer to this question depends on many empirical factors. As we shall see, the difference principle contains an incentive clause, and the working of an incentive system involves many ill-defined empirical factors such as the motivational structure of different social classes, their attitudes toward work and leisure, earning and spending, and even their concern for others. Moreover, the efficacy of incentive factors varies from individual to individual, from class to class, from society to society, and from one historical stage to another. For these reasons, the difference principle is practically indeterminate, perhaps more indeterminate than the concept of a social minimum.

In his critique of utilitarianism, Rawls employs the pluralistic scheme of procedural comparison. He does not claim that the principle of utility would not be chosen in the original position. He knows that its choice is precluded by the original position. Hence the merit of utilitarianism cannot be assessed inside the original position. So he proposes to compare the original position with the impartial observer, which justifies the utilitarian conception of justice, and then wants to prove the superiority of the original position to the impartial observer as a choice procedure. In this case, Rawls is using the pluralistic scheme of comparison.

Rawls's attempt to demonstrate the superiority of his two principles to other conceptions of justice raises some serious methodological problems. If he takes his original position as the universal vantage point for comparing all competing theories of justice, he appears to do injustice to many of them. His original position is clearly inadequate on the ground of available information. It is blind to many factors that are considered essential and relevant to the question of justice in other theories. This point concerns what I called the indeterminacy of relevance in chapter 1, and Rawls wants to settle this problem of indeterminacy by fixing his moral perspective on the original position. But he has yet to justify his original position as a point of universal perspective.

The pluralistic scheme has its own difficulty. Rawls has said that the different contract situations represent different moral points of view. In that case, to compare different contract situations is to compare different moral points of view. Which moral point of view does he take in his comparison of different contract situations? He cannot make the comparison from a morally neutral perspective; a neutral perspective gives no criteria for ranking competing theories of justice. He must appeal to his intuitive idea of justice. For illustration, let us consider Rawls's comparison of the original position with the impartial observer (*TJ* 184–92). He locates the fatal defect of an impartial observer in its blindness to the separateness of individuals, which overlooks the most essential feature of justice. Hence the use of an impartial observer is an offense to the very idea of justice. The virtue of the original position is that it avoids this mistake by taking seriously the separateness of individuals. Hence the original position is a better formal procedure than the impartial observer.

This comparison is made by consulting our intuitive idea of justice. Rawls has no conclusive procedural argument for the superiority of his two principles to other conceptions of justice. To that extent, his formal proceduralism is incomplete. He can make it complete only by demonstrating that the original position can indeed offer a truly universal perspective for comparing all competing theories of justice. But he never makes this demonstration.

Pure and Impure Procedures

Rawls distinguishes pure procedures from perfect and imperfect procedures (*TJ* 85–86). Perfect and imperfect procedures are alike in one regard: they are instruments for implementing independent standards of justice. A criminal trial is such an instrument; it is a procedure for determining whether the defendant has committed a crime. It presupposes an independent criterion of criminal justice: one ought to be convicted of a crime and be punished for it if and only if one has committed it. But the procedure is far from perfect; it often produces a miscarriage of justice. Such a procedure is called an imperfect procedure in Rawls's classification.[3]

For certain standards of justice, Rawls says, it is possible to devise a perfect procedure. For example, a perfect procedure for dividing a cake equally between two persons is to have one of them cut it in half and the other pick one of the pieces before the cutter does. This procedure can produce an equal division of the cake, if the cutter has the skill to divide the cake into equal halves and if he has the desire to have as large a piece as he can get. Rawls calls it a perfect procedure because it can almost perfectly implement the independent standard of equal division.

A pure procedure is different from these instrumental procedures. "By contrast," Rawls states, "pure procedural justice obtains when there is no independent criterion for the right result: instead there is a correct or fair procedure such that the outcome is likewise correct or fair, whatever it is, provided that the procedure has been properly followed." Whatever comes out of a pure procedure is just if it is a fair procedure; there are no independent criteria of fairness for assessing the outcome. Rawls cites gambling as an example. Whatever comes out of a betting procedure is just, as long as the betting procedure is fair and all the participants follow its rules. The fairness of a gamble lies in its procedure, and the fairness of its procedure assures the fairness of its outcome.

3. This account of criminal justice as an imperfect procedure assumes that the conviction of a criminal is the sole purpose of the procedure. But the procedure of criminal justice is also meant to protect the rights of those on trial. Since the protection of their rights is also a question of justice, a criminal trial has to be controlled by more than one criteria of justice.

The triadic distinction of pure, perfect, and imperfect procedures is not so important for Rawls's purpose as the dyadic distinction between pure and impure procedures. Although he does not use the expression "impure procedure," I am using it to refer to both perfect and imperfect procedures. They are alike in being instruments for executing some independently existing standards of justice. They should be called impure procedures in contrast to pure procedures, which are defined as those having no independently existing standards of justice. Pure procedures are truly perfect procedures. Whatever comes out of them is always perfectly just as long as their rules are faithfully obeyed. This sort of guarantee does not obtain even for the so-called perfect procedure, such as cutting a cake into equal halves. There is no truly perfect device for making an equal division of a cake.

If Rawls is correct, there are two different ideas of justice. One is outcome-oriented and the other is process-oriented. Our idea of criminal justice is definitely outcome-oriented; the procedure of a criminal trial is to achieve the desired outcome and to safeguard the rights of the defendant. But the idea of justice for gambling is completely process-oriented; it has nothing to do with the outcome. Process-oriented justice is procedural; outcome-oriented justice is substantive.

Now the question of distributive justice can be looked at from the perspective of procedure as well as of outcome. Who should get what? or Who should get how much? are questions of outcome, which presupposes an independent criterion of fairness. But that criterion is often indeterminate because it is intuitive. It may be possible to avoid the indeterminacy of intuitions by restating the question of distributive justice as a question of procedure. If we can set up the right procedure of distribution, whatever comes out of it can be accepted as fair. In fact, this has been the rationale for the tradition of social contract and the doctrine of consensual justice. They stand on the common premise that whatever is done by mutual consent is just. The device of mutual consent is a pure procedure, and it can settle many questions of justice.

A pure procedure in general appears to have a certain magic power of producing justice all by itself. And it also appears to have the advantage of circumventing the indeterminacy of our substantive intuitions about fairness. But not all pure procedures are fair procedures. Rawls appears to take it for granted that there is a distinction between fair and unfair pure procedures, and that only fair procedures can produce just outcomes. What then constitutes the fairness of a pure procedure? This is perhaps the most difficult question for his theory of procedural justice. He tries to answer it by the example of gambling (*TJ* 86): "If a number of persons engage in a series of fair bets, the distribution of cash after the last bet is fair, or at least not unfair, whatever this distribution is. I assume here that fair bets are those having a zero expectation of gain, that the bets are made voluntarily, that no one cheats, and so on. The betting procedure is fair and freely entered into under conditions that are fair. Thus the background circumstances define a fair procedure."

In this description of a fair procedure, Rawls does not specify the defining characteristics of a fair procedure. Instead, he gives a series of background conditions, each of which can be characterized as fair or unfair. What is the criterion for determining the fairness of those background conditions? There are two ways of accounting for this criterion: procedural and substantive. A background condition is fair just in case it is an outcome of a fair pure procedure. This is the procedural account. The substantive account appeals to a substantive standard of fairness; a background condition can be said to be fair or unfair in reference to an independent standard of fairness.

The procedural account leads to an infinite regress. The fairness of a pure procedure can be derived only as an outcome of a prior procedure; there is no pure procedure whose outcome can warrant its own fairness. The fairness of a first procedure depends on the fairness of a second procedure, which in turn depends on the fairness of a third procedure, and ad infinitum. We can avoid such an infinite regress only by accepting the substantive account of procedural fairness. Ronald Dworkin offers one plausible version of the substantive account. He holds that Rawls's contract theory of justice presupposes a deep theory that assumes natural rights, and that these rights are the right to liberty and the right to equal concern and respect.[4] The parties in the original position exercise these natural rights in designing the basic structure of their society. The procedural fairness of the original position lies in the exercise of these natural rights.

Dworkin's account of procedural fairness for the original position does not correctly reflect the idea of fairness Rawls tries to express with his examples of betting and gambling. Those examples appear to have no reference at all to any notion of rights. Rawls seems to say that fair procedures are fair by their very nature. Perhaps we can distinguish between internal and external theories of fairness. Dworkin's account is an external theory; it accounts for the fairness of a pure procedure in reference to natural rights, which lie outside the pure procedure. An internal account is to explain the fairness of a pure procedure solely in terms of its own properties.

The distinction between internal and external accounts of procedural fairness is expressed in William Nelson's two ways of reading Rawls's idea of a pure procedure.[5] On the weak interpretation, a pure procedural justice can be explained in terms of entitlement and its free exercise. Any transaction between two or more people is a case of pure procedure as long as they freely exer-

4. Dworkin, *Taking Rights Seriously* (Cambridge, Mass., 1977), 177–81.
5. William Nelson, "The Very Idea of Pure Procedural Justice," *Ethics* 90 (1980): 502–11.

cise their rights. A pure procedure is none other than the procedure of freely exercising entitlements. On the strong interpretation, a pure procedure has a certain property F such that this property enables the procedure to produce just results. This property belongs to the procedure itself; it is something other than the participants' exercise of their entitlements. The weak interpretation is a general formulation of Dworkin's view, and the strong interpretation appears to capture Rawls's idea of procedural fairness as sketched in his examples.

For an illustration of these two interpretations, we can go back to Rawls's example of gambling. It has two different elements of fairness: the notion of fair bets and that of voluntary participation. The fairness of the latter is derived from the participants' entitlements; the fairness of the former belongs to the betting procedure. These two features of procedural fairness are independent. Voluntary participation need not be limited to fair bets; one can voluntarily participate in an unfair bet. Conversely, the fairness of a fair bet has nothing to do with the question of whether participation is voluntary or involuntary. One can be forced, against one's will, to participate in a fair bet.

Since a gamble involves these two features of fairness, it can be regarded as fair or unfair on two different grounds. These two different grounds are separated in Nelson's weak and strong interpretations of the idea of a pure procedure. On the weak interpretation, pure procedural justice is reducible to substantive justice; it is based on entitlements or some other prior rights. Only on the strong interpretation, Nelson says, does a theory of pure procedural justice gain its unique significance. But he rejects the strong interpretation on the ground that he cannot identify the intrinsic features of a game that make it a fair procedure, apart from the conditions of voluntary participation.

To reinforce this point, Nelson maintains that what appears to be a pure procedure in its strong sense usually turns out to be something else. For example, a fair lottery is often taken as an example of a fair procedure. But its function is to allocate an equal chance to everyone concerned, and the allocation of an equal chance is the independent criterion of fairness that governs the operation of a fair lottery as a procedure of justice. Moreover, a fair lottery can perfectly accomplish the independent criterion of allocating an equal chance to everyone. Hence, Nelson maintains, a fair lottery should, by Rawls's definition, be classified as a perfect procedure.[6]

Rawls has indeed given us a fair bet as an example of a fair procedure, and the fairness of a betting procedure appears to lie in its allocation of even chances of winning to everyone. In that case, the procedural fairness of a lottery is determined by a substantive idea of fairness. The same point can be made in terms of the procedural fairness for making a contract. The law of contract recognizes procedural constraints that do not allow the signing of a contract under duress,

6. Nelson, "The Very Idea of Pure Procedural Justice," 506.

misrepresentation, with the mentally unsound or a minor. Such constraints are meant to safeguard the procedural fairness of contract.

What constitutes the procedural fairness of a contract? It can be defined as a procedure that does not allow one contracting party to take an unfair advantage of the other party. The making of a contract with a mentally retarded person or with a minor is an unfair procedure because it allows such a person to be taken advantage of. The question of whether such a person can indeed be taken advantage of can be settled only by looking at the sort of substantive agreement he could make. Hence it is impossible to distinguish between fair and unfair procedures without presupposing the criteria of fairness for substantive contractual terms. To be sure, fair procedures for making contracts can be instituted as independent requirements, but they can be justified only as instruments for guarding against unfair contracts. Hence the substantive criteria of fairness in contract are presupposed for its procedural fairness. This is true also of the original position as a fair procedure.

The fairness of a pure procedure may initially seem totally procedure-bound because the procedure can be installed as an independent requirement. In substance, however, its fairness is outcome-oriented; it can be defined only in reference to possible outcomes. Hence the fairness of a pure procedure appears to be both process-oriented and outcome-oriented. These two conflicting views can be found even in Rawls's descriptions of the original position. When he stresses its procedural independence, he says that whatever is adopted in the original position is just and that there is a set of shared presumptions for the constraints to be placed on the original position (*TJ* 18). He also expresses an outcome-oriented view of the original position when he claims that the original position should be designed in such a manner as to yield the principles of justice that can converge with our considered judgments of justice (*TJ* 45). More emphatically, he writes, "We want to define the original position so that we get the desired solution" (*TJ* 141).

In the end, we may have to admit the impossibility of characterizing the nature of the original position as a pure procedure. But it is too early to concede defeat because we have considered only his remarks in *A Theory of Justice*. In his John Dewey Lectures, though he does not make the original position a special topic for discussion, he gives an illuminating account of its relation to Kantian ideals, which constitute the Archimedean point for Rawls's conception of justice as fairness.

Direct and Indirect Derivations

In his John Dewey Lectures, Rawls names two basic model-conceptions for his theory: the concepts of a well-ordered society and of a moral person (*KC* 520). The Kantian conception of moral persons as being free and equal is the most basic concept for his theory, and the conception of a well-ordered society is to be articulated in reference to this basic concept. For this articulation, he introduces a third concept, the idea of the original position. He calls it the "mediation model-conception: its role is to establish the connection between the model-conception of a moral person and the principles of justice that characterize the relations of citizens in the model-conception of a well-ordered society" (*KC* 520).

The three model-conceptions are three tiers in Rawls's project, which begins with the Kantian conception of moral persons and translates it into a set of principles for the basic structure of a well-ordered society. The original position is a procedural device for mediating this translation. The Kantian conception of moral persons is the ultimate basis for his three-tiered project. For this reason, Rawls in *A Theory of Justice* called this Kantian conception the Archimedean point for his entire theory (*TJ* 584).

The three-tiered project is a project of derivation; it is for deriving principles of justice from the Kantian ideals of liberty and equality. On the surface, these ideals may appear to be semantically different from the Kantian conception of a moral person as being free and equal. The latter seems to refer to the personal attributes of an individual, while the former names social relations. But the ideas of liberty and equality can be stated in both ways because they are relational attributes. 'John is free' (or 'John has freedom') and 'John is equal' (or 'John has equality') are not complete statements. They can be completed by spelling out John's relation to others.

The Kantian conception of a moral person as being free and equal sums up the social ideals of liberty and equality. Rawls's two principles of justice are derived from these two Kantian ideals. Their derivation can be made in two modes: direct and indirect. The direct mode is the intuitive approach; the indirect mode is the procedural approach. The original position is required for the indirect mode of derivation; it functions as the mediator between the Kantian ideals and the two principles of justice. The direct mode of derivation does not require such mediation; the principles of justice are directly derived from the Kantian ideals. In chapter 1, I discussed the operation of a direct mode in Rawls's intuitionist arguments for the two principles. Since the direct mode dispenses with the mediation by the original position, it has a two-tiered structure instead of a three-tiered one.

In the indirect mode of derivation, the Kantian ideals of liberty and equality do not directly determine the two principles of justice. Instead, they determine the procedural constraints to be placed on the original position, which will decide the adoption of principles. Hence the question of procedural constraints should be settled by appealing to the Kantian conception of moral persons. This way of characterizing the nature of those constraints appears to make much better sense than the vague appeal to commonly shared presumptions.

How can one derive the procedural constraints for the original position from the Archimedean point? There are two ways, procedural and intuitive. The procedural approach is to imagine what sort of procedural constraints free and equal persons would accept for the constitution of the original position. But this decision should also be made under suitable conditions, and we have to find a way to determine what they should be. What sort of procedural constraints should be placed on the original position can be settled by constituting another original position, which requires its own procedural constraints. The procedural derivation of the constraints will lead to an infinite regress of procedures. We have already encountered this unsavory consequence of Rawls's formal proceduralism.

This unsavory consequence can be averted by an intuitive approach. We appeal to our intuitions in answering the question: Under what conditions should free and equal persons adopt the principles of justice? Rawls takes this intuitive approach in his appeal to commonly shared presumptions. But do we really have commonly shared presumptions for the procedural constraints to be placed on the original position? Though each of us may have some, we may not share all of them. We may have some shared presumptions about the need for a veil of ignorance but may not agree on its thickness or thinness. We may have some presumptions about the concept of primary goods but may not agree on what they should be. There is an unavoidable indeterminacy of presumed intuitions for every procedural constraint.

We cannot escape the indeterminacy of our presumed intuitions, even if all of us subscribe to the same Kantian idea of moral persons as being free and equal. John Rawls has lived in the pious hope of finding a formal procedure that can eliminate or reduce the indeterminacy of intuitions. He wants to give a theoretical basis to this pious hope in his theory of pure procedural justice. But there is no way of constituting a formal procedure without the use of intuitive ideas. If we do not use them, our formal procedures will have nothing to do with our normative concerns. On the other hand, if we do use those intuitive ideas, they inevitably carry their indeterminacy into the formal procedures they constitute. Hence we do not gain much by adopting the indirect method of derivation. For the demonstration of this point, we should compare the result of an indirect derivation with that of a direct derivation.

In chapter 1, I noted Rawls's effort to make a direct derivation, his attempt at giving the best interpretation of the two principles without taking his arguments to the original position. Let us see how far he can go in this direct mode of derivation. On the intuitive level, we can accept his interpretation of the first principle. But we have to agree with him that natural and social contingencies unequally affecting our life prospects are incompatible with the Kantian ideal of equality. Rawls recognizes two ways of dealing with the problem of inequality. One is to adopt some political means to make everybody alike and equal and the other is to use unequal talents and abilities for the benefit of all under the constraint of equality. The latter is to link the fair equality of opportunity with the difference principle. Let us see how the conjunction of these two principles can work for the Kantian ideal of equality.

Imagine a society whose production makes use of all the talents and abilities developed under the fair equality of opportunity. Further suppose that this society adopts one uniform payment schedule for all its members. But such an egalitarian system can kill incentives and severely damage productivity. This problem can be solved by establishing a separate schedule of payments for incentives. We can have two payment schedules: the basic and the incentive schedules. The combination of these two schedules produces the maximin schedule. Thus the maximin combines two ideas: the equality of outcome and efficiency.

Figure 3

	A	B	C
d_1	10	30	50
d_2	15	28	40
d_3	20	25	30

In figure 3, the third row gives the maximin solution. The distributive shares in this row (d_3) are composed of two parts (d_3' and d_3''):

Figure 4

	A	B	C
d_3	20	25	30
d_3'	20	20	20
d_3''	0	5	10

The middle row, d_3', indicates the uniform basic payment; everyone receives 20 units. The bottom row indicates the incentives; B and C receive the extra payments of 5 and 10 units, respectively. The notion of incentives should be taken in a broad sense; it includes the incentive not only to work, but also to get trained. Rawls says that inequalities in income and distribution can be justified only to cover the cost of training and education and to encourage effective performance (TJ 102, 151). People deserve extra rewards not for having talents, but only for the trouble of getting them developed and putting them to work. The notion of incentives may even cover the trouble of taking risks. Without a prospect of some reward, potential innovators and entrepreneurs may not be induced to take risks. This broad notion of incentives can justify the inequalities in d_3, but not those in d_1 and d_2.

The notion of incentives also determines the identity of the least well-off. According to figure 4, the least well-off receive no incentive payments. Why are they not entitled to any incentive payments? Incentives make no difference for those totally crippled in mind or body because they can play no productive social role. They are the worst-off in any society. This notion of the worst-off is not exactly the same as Rawls's notion. He offers two methods of identifying the least advantaged: the index of primary goods and social standings. By the second method, the least advantaged is the lowest social class, unskilled labor (*TJ* 98). By the first method, the least advantaged is the group with the lowest index of primary goods (*TJ* 320). Rawls appears to assume the identity of these two classes, but they are different. The people with the lowest primary goods are not the class of unskilled labor, but the crippled, who cannot participate in any mode of production.

In his discussion of the difference principle, Rawls is chiefly concerned with the welfare of unskilled labor. He wants to set aside the problem of the crippled and the disabled and consider the question of justice primarily in the context of fully cooperating members of society (*KC* 546). But this is an un-Kantian approach. By the Kantian principle, all human beings have equal dignity, whether they are healthy or crippled. Moreover, as Rawls so often insists, the mental and physical condition of every human being is a consequence of natural and social contingencies. The same forces of contingency that assign some people to the class of unskilled labor also incapacitate some people for life. The difference between productive and unproductive people is arbitrary from a moral point of view.

It has been said that the difference principle can justify even gross inequalities in income and wealth. In its defense, it should be noted that the difference principle can justify gross inequalities only to the extent that they are necessary for incentive and inducement. The difference principle sets a limit to gross inequalities, but that limit is determined by human motivation and psychology. Without incentive payments, the level of base payments for all will be lowered. In spite of inequalities due to incentive payments, the difference principle always delivers the same base payment for all. If the maximin rule is understood in this manner, the difference principle is a strict egalitarian principle, buttressed by a special schedule of payoffs for incentives.

The difference principle combines two ideas: the equality of outcome and the best productive efficiency. The former is represented by the equal base payment, and the latter by the unequal incentive payments. These two correspond to the Kantian conception of human beings. Every human being is composed of the noumenal and the phenomenal selves; the noumenal self is morally free and equal whereas the phenomenal self is subject to natural and social contingencies. The Kantian distinction between the noumenal and the phenomenal self is appropriated by Rawls in his distinction between the moral and the natural selves. Because all moral persons are free and equal, he holds, they are entitled to equal life prospects without being influenced by the arbitrariness of fortune. Natural persons are neither free nor equal.

Let us reconsider the distributive scheme in figure 4 in reference to the distinction between the natural and the moral selves.

Figure 5

	A	B	C
d_3	20	25	30
d_3'	20	20	20
d_3''	0	5	10

The distributive schedule d_3 is the maximin schedule, which consists of the equal base payment (d_3') for everyone and of the unequal incentive payments (d_3') for the advantaged. These two components in the distributive schedule correspond to the two components of every individual: the moral and the natural self. The basic payments are given to A, B, and C as moral persons; these payments are equal because all moral persons are equal. The incentive payments are given to A, B, and C as natural persons; these payments are unequal because natural persons are unequal. The incentive payments can now be regarded as the concession moral persons make to natural persons.

The argument from equality can be made without the veil of ignorance; the difference principle can be derived directly from the equality of noumenal selves and the necessity of incentives for phenomenal selves. In the argument from equality, there is a deductive connection between the difference principle and the principle of equality. But no such deductive connection obtains between the principle of equality and the argument from security that is made behind the thick veil of ignorance. If the parties in the original position regard it as rational to adopt the maximin rule for their security, they are directly concerned with their security and not at all with their equality. The concept of equality affects their deliberation only indirectly; they are equally ignorant about their security level behind the veil of ignorance.

Whereas the principle of equality is a premise for the argument from equality, it functions as a procedural constraint (equal ignorance) for the argument from security. Hence the connection between the argument from security and the principle of equality is indirect. Because of this indirect connection, the argument from security produces uncertain results. Even if the parties in the original position are concerned with their security, they may not accept the difference principle. On the other hand, the argument from equality is absolutely certain as long as its premises are accepted. If we accept the premises, we have to accept the difference principle as a logical consequence.

When we compare the results of these two derivation methods, the indirect method does not deliver any more determinate results than the direct method, as Rawls has hoped. On the contrary, the direct method has given us a much more conclusive argument for the difference principle than the indirect method. This should be sufficient proof that the original position is an undesirable detour for Rawls's theory of justice.

The Archimedean Point

Whether we take the direct or the indirect method of derivation, we have to stand on the Kantian conception of moral persons. It is the Archimedean point for the whole theory. But the Kantian ideal of moral persons as being free and equal has serious metaphysical implications because it involves his metaphysical demarcation between the noumenal and the phenomenal selves. Is Rawls willing to accept the metaphysical implications? On this question, he has given two conflicting answers.

The Kantian ideal can be understood in two ways; it can be taken either as a transcendent ideal or as a mere product of our culture. These two views can be called Kantian transcendentalism and Kantian conventionalism. Kantian transcendentalism says that Kantian ideals transcend all cultural boundaries; Kantian conventionalism claims that they are only our conventions, which emerge as products of history. In *A Theory of Justice*, Rawls assigns a transcendental perspective to the original position (*TJ* 255):

> My suggestion is that we think of the original position as the point of view from which noumenal selves see the world. The parties qua noumenal selves have complete freedom to choose whatever principles they wish; but they also have a desire to express their nature as rational and equal members of the intelligible realm with precisely this liberty to choose, that is, as beings who can look at the world in this way and express their perspective in their life as members of society.

This transcendental perspective is stated in terms of Kant's distinction between the two worlds of noumena and phenomena. The world of phenomena is the world of appearances; it is the world as it appears to us as human beings. It is the world bound by space and time because we can know the world only in a space–time framework. The world of noumena is the real world; it is the world as it really is. It transcends space and time. These two worlds determine two dimensions of human existence because human beings exist in both worlds. The two dimensions are the noumenal and the phenomenal selves.

In Kant's view, only the noumenal selves are truly free and equal. The phenomenal selves are not free; they are subject to the causal laws of the phenomenal world. Hence Kant says that human beings are free only when they are viewed from the noumenal perspective. From the phenomenal perspective, he says, human behaviors are as causally determined as any other events in the phenomenal world. The same dual perspective obtains for human equality. From the phenomenal perspective, there is no reason to claim human equality. The phenomenal selves are obviously unequal; they are endowed with clearly different powers and talents, which belong to the world of phenomena. In the noumenal world, however, there is nothing to distinguish one noumenal self from another. They are truly equal.

The concept of moral persons as being free and equal makes no sense from the phenomenal perspective; the phenomenal world has no place for any moral concept because it is a world devoid of norms and values. It is mainly the world of physical objects and their relations. Even Rawls appeals to the idea of noumenal selves in his claim that all human beings are entitled to equal life prospects without being subject to natural and social contingencies (*TJ* 255). To be subject to natural and social contingencies is neither just nor unjust for the phenomenal self because the phenomenal world knows nothing about justice and injustice. Moreover, it is the unavoidable fate of every phenomenal self to be subject to natural and social contingencies.

As I pointed out in chapter 1, Rawls's idea of equality is the idea of equal life prospects; any natural and social contingencies that adversely affect this equality are unfair and unacceptable from a moral point of view. This assertion has been disputed by many for good reasons, but it gains a compelling force if it is given from the Kantian premise. Yet Rawls cannot have this premise without accepting Kant's concept of the noumenal self. He has to endorse the metaphysical foundation of Kant's philosophy. In *A Theory of Justice*, however, he never concerns himself with the metaphysical implications of his theory of liberty and equality.

In his John Dewey Lectures, Rawls does turn his attention to metaphysical questions. He wants to make sure that his Kantian constructivism evades all the metaphysical problems associated with rational intuitionism. This cannot be done without dropping the doctrine of noumenal selves, which is as metaphysical as anything can be. So he abandons the transcendental perspective and restates the ontological basis for his Archimedean point. He says that the concept of moral persons as being free and equal is located in the public culture of our democratic society (*KC* 518).

Although he is still hanging on here to the Kantian ideal of moral persons, he is now giving it a different ontological status. In *A Theory of Justice*, he located that ideal in the noumenal world. Now he is relocating it in the world of culture, the phenomenal world. As a phenomenal entity, the Kantian ideal is only a historical and cultural product and thus cannot provide a timeless moral perspective. As a noumenal entity, it was claimed to offer such a timeless perspective (*TJ* 587): "Thus to see our place in society from the perspective of this position [the original position] is to see it *sub specie aeternitatis:* it is to regard the human situation not only from all social but also all temporal points of view."

Arguing from a timeless Kantian perspective, Rawls had maintained that the original position could justify not only the principles of justice but all natural duties (*TJ* 114–17). After dropping such a comprehensive perspective, he restates his objective in much more modest terms: to elaborate the basic political ideas of liberal democracies. Even in his *Theory of Justice*, to be sure, he had been eager to detach Kant's idealism from its "metaphysical surroundings" (*TJ* 264). But nevertheless he stressed the affinity and resemblance of his program to Kant's idealism. Fourteen years later, however, he openly dissociates his conception of justice from Kant's metaphysics, saying that his program is not metaphysical but political.[7]

Rawls's program should not be regarded as settling any metaphysical issues in political philosophy because it is addressed to the practical problem of establishing some consensus in a pluralistic liberal society. Even his conception of moral persons as being free and equal is no longer metaphysical, but political. This political approach recognizes no important difference between Kant and Mill.[8] This antimetaphysical, practical posture is more suitable to our ethos of normative skepticism than is Kant's transcendental idealism. In his John Dewey Lectures, Rawls accentuates his antimetaphysical stance by advocating the special advantage of his Kantian constructivism over rational intuitionism.

By *rational intuitionism* Rawls understands the long tradition that has come down from Plato and Aristotle and has thrived in the works of Henry Sidgwick, G. E. Moore, and W. D. Ross. He names two essential features of rational intuitionism (*KC* 557). First, the three basic moral concepts of the right, the good, and the moral worth of persons are not analyzable in terms of nonmoral concepts. Second, the first principles of morality are self-evident, and these self-evident propositions provide the reasons for applying the three basic moral concepts to moral situations. These reasons are fixed by a moral order that is prior to and independent of our conception of a person and the social role of morality. The independent existence of a moral order is the ontological premise of rational intuitionism.[9]

Whereas rational intuitionism presupposes the independent existence of moral order and truth, Rawls says, Kantian constructivism begins with the concept of

---

7. Rawls, "Justice as Fairness: Political not Metaphysical," *Philosophy and Public Affairs* 14 (1985): 223–51.

8. Rawls, "Justice as Fairness: Political and Not Metaphysical," 246.

9. Rawls cites the independent existence of a moral order as the third feature of rational intuitionism in his "Themes in Kant's Moral Philosophy," in Eckart Foerster, ed., *Kant's Transcendental Deductions* (Stanford, 1989), 95.

moral persons, who are taken to be free and equal (*KC* 560). Instead of discovering moral principles in the domain of truth, moral persons are to decide what principles they can accept as the basic principles of their social order. Since Kantian constructivism is an affair of mutual agreement and acceptance, it is a version of social contract theory. Rawls writes, "On a contract doctrine the moral facts are determined by the principles which would be chosen in the original position" (*TJ* 45). In Kantian constructivism, there are no moral facts or moral order prior to the constructive procedure, which produces moral principles. And the constructive procedure is determined by the concept of the moral person. Hence Rawls regards the concept of the moral person as an Archimedean point for his theory of justice (*TJ* 584).

Which is prior, moral principles or the concept of moral persons? This is the question that is supposed to divide rational intuitionism and Kantian constructivism. But this divide becomes meaningful only on the supposition that the concept of moral persons is quite different from moral principles. I have already questioned this supposition by noting that the concept of moral persons is another way of stating moral ideals. The concept of moral persons as being free and equal is none other than the Kantian ideals of liberty and equality, which can be stated as two general principles of liberty and equality. The moral conception of persons and moral principles are interchangeable. In that case, how should we understand the methodological advantage Rawls's Kantian constructivism supposedly has over rational intuitionism?

Let us take a close look at the alleged advantage of Kantian constructivism. Since rational intuitionism recognizes the objective truth of moral principles and the objective existence of a moral order, Rawls says, it gets entangled in the metaphysical question of moral truth. The difficulties of this metaphysical question are manifold. First, there is the semantic problem of accounting for the meaning of moral concepts. Naturalists try to explain their meaning in terms of nonmoral concepts. But rational intuitionists want to avoid such a reductive account. They can do so only by postulating supersensible entities. This is the ontological problem, which leads to the epistemological problem. Rawls says that the recognition of these entities requires a special mental telescope (*KC* 558). All these maneuvers are the familiar features of Platonism. Kantian constructivism can dispense with these dubious semantic and epistemic claims of Platonism.

The methodological advantage of Kantian constructivism is to deliver the principles of justice without getting bogged down in metaphysical problems. Kantian constructivism can do it, according to Rawls, because it constructs the principles instead of discovering them in an independent moral order. But the construction cannot begin without presupposing the conception of moral persons as being free and equal, which are none other than the Kantian ideals of liberty and equality. And those ideals are in their own right moral principles, which raise the metaphysical question of their truths.

Rawls can evade the metaphysical question only by taking the antimetaphysical and antirealistic position, that is, the concept of moral persons is not a metaphysical entity but only a product of our culture, or rather the Kantian ideals of liberty and equality have no significance outside our tradition of liberal democracy. In that case, the original position and the two principles of justice can make normative claims only for those who happen to share the same Kantian ideals. There is no reason to say that the conception of justice as fairness is objectively better than any other conception. This is the consequence of Kantian conventionalism; Rawls's entire program becomes enchained to cultural relativism.

Rawlsian cultural relativism leads to some serious methodological problems. He said that different contract situations represent different moral points of view. When he says that the original position is better than any other, what point of view does he take? From what perspective does he compare the perspective of the original position with that of an impartial observer? These are the questions of comparative justification we have set aside for some time. Cultural and moral relativism have important implications for these questions.

If each culture has its own moral point of view, different contract situations may represent the normative ideals of different cultures. The Kantian and the utilitarian ideals may belong to two incommensurate cultures; they can be represented by two different contract situations, the original position and the impartial observer. In that case, there can be no comparative justification. It is impossible to compare and rank different contract situations because there is no common ground for comparing them.

When Rawls argues for the superiority of the original position to the impartial spectator on the ground that the latter offends our sense of justice by eliminating the distinction of persons, he must be speaking either from his Kantian perspective or from a neutral perspective. If he takes the Kantian perspective, the utilitarians can only return his compliment. They can say that the Kantian perspective is faulty because it offends their sense of justice. If he takes a neutral perspective, he cannot say that one contract situation is better than another. From a morally neutral perspective, contract situations are neither good nor bad. None can be better or worse than another.

In his devastating critique of utilitarianism, I am sure, Rawls does not sound like a cultural or moral relativist. When he says that utilitarianism offends our basic sense of justice by disregarding the separateness of individuals, he does not seem to be saying that the offense is limited to our public culture. He appears to believe that the offense is against the Kantian idea of moral persons, which transcends all cultural boundaries. In that case, he is taking not a provincial, but a transcendental perspective.

We can readily understand Rawls's reluctance to embrace moral realism. Some versions of moral realism talk about moral facts and properties, as if they were as solid and secure as physical facts and properties. Surely, moral facts and moral ideals are not on a par with physical facts and physical properties. So Rawls wants to regard moral facts and moral ideals as social or cultural entities. That amounts to a surrender to normative positivism: moral norms and ideals are no more than social or cultural facts. Normative positivism inevitably leads to moral and cultural relativism. Kant took the transcendental perspective chiefly to avoid the evils of normative positivism and moral relativism. In that regard, Rawls's Kantian conventionalism goes against the spirit of Kant's own philosophy.

CHAPTER THREE

Reflective Equilibrium

The justification of principles begins in the original position but ends in reflective equilibrium. This last stage in the justification procedure, however, is a big mystery in Rawls's theory of justice. It never becomes a formal topic of extended discussion. *A Theory of Justice* contains only two short passages that mention the role of reflective equilibrium (*TJ* 20–21, 48–51). Not one of the titles of the nine chapters and eighty-seven sections of this book refers to reflective equilibrium. And Rawls did not pay any more attention to the topic in his papers that have followed his great book. Here lies the mystery of reflective equilibrium; he appears to be reluctant to share its secret with his readers.

The only exception to this baffling tendency appears to be his earliest paper, "Outline of a Decision Procedure for Ethics." [1] But this article is not really an exception; it predates his theory of justice as fairness. And the aim of this paper was not to present a theory of reflective equilibrium. It was addressed to the following question: Is there any reasonable and reliable decision procedure for settling moral and political issues? In his attempt to answer this question, he proposed the idea of constructing moral principles that can match our considered judgments. The idea of reflective equilibrium can be traced back to this matching relation.

The matching relation between moral principles and considered judgments is quite different from the sort of reflective equilibrium required for his theory of justice as fairness. Rawls has recognized two types of reflective equilibrium: narrow and wide. [2] Reflective equilibrium between moral principles and considered judgments is called narrow when the principles are directly generated from considered judgments. It is called wide reflective equilibrium when

---

1. "Outline of a Decision Procedure for Ethics," *The Philosophical Review* 60 (1951): 177–97. It will be referred to as *ODP*.
2. Rawls, "The Independence of Moral Theory," *Proceedings and Addresses of the American Philosophical Association* 48 (November 1975): 5–22. For a good discussion of the two types of reflective equilibrium, see Norman Daniels, "Wide Reflective Equilibrium and Theory Acceptance in Ethics," *The Journal of Philosophy* 76 (1979): 256–82.

the principles are generated not from considered judgments, but from some other source, such as the original position. The two principles of justice are supposed to be matched with considered judgments in a wide reflective equilibrium. Since Rawls has never given an adequate exposition of the nature and function of wide reflective equilibrium, I want to get some help from his theory of narrow reflective equilibrium.

Narrow Reflective Equilibrium

In "Outline of a Decision Procedure for Ethics," Rawls constructs a reasonable moral decision procedure in an analogy to the scientific method. He believes that the objectivity of scientific propositions is established by the rules and procedures of inductive logic. By "inductive method" he means the two-stage process of assembling observational data and formulating a theory that can explain them.[3] Modeling his proposals on this method, he posits the following two-stage procedure for ethics. In the first stage, he defines a class of competent moral judges and a class of their considered moral judgments. Given these definitions, we can collect the considered judgments of competent moral judges and then find a set of moral principles that can explicate these considered judgments. This is the second stage.

There are complications in executing these two stages. First, there is the problem of defining competent moral judges. Second, it is equally difficult to define their considered judgments. They can be characterized as those judgments that are not distorted by such irrelevant considerations as self-interest, partiality, or emotional disturbances and that are shared by the class of competent judges. They constitute a body of consensus among competent judges, and Rawls uses them as the basis for formulating justifiable moral principles.

Rawls defines justifiable principles as reasonable ones and gives four criteria for determining their reasonableness (*ODP* 187–88). First, moral principles are reasonable if they can explicate the considered judgments of competent moral judges. Second, a principle is reasonable if it can be accepted by competent moral judges after critical and open discussion. Third, a principle is reasonable if it can resolve a controversial issue like punishment to the satisfaction of all competent judges. Fourth, a principle is reasonable if it has the power to repudiate a subclass of considered judgments. This may be evidenced "by our intuitive conviction that the considered judgments are incorrect rather than the principle" (*ODP* 188).

3. To call this method an inductive one is misleading. The inductive method is to formulate a general proposition ("All swans are white") from particular propositions ("Some swans are white"). Rawls's idea of scientific method is what Charles Peirce called the method of abduction, the method of formulating a hypothesis for explaining observable phenomena.

Of these four criteria, the second one is quite different from the rest. It is directly concerned with the question of acceptability: whether a principle is acceptable to competent judges. This criterion does not give reasons for the acceptance of a principle, as the other three do. The other three criteria are three reasons for accepting a principle. It is possible that a moral principle is acceptable to competent judges for one of these reasons. In that case, the second criterion is redundant. It is also possible that a moral principle is acceptable for reasons other than those three. In that case, those reasons should be spelled out to complete the list of criteria.

Of the three reason-giving criteria, it is the first and the last that establish reflective equilibrium between moral principles and considered judgments. The first criterion requires that considered judgments be explicated by principles. Rawls does not expect that moral principles can explicate all considered judgments. He says that some of them may "contain deviations, or confusions, which are best discovered by comparing considered judgments with principles" (*ODP* 189). The fourth criterion requires that deviant or confused judgments be exposed and rejected. When these two criteria are fulfilled, moral principles will be in reflective equilibrium with considered judgments.

The second criterion cannot participate in this process of establishing reflective equilibrium. It demands that moral principles be used for resolving controversial issues. Judgments on controversial issues are not even considered in the formulation of moral principles. Their formulation is based solely on shared considered judgments. Since considered judgments are judgments of consensus by definition, judgments on controversial issues cannot qualify as considered judgments. Hence they are excluded from the second stage of Rawls's decision procedure, namely, the formulation of principles and their fit with considered judgments.

The second criterion becomes important for the third stage of Rawls's decision procedure. This is the stage he does not mention. His decision procedure cannot end with the second stage of formulating moral principles because its ultimate end is to find a method of settling moral and political disputes. This ultimate end cannot be fulfilled even in a reflective equilibrium between moral principles and considered judgments. Such an equilibrium is restricted to the domain of shared stable judgments that are far removed from controversial issues. Rawls has yet to show how moral principles can be used for resolving controversial issues. This is the third and final stage of his projected decision procedure, and a counterpart to it does not exist in the scientific procedure. As Rawls says, the scientific procedure consists of two stages.

The third stage of Rawls's decision procedure can be achieved by finding a moral principle that meets the requirement of the second criterion. It is a much stronger criterion of reasonableness than the first one. If moral principles are formulated on the basis of shared considered judgments, the former are expected to explicate the latter. But what reason do we have to expect those principles to settle controversial moral issues? Let us consider Rawls's example of a controversial case, punishment. The dispute on this issue is generated by conflicting rationales for punishment. These conflicting rationales and the judgments based on them cannot be included in the set of considered judgments to be used as the basis for the formulation of moral principles. If those conflicting rationales are not taken into account in the formulation of moral principles, it is highly unlikely that those principles will have any relevance to a resolution of their conflict. Rawls has not given a theoretical account of why the second criterion of reasonableness should be applicable to moral principles.

After specifying these criteria of reasonableness, Rawls proposes seven principles of justice that can meet them. Except for the first one, each of these principles consists of two or more propositions. All of them are formal principles. They lay down formal requirements for settling conflicting claims, for example, "Each claim in a set of conflicting claims shall be evaluated by the same principles"; "No claim shall be denied possible satisfaction without a reason"; "Claims shall be ordered according to their strength"; "Given a set of equal claims, as determined by their strength, all shall be satisfied equally, if that is possible" (*ODP* 192–93).

These formal principles of justice are offered "as an explication of the considered judgments of competent judges" (*ODP* 104). This is rather surprising and disappointing, for one has expected to see the formulation of substantive rather than formal principles on the basis of considered judgments. The concept of explication is substantive rather than formal. The natural phenomena of thunder and lightning can be explicated by the scientific laws of electricity, but not by the formal procedures governing scientific observation and inference. Likewise, considered judgments on the questions of justice can be explicated not by any formal principles of justice, but by some substantive principles. In fact, there is no need to take the detour of considered judgments to find formal principles because we can recognize them as necessary conditions for all sound moral judgments. Hence they should be regarded as formal conditions required for all considered judgments rather than as principles for their explication.

The formal principles of justice are even more disappointing in the third stage of Rawls's decision procedure. They are useless for settling controversial issues because the controversy over these issues arises mostly from their substantive content rather than their formal framework. By the time Rawls writes "Justice as Fairness,"[4] he appears to have recognized the futility of marshaling formal principles to settle substantive issues. Since then he has never repeated the

4. *The Philosophical Review* 67 (1958): 164–94.

Kantian mistake of overestimating the power of formal conditions. He says, "The formal conditions are, I think, best viewed as simply very general properties that it seems natural to impose on moral conceptions for various reasons." [5] Even in giving a Kantian account of his principles, he begins by downgrading Kant's formalism (*TJ* 251):

> It is a mistake, I believe, to emphasize the place of generality and universality in Kant's ethics. That moral principles are general and universal is hardly new with him; and as we have seen these conditions do not take us very far. It is impossible to construct a moral theory on so slender a basis, and therefore to limit the discussion of Kant's doctrine to these notions is to reduce it to triviality. The real force of his view lies elsewhere.

Indeed, the formal concepts of generality and universality are not new with Kant. What is new is the claim that his formalism can take us not only very far, but all the way to the promised land, the kingdom of morals. This glorious Kantian journey, however, is feasible only if Kant succeeds in his program of transforming formal ideas into material principles. But Rawls does not believe in the Kantian program of transformation; he says it does not "take us very far." Although he never adopts Kant's program of transformation, his program of pure procedural justice is an adaptation of it. Whereas Kant's formal principle is free of substantive content, Rawls's formal procedure is guided by the substantive ideals of liberty and equality. Rawls's program is not Kantian in the traditional sense; it is Kantian because it stands on the Kantian ideals of liberty and equality. His program is Kantian on the substantive level.

The difference between Kant's formalism and Rawls's proceduralism has been the chief source of many Kant scholars' complaint that Rawls's Kantian constructivism is not truly Kantian.[6] Their view is obviously correct if Kantianism is understood as a purely formal program. Rawls's constructivism has too many substantive ideas to meet the stringent requirements of Kant's formal program. Furthermore, as we shall see later, Kant's execution of his program falls far short of its own formal requirements. In fact, his formal requirements are impossible to fulfill. There is no point in demanding the impossible. The standard Kantian complaint makes sense only for those pious Kantians who still believe in the Kantian project of transforming formal into material principles.

Wide Reflective Equilibrium

In "Justice as Fairness," Rawls decides to seek a substantive decision procedure and proposes two substantive principles of justice: their elaboration is to

5. Rawls, "The Independence of Moral Theory," 10.
6. For example, Oliver A. Johnson, "The Kantian Interpretation," *Ethics* 85 (1974): 58–66; Andrew Levine, "Rawls' Kantianism," *Social Theory and Practice* 3 (1974): 47–64.

occupy the rest of his career. In taking this substantive step, he seems to leave behind the considered judgments of competent judges; he neither claims to use them in formulating the two principles of justice nor appeals to them for the justification of the two principles. Instead he tries to justify the two principles by reviving and revamping contractarian arguments, and these culminate in his theory of the original position.

The original position breaks the direct link between considered judgments and moral principles that obtains in the inductive model. The principles of justice are not directly derived from considered judgments, but adopted in the original position. The elimination of the direct link between them makes room for a wide reflective equilibrium. Moreover, considered judgments are defined differently; their definition requires no reference to competent moral judges. And they are not restricted to particular intuitive judgments. Rawls equates considered judgments with well-established moral intuitions and convictions on all levels. This equation considerably extends the meaning of the term *considered judgment*. He writes, "People have considered judgments at all levels of generality, from those about particular situations and institutions up through broad standards and first principles to formal and abstract conditions on moral conceptions." [7]

How should one characterize the relation of considered judgments and moral principles in wide reflective equilibrium? This has been a thorny question for Rawls's readers, not only because his explanation is too sketchy, but because it is open to different interpretations. Norman Daniels has stressed the independence constraint, [8] which requires that the constitution of the original position and the adoption of principles be independent of considered judgments. According to this requirement, considered judgments make their appearance not before, but only after the adoption of principles in the original position.

The independence constraint appears to be impossible to fulfill. As I have remarked in the last two chapters, the constitution of the original position is determined by moral presumptions and considerations, which are considered judgments. Rawls's definition of considered judgments has changed. It used to be restricted to particular intuitive judgments, which need not affect the adoption of principles in the original position. But this restriction has been relaxed in *A Theory of Justice*, and we should take considered judgments in their broad sense, which includes even the Kantian ideals of liberty and equality. In that case, the constitution of the original position and the adoption of principles can never be independent of considered judgments.

There may be no difference between narrow and wide reflective equilibria,

7. Rawls, "The Independence of Moral Theory," 8.
8. Daniels, "Reflective Equilibrium and Archimedean Points," *Canadian Journal of Philosophy* 10 (1980): 90.

insofar as considered judgments are required from beginning to end. But we can make the distinction between considered judgments that come into reflective equilibrium after the adoption of principles and considered judgments used in the constitution of the original position. If these two groups of considered judgments are the same, the equilibrium between the principles of justice and considered judgments will be circular. Such circularity, which is permitted in a narrow reflective equilibrium, can be avoided by keeping apart the two groups of considered judgments. This is most likely what is required by the independence constraint.

How should one understand the nature of equilibrium between principles and considered judgments? To answer this question, I want to consider Ronald Dworkin's distinction between a natural and a constructive model.[9] The natural model is the model of natural science. In a natural model, moral principles represent an objective moral reality, just as physical laws represent an objective physical reality. Moral principles are discovered by a moral faculty, and moral intuitions are clues to their discovery, just as physical observations are clues to the discovery of physical laws.

The constructive model treats moral intuitions not as clues to the existence of independent principles, but as stipulated features of a general theory to be constructed. This model does not assume the independent existence of moral principles. The constructive model is analogous to one model of common law adjudication. A judge tries to construct a common principle that can cover divergent rulings in related precedents. The precedents and their rulings correspond to moral intuitions or considered judgments, and the common principle to moral principles.

Now suppose that the judge cannot reconcile conflicting rulings in precedents with a set of principles. The two models give him different advice, Dworkin says. If the judge follows the natural model, he will uphold his intuitions and submerge the apparent contradiction between divergent rulings. He may at best hope to discover a better set of principles that can reconcile the conflicting intuitions. He is in the position of an astronomer who has clear observational data but has not been able to find physical laws that explain those data. His observations have outstripped his power of explanation.

The constructive model does not allow the judge to uphold the conflicting intuitions. "On the contrary," Dworkin says, "it demands that decisions taken in the name of justice must never outstrip an official's ability to account for these decisions in a theory of justice, even when such a theory of justice must compromise some of his intuitions."[10] Since the judge must account for his decisions by means of principles, he must always act on principles. In case of

9. Dworkin, *Taking Rights Seriously* (Cambridge, Mass., 1977), 159–68.
10. Ibid., 162.

conflict between intuitions and principles, he should maintain his consistency by sacrificing intuitions for the sake of principles.

The two models appear to be dedicated to two different types of integrity. The natural model advocates the integrity of intuitions; the constructive model, the integrity of principles. When principles and intuitions misfit, the two models require two different methods of adjustment. One recommends the sacrifice of intuitions for the sake of principles, and the other recommends the opposite. But neither of these two procedures agrees with what Rawls recommends for reaching reflective equilibrium. Both of them are one-way procedures, whereas Rawls recommends a two-way procedure of mutual adjustment between principles and considered judgments.

In reflective equilibrium, the principles generated from the original positions are tested by being matched against considered judgments. An unsatisfactory match can be improved either by altering the constitutive conditions of the original position or by revising considered judgments. By going back and forth between the two methods, Rawls says, one can find a description of the original position that yields principles that match our considered judgments duly pruned and adjusted. He says, "This state of affairs I refer to as reflective equilibrium" (*TJ* 20).

This account of mutual adjustments seems to jeopardize the independence constraint, which requires that the constitution of the original position and the adoption of principles be independent of considered judgments. Rawls cannot fulfill this requirement if he really alters the conditions of the original position for the purpose of producing principles that fit better with considered judgments. He sometimes talks as though the expected fit between principles and considered judgments really controlled his construction of the original position: "We want to define the original position so that we get the desired solution" (*TJ* 141). This and similar remarks have provoked R. M. Hare's charge that Rawls has rigged his social contract.[11]

Has Rawls rigged the social contract in the constitution of the original position? The question is hard to answer. After proposing the method of mutual adjustment between the conditions of the original position and considered judgments, he writes, "I shall not, of course, actually work through this process. Still, we may think of the interpretation of the original position that I shall present as the result of such a hypothetical course of reflection" (*TJ* 21). This is a highly ambiguous statement. The first sentence says that he is not going to use the method of mutual adjustment at all; but the second sentence states that his interpretation of the original position is the result of "such a hypothetical course of reflection." The hypothetical course of reflection may be none

---

11. Hare, "Rawls' Theory of Justice," *Philosophical Quarterly* 23 (1973): 144–55, 241–51; reprinted in Norman Daniels, ed., *Reading Rawls* (New York, 1975): 81–107.

other than the thought-experiment of mutual adjustment between the original position and considered judgments.

In chapter 2, I entertained the possibility that Rawls constructed the original position by improving upon the theory of an impartial observer. It is likely that he began with a contract situation that installed an impartial observer behind a thin veil of ignorance. Then he saw that such a contract situation justifies the principle of utility and that the utilitarian conception of justice does not fit our considered judgments. The principle of utility condones even slavery if it can produce greater utility than nonslavery. This goes against our considered judgment that slavery is wrong under any circumstances. Since the fault of utilitarianism can be traced back to the thin veil of ignorance, which disregards the separateness of individuals, he may have decided to replace the thin veil with a thick one. This may be the hypothetical course of reflection that he relied on in constructing the original position.

Is there any way to defend such a hypothetical course of reflection against Hare's charge? To defend Rawls, I have to consider two ways of interpreting the independence constraint. This constraint can be taken in a stringent way: the conditions of the original position should never be altered by the pressure of considered judgments. This stringent interpretation cannot allow the method of mutual adjustment. But the independence constraint can also be taken in a moderate way: the independence of the original position is limited to the initial and basic considerations for its constitution. After the initial constitution of the original position, the moderate interpretation of the independence constraint can allow it to be altered insofar as the alteration is compatible with the initial and basic ideas for its initial constitution.

What are the initial and basic considerations for the constitution of the original position? They are the conception of moral persons as being free and equal and the conception of a well-ordered society. These considerations lead to the initial interpretation of the original position. It may be necessary to alter this initial interpretation if the principles generated from it do not match some of our considered judgments. But its alteration need not run afoul of the independence constraint, as long as it can be made without rejecting the initial and basic considerations for the constitution of the original position. Such an alteration is possible chiefly because the general ideas governing the constraints on the original position are indeterminate. There is more than one way of translating them into the procedural constraints to be placed on the original position.

The Ground of Equilibrium

The theory of mutual adjustment raises a difficult metaphysical problem. The two-way process of mutual adjustment presupposes the mutual independence of general principles and considered judgments from each other. For illustration, let us go back to Dworkin's two models. In the case of a misfit between principles and observations, the natural model dictates that principles be sacrificed for the integrity of observations. In the natural model, principles are dependent on observations; there is no independent source for their derivation. On the other hand, the constructive model can dictate the sacrifice of particular rulings for the sake of principles because principles have a measure of independence. They are not always derived from particular rulings.

Each of Dworkin's two models dictates a one-way adjustment because each of them consists of one independent and one dependent element. The two-way process of mutual adjustment appears to presuppose that general principles and considered judgments are mutually independent and dependent on each other at the same time. If they are independent, they should come from different sources. If they are dependent, they should come from the same source. These two views may be called the single source thesis and the double source thesis. Dworkin's two models each accept a single source thesis.

The distinction between the single and the double source thesis is important for understanding the nature of reflective equilibrium. If the principles and considered judgments come from two independent sources, there appears to be no reason for them to be in reflective equilibrium. If they do fit with each other, they will do so only by accident. Their being in equilibrium can be only accidental and never essential if they come from two different sources. It becomes artificial if it has to be achieved by revising principles or altering intuitions. What is the point of having an accidental or artificial fit between particular intuitions and general principles?

This point can be further illustrated by the scientific model. We expect a fit between our observations and scientific laws because both of them are meant to describe the same physical reality and because they come from the same source. Scientific observations are derived from physical reality, and scientific laws are based on scientific observations. Scientific laws are linked to physical reality via scientific observations. Because they come from the same source, their fit is not accidental, but essential.[12] This is true of rational intuitionism. Moral principles must fit the intuitions of commonsense morality, a rational intuitionist would say, because they represent the same moral order. The only difference between them lies in their different levels of representation. This way of accounting for the fit may be called the common source thesis.

Rawls cannot accept the common source thesis because it is incompatible

12. The difference between the accidental and the essential fit can be illustrated by the relation of Kepler's planetary orbits and Brahe's observational data. Imagine that Kepler had constructed the planetary orbits without using the observational data. Then the fit of the orbits to the data would have been accidental. Their fit is not accidental if the orbits are constructed on the basis of observational data.

with the two-way process of mutual adjustment. Neither can he accept a double source thesis because it does not allow him to account for the fit of general principles and considered judgments except by accident. These considerations lead to a serious dilemma in his theory of reflective equilibrium. He really needs both a single and a double source thesis.

Rawls sometimes advocates a single source thesis. On this thesis, the original position is the only ultimate source of all moral assertions, ranging from the principles of justice to particular considered judgments. The latter may appear to be independent of the original position only because they are subconscious or unconscious products of the principles of justice. Because the original position is the common source of principles and particular considered judgments their fit is not accidental but essential.

In this interpretation of reflective equilibrium, the original position plays the role of Kant's categorical imperative. Although the commonsense moral rules and intuitions appear to be independent of any general principles, Kant maintains, their genesis can be accounted for by the categorical imperative because they coincide with dictates of the categorical imperative. For that reason, he holds, the analysis of popular moral consciousness is the right basis for the recognition of the categorical imperative.[13] Prior to the prescriptions of the categorical imperative, our moral sense is a tabula rasa. This is the premise of Kant's constructivism: the categorical imperative generates all moral rules and maxims out of nothing.

Rawls often expresses this view of a Kantian tabula rasa. Apart from the procedure of constructing the principles of justice, he repeatedly says, there are no moral facts (*KC* 519, 568). "On a contract doctrine the moral facts are determined by the principles which would be chosen in the original position" (*TJ* 45). He also writes, "The concept of something's being right is the same as, or better, may be replaced by, the concept of its being in accordance with the principles that in the original position would be acknowledged to apply to things of its kind" (*TJ* 111). To be sure, he says, he is not giving an analysis of the meaning of the term *right* or of the concept of right in the traditional sense. He is giving a satisfactory substitute for the ordinary concept of right, just as set theory provides a satisfactory substitute for the ordinary concepts of arithmetic. In support of this procedure of substitution, he quotes W. V. Quine's adage "Explication is elimination" (*TJ* 111).

Rawls's analogy of his theory to set theory is important for understanding the

13. The relation of commonsense morality and the categorical imperative is the main theme of Kant's *Groundwork of the Metaphysics of Morals*. This theme is highlighted even in the titles of the first two sections: "Transition from the Common Rational Knowledge of Morals to the Philosophical" and "Transition from the Popular Moral Philosophy to the Metaphysics of Morals."

relation of his principles of justice to commonsense moral ideas. If all arithmetic concepts can be defined in terms of set theory, we can assume that arithmetic has no existence independent from set theory. If all our commonsense moral concepts can be restated in terms of the two principles of justice, we can assume that our commonsense morality is derived from the two principles. In this sense, Rawls maintains, the two principles are the ultimate principles not only for our commonsense concepts of right and wrong, but also for our moral sense or the sense of justice (*TJ* 46):

> One may regard a theory of justice as describing our sense of justice. This enterprise is very difficult. For by such a description is not meant simply a list of the judgments on institutions and actions that we are prepared to render, accompanied with supporting reasons when these are offered. Rather, what is required is a formulation of a set of principles which, when conjoined to our beliefs and knowledge of the circumstances, would lead us to make these judgments with their supporting reasons were we to apply these principles conscientiously and intelligently. A conception of justice characterizes our moral sensibility when the everyday judgments we do make are in accordance with its principles.

The last sentence of this passage stresses the unity of principles and considered judgments in a conception of justice. Sometimes Rawls asserts their identity. He holds that "justice as fairness is the hypothesis that the principles which would be chosen in the original position are identical with those that match our considered judgments and so these principles describe our sense of justice" (*TJ* 48). If they are identical, how can he explain even the possibility of their conflict? The following appears to be his explanation (*TJ* 48): "In describing our sense of justice an allowance must be made for the likelihood that considered judgments are no doubt subject to certain irregularities and distortions despite the fact that they are rendered under favorable circumstances."

Considered judgments can be faulty because they are subject to irregularities and distortions. How can we detect and recognize those irregularities and distortions? We can detect irregular and distorted considered judgments if we can appeal to regular and undistorted ones. But Rawls has not offered a theory of regular and undistorted considered judgments. On his theory, it is possible to detect the irregularities and distortions of considered judgments by appealing to one's sense of justice. But the sense of justice is constituted by the principles of justice. Rawls runs these ideas together in the following remark (*TJ* 48): "When a person is presented with an intuitively appealing account of his sense of justice, he may well revise his judgments to conform to its principles even though the theory does not fit his existing judgments exactly."

In the case of a discrepancy between the principles and the considered judgments, Rawls is giving primacy to the principles if the principles are intuitively appealing. When Rawls advocates this view of reflective equilibrium, he compares his enterprise to logic, mathematics, and linguistics (*TJ* 47–52). At the same time, he stresses its difference from physics. He appears to presuppose Charles Peirce's distinction between normative and positive sciences.[14] Positive science is the science of fact; it includes all natural and social sciences. Since the world of fact is the object of positive science, the observation of fact is its ultimate basis. This is why positive science cannot ignore or alter the observed facts to make a better fit with its theories. Theories have to be faithful to facts. This picture of positive science fits Dworkin's idea of a natural model.

Normative science is the science of norms and standards; it includes logic, mathematics, ethics, and aesthetics. It can neither begin with facts nor end with them. The science of logic cannot formulate its principles by observing how people think. If we want to formulate the laws of logic by induction from people's actual thought processes, we have to begin by discriminating sound from faulty processes. The laws of logic cannot inductively be derived from faulty processes. But the discrimination of sound from faulty processes is a normative decision; it requires the use of norms for sound thought process. This sort of normative decision is not required for the observations of positive science.[15] Since the norms of normative science cannot be inductively derived from facts, normative science must begin with its norms and then construct its principles. Norms and principles have their own integrity and independence from the world of facts. This picture of normative science fits Dworkin's idea of a constructive model.

Two Dimensions of Normative Science

The important difference between the natural and the constructive models lies in the relation between general principles and particular rulings, universals and particulars. In the natural model, there is no other way of constructing general principles except by induction from particular rulings. In the constructive model, Dworkin implies, a judge has a way of constructing a general principle that even goes against some particular rulings. Although he never explains how this can be done, he assumes that the formulation of general principles need not depend on particular rulings. I shall call this the independence requirement of general principles.

I propose that the independence requirement is a unique feature of normative sciences that cannot be found in empirical sciences. In empirical sciences,

14. This distinction is discussed by Peirce in *Collected Papers of Charles Sanders Peirce*, ed. Charles Hartshorne and Paul Weiss (Cambridge, Mass., 1960), 1:573–84, 5:120–50.
15. There are normative requirements for the method of observation that are quite different from the normative requirements for the content of observations.

the independence requirement cannot be admitted; the formulation of general principles must be faithful to observed facts. The natural model does not permit the independence requirement. In normative sciences, however, we do not formulate general principles only by induction from observed facts. We do not always develop general normative ideas by abstracting from particular ones. In the normative world, the independence requirement means that general ideas are independent of particular ones.

The independence of generality from particularity makes possible the constructive model for normative discourse. On the other hand, the dependence of generality on particularity dictates the natural model for empirical sciences. The difference between the two models stems from the different relations between universals and particulars, and between higher and lower universals. To illustrate, let me compare the normative science of mathematics and the empirical science of physics. In physics, for example, the concept of force is formulated by induction from particular phenomena of forces. In mathematics, the concept of equality is not produced by induction. It is independent of particular objects, which may exemplify the relation of equality.

In the normative world, we can have an independent access to general ideas because those ideas are independent of particular ideas or judgments. The independent access makes possible what Norman Daniels calls the independence constraint. The independence requirement is one of the important improvements Rawls makes for normative discourse. In his younger days, he tried to understand the relation of universals and particulars in the normative world by uncritically accepting the model of the empirical sciences. By recognizing our independent access to general ideas in the normative world, he has rejected the natural model and adopted the constructive model.

The constructive model is not limited to Kantian constructivism. It is even better suited to rational intuitionism and Platonism, which regard normative universals as more real than normative particulars. If universals are more real than particulars, they are also more accessible. The reality of universals ensures the independence requirement. Kantian constructivism also ensures the independence requirement. But it does so by virtue of the fact that its highest ideals—the concept of moral persons, for example—are independent of any particular considered judgments.

Though the constructive model of normative science may explain the independence constraint, it does not explain the two-way process of mutual adjustment in reflective equilibrium. We have already seen that the constructive model recommends the one-way adjustment from universals to particulars. We may be able to explain the two-way adjustment by taking note of the fact that norms or normative standards are composed of two dimensions, positivity and ideality.

Every normative science has two dimensions, theoretical and practical. Let us consider natural numbers, which can be generated from the basic ideas of set theory. There are different ways of organizing natural numbers: by a binary, ternary, octal, decimal, hexadecimal, or sexagesimal system. These different systems of natural numbers belong to the practical dimension of arithmetic. Their difference is important for practical purposes. It is easier to use the binary system for computers than the decimal system. The latter is more useful for human beings, who count with ten fingers. The numerals that express natural numbers also belong to the practical dimension of arithmetic. The difference between Roman and Arabic numerals has practical significance. These practical features do not belong to Platonic Heaven, which contains only the basic concepts of set theory. These basic concepts and the generation of natural numbers belong to the theoretical dimension of arithmetic as a normative science, while its practical features constitute its practical dimension.

Even such an austerely abstract normative science as set theory can have a practical dimension. Peter Aczel has recently proposed a theory of circular sets primarily for practical considerations. In the standard theory, the hierarchy of sets is constructed from the bottom to the top. This linear construction follows the axiom of foundation, which prohibits the definition of sets in reference to themselves. But circular sets loop back to themselves; their definition is circular. A system of circular sets has no foundation in the normal sense; it violates the axiom of foundation. But Aczel says that his theory of circular sets has been designed to meet the practical needs of computer science and situation semantics. In these practical sciences, the definition of some basic terms cannot avoid circularity.[16]

The two dimensions of normative science reflect the two levels of norms or normative standards. Let us consider linguistic norms. They can be divided into empirical (or positive) norms and transcendent (or ideal) norms. The system of vowels and consonants of a given language belongs to the empirical or positive norms. The permissible ways of combining them into words also belong to empirical or positive norms, as does the word order of a sentence, clause, or phrase. All these positive or empirical norms serve the practical purpose of linguistic expression and communication. But they all presuppose the ideal or transcendent norms of all languages, namely, rules and principles of logic.

Positive norms vary from one natural language to another; transcendent norms are invariant for all natural languages. Positive norms can be discovered by the empirical investigation of linguistic usages and conventions. But transcendent norms are the objects of normative investigations. Empirical linguistics can be defined as the study of positive norms in a natural language, and normative linguistics as the study of the transcendent norms of all possible languages. Normative linguistics belongs to what I called the theoretical dimension of normative science; empirical linguistics belongs to the practical dimension. To

16. Aczel, *Non-Well-Founded Sets* (Stanford, 1988).

be sure, empirical linguistics has its own theories, but they are descriptive or practical theories.

The relation between these two levels of norms can be understood as that of articulation or realization. The positive norms of English realize or articulate the transcendent norms in a certain cultural or social context. To articulate a transcendent norm is to give it a particular concrete shape in a particular context; it always introduces the empirical and historical dimension of language. Words and sentences have to be given physical shapes. As long as transcendent norms remain in Platonic Heaven, they are totally free of empirical and historical elements. As soon as they are brought down to the practical world, they have to be mixed with empirical elements. The practical world is always empirical, and positive norms can be realized only in the empirical world.

The normative science of ethics or political philosophy also has these two theoretical and practical dimensions. Every society has its own positive ethical norms, just as every language has its own positive linguistic norms. The relations of articulation and realization also obtain between the positive and the ideal norms of ethics. The positive ethical norms of every society articulate and realize the ideal norms. Rawls's project can be taken as an enterprise of articulation and realization. As I indicated in the last chapter, Rawls's program is a procedure of derivation; it is to derive the principles of justice from the most general ideals. The procedure of derivation is the procedure of specification, articulation, and realization.[17]

The project of articulation and realization is always context-relative. The social ideals of liberty and equality can and should be articulated differently for different social contexts. The project of articulation and realization should also be faithful to the ideals themselves. Hence there are two different pressures and demands placed on the project of articulation and realization. One of them comes from the need to be sensitive to the empirical dimension of the normative world, and the other comes from the need to be faithful to the transcendent ideals. This is the dual pressure of normative discourse, which dictates the thesis of dual consideration.

The idea of dual consideration applies to all normative judgments, whether they are matters of general principles or particular programs. For any particular

17. The procedure of specification, articulation, and realization underlies Rawls's distinction between "concept" and "conception." The concept of justice is a general idea that can be articulated and realized in different conceptions of justice. Conceptions of justice take into account the empirical and historical circumstances of a society, while the concept of justice abstracts from those particular circumstances. The former is more specific or particular than the latter. A particular conception of justice articulates or realizes the general concept of justice in a specified context of empirical and historical contingencies. Ronald Dworkin employs the concept–conception distinction in his theory of legal interpretation. For details, see Law's Empire (Cambridge, Mass., 1986), 70–76.

judgment or practical principle, we have to see how faithfully it reflects ideal norms and how adequate it is for a particular context. This dual consideration is also important for resolving the conflict of competing judgments or principles. We can resolve the conflict by considering their fidelity to ideals and their sensitivity to facts. To resolve such a conflict is the basic procedure for ordering our moral intuitions and principles. To resolve the conflict between the principles of justice and considered judgments is a special case of this general procedure.

In this special case, we can have a division of labor. If considered judgments are particular judgments, it is easier to assess their contextual sensitivity than that of general principles because particular judgments are closer to the context of practice than principles. Conversely, it is easier to assess the fidelity of principles to transcendent ideals than that of considered judgments because the principles are closer to transcendent ideals than particular judgments. But considered judgments are not always particular judgments; they can be convictions of a highly general level. If considered judgments are more general than principles, their division of labor will be reversed. Whichever direction the division of labor may take, it can facilitate the mutual adjustment between principles and considered judgments.

The dual pressure of normative discourse can account for the two-way process of mutual adjustment in reflective equilibrium. The original position can be taken as a procedural device for protecting our fidelity to transcendent ideals. If the original position is well constructed, it can meet the pressure coming from the transcendent ideals. On the other hand, particular considered judgments are much closer to the practical dimension of our normative world. Hence, if we have confidence in those particular judgments, we can take them as our guide for meeting the pressure coming from the empirical world. Since we want not only to be faithful to our ideals, but also to be sensitive to the practical world, we have to pay equal attention to general principles and to particular judgments in adjusting them to each other.

The consideration of dual pressure in normative discourse can also account for one special type of important criticism of Rawls's theory of justice, and this can be summed up as his neglect of the empirical dimension of human existence. Michael Sandel says that the conception of moral persons in Rawls's theory is too deontological and too unencumbered, that is, it ignores all the important natural and emotional ties human beings have with each other and their allegiance to institutions and traditions.[18] This criticism is true to the extent that the parties in the original position operate behind a thick veil of ignorance that blocks out all information on their empirical selfhood.

Michael Walzer's complaint is also concerned with the empirical dimension

18. Sandel, *Liberalism and the Limits of Justice* (Cambridge, 1982).

of human existence. He maintains that we should not try to apply the same principles of justice to different spheres of justice. The question of justice involving the distribution of public offices is different from the question of justice involving the distribution of commodities. There are different spheres of justice, and each of them demands its own principles of justice.[19] Hence the most important task in a theory of justice is to make a correct demarcation of different spheres and formulate suitable principles for each sphere.

These two critics are calling attention to the importance of empirical factors in our conception of justice. Those factors are indeed shut out by Rawls's thick veil of ignorance; and their criticisms can be taken as complaints against the Kantian veil. Walzer and Sandel, who have a tendency to go to the other extreme, do not stop with these criticisms: they further maintain that empirical factors are, duly considered, sufficient for settling all questions of justice. For example, our natural and social ties to other human beings can give us adequate criteria of justice. But this is a naive view. We have to know which of our natural and social ties can make legitimate claims on the question of justice. We may be tempted to settle this question by relying on the positive norms of our society, as Walzer recommends.[20] But that is a sure way to normative positivism and relativism, which can be averted only by appealing to transcendent norms.

Two Ways of Reading Rawls

So far I have assumed the existence of transcendent norms and ideals. But Rawls feels uneasy with that assumption. By rejecting transcendental ideals, we saw in the last chapter, Rawls has advocated Kantian conventionalism. If the Kantian ideals are not in Platonic Heaven, they are only our positive norms. How should we understand the role of reflective equilibrium in this context of normative positivism? In such a context, the function of reflective equilibrium is to secure a coherence of all positive norms.

All our positive norms come from the same source, namely, our culture, regardless of their levels of generality and specificity. Some of our cultural ideals will be used to constitute the original position and others will be used for testing the principles derived from the original position. Since all of them come from the same source, their fit in a reflective equilibrium can readily be secured unless there is a serious conflict between our ideals and norms. This assurance is bought at the cost of abandoning the independence constraint. Because the original position is constituted by our cultural ideals, it cannot be independent of considered judgments that belong to the same cultural ideals. The indepen-

19. Walzer, *Spheres of Justice* (New York, 1983).
20. Walzer, *Interpretation and Social Criticism* (Cambridge, Mass., 1987).

dence constraint gains its unique significance only from the possibility that the original position can be constructed under the guidance of transcendent norms and ideals.

Without the independence constraint, Rawls has to resort to a positivistic justification of the original position. In describing the conditions for the original position, Rawls says they are appropriate because they are widely accepted views or commonly shared presumptions (*TJ* 18, 21, 587). The widely accepted views or commonly shared presumptions are none other than those ideas or intuitions embedded in our culture. Hence R. M. Hare charged that *A Theory of Justice* is based on commonsense intuitions, although those intuitions are called by many different names, for example, considered judgments or convictions. Hare writes, "Intuitionism is nearly always a form of disguised subjectivism. Rawls does not call himself an intuitionist; but he certainly is one in the usual sense." [21]

If the original position is justified on the ground that its constitution is based on widely shared ideas in our culture, Michael Sandel says, the justification is question-begging.[22] For it is an empirical or positivistic justification, which has no compelling normative force. If the theory of the original position stands on Kantian conventionalism, it can be given no other justification than an empirical one. Positivism knows no other justification, and conventionalism is a form of positivism.

Taken in the positivistic mode, Rawls's program is basically Hobbesian rather than Kantian. The Kantian project begins with ideals; the Hobbesian approach begins with agreements. When Rawls says that the conception of moral persons as being free and equal is the Archimedean point, he appears to begin with an ideal. But when he says that he begins with the ideal because it is well accepted in our culture, he is shifting his point of departure from ideals to acceptance and agreement, from the Kantian to the Hobbesian basis.

The positivistic stance does not adversely affect the efficacy of the original position as an instrument for achieving coherence in the world of positive norms. If we achieve reflective equilibrium between widely scattered considered judgments and the principles of justice, we may achieve a high degree of coherence in our moral intuitions.[23] Such a system of coherent intuitions may require what Robert Paul Wolff calls "a rational reconstruction" or "a systematization." [24] Rawls has confirmed this view of his program: it "may

---

21. Hare, "Rawls' Theory of Justice," in *Reading Rawls*, 83.
22. Sandel, *Liberalism and the Limits of Justice*, 45.
23. This is David Lyons's coherence account of reflective equilibrium in "The Nature and Soundness of the Contract and Coherence Arguments," ed. Norman Daniels, *Reading Rawls*, 141–68.
24. Wolff, *Understanding Rawls* (Princeton, 1977), 181.

only articulate familiar intuitive ideas and principles" and "may organize these familiar ideas and principles by means of a more fundamental intuitive idea within the complex structure of which the other familiar intuitive ideas are then systematically connected and related." [25]

If Rawls's program is limited to the rational systematization of our familiar ideas, it is very much like the program of the American Law Institute, which has drawn up the Model Penal Code and the Uniform Commercial Code. Just as the American Law Institute has smoothed out many wrinkles in our legal system, so Rawls's theory of justice will reorganize our commonsense intuitions of social justice. It is a program of harmonization and emendation that can never take us out of our provincial perspective. Such a perspective is always internal; we can examine our familiar ideas only by checking them against each other. We can make only internal criticisms of our intuitions. But our original intuitions may be no more than our social prejudices, however coherent they may be. In that case, their reflective equilibrium can deliver only an articulated harmony of our initial prejudices.[26]

To limit the function of pure procedural justice to the systematization of our initial intuitions appears to trivialize Rawls's grand project. There is only one way to save it from this invidious restriction, and that is to unify his two views: Kantian transcendentalism and Kantian conventionalism. To say that the Kantian ideals are embedded in our political culture does not automatically deny their transcendence. To say that the idea of natural numbers is embedded in our culture does not automatically assert that this idea is no more than our provincial cultural product. The Kantian ideas can have two modes of existence; they can be not only transcendent but also immanent in our culture. In his two different accounts of Kantian ideals, I venture to propose, Rawls is describing them in two modes of transcendence and immanence. Let us call this way of reading Rawls the dual perspective thesis.

Even the project of the American Law Institute was twofold; its aim was not limited to the articulation and systematization of existing laws. It also proposed the ideal code that goes well beyond existing laws. Its project has two dimensions: the pull of ideality (ideal norms) and the push of positivity (positive norms). The latter demands the systematization of the existing laws; the former encourages their improvement beyond their systematization. These two dimensions of a normative project also obtained in the operation of the Academie Française for the improvement of the French language.

To recognize the same two dimensions in Rawls's project is the dual perspective thesis. What sort of textual evidence can be found for this way of reading

25. Rawls, "Justice as Fairness: Political and Not Metaphysical," 229.
26. This is Richard Brandt's criticism of reflective equilibrium in *A Theory of the Good and the Right* (Oxford, 1979), 19–20.

Rawls? The answer to this question largely turns on the question of whether there is an important break between *A Theory of Justice* and Rawls's subsequent papers. Many commentators have claimed to have recognized such a break. *A Theory of Justice* supposedly advocates Kantian transcendentalism, whereas his subsequent papers espouse Kantian conventionalism. But this widespread view appears to be a hasty, careless conclusion based on incomplete textual evidence. In all his writings, on the contrary, Rawls appears to express both Kantian transcendentalism and Kantian conventionalism.

In *A Theory of Justice* one can find many passages that appear to express Kantian conventionalism. When Rawls describes the conditions for the original position, he says that they are appropriate because they are widely accepted views or commonly shared presumptions (*TJ* 18, 21, 587). On the basis of this statement, as I just observed, Hare and Sandel leveled the charge of subjectivism and positivism against Rawls. Their charges, however, are valid only on the condition that those expressions state Rawls's whole view. But nobody ever questions that the same book espouses Kantian transcendentalism. Given this textual fact, there are two ways of reading the same book: Rawls contradicts himself by advocating two incompatible views, and the two view express the two dimensions of the same Kantian ideals: immanent and transcendental. The choice is obvious.

In his Dewey Lectures, likewise, Rawls expresses not only Kantian conventionalism, but also Kantian transcendentalism. He repeats the familiar assertion that there are no moral facts apart from the principles adopted in the original position (*KC* 519, 568). This problematic assertion appears to presuppose Kantian transcendentalism. Until the Kantian ideals are brought down from the noumenal to the phenomenal world, there can be no moral rules or facts. This assertion makes no sense whatsoever, if it is taken in the context of Kantian conventionalism. On this view, our shared moral ideas or intuitions are everywhere because they are embedded in our culture. The existence of our culture and its positive norms does not depend on the constitution of the original position and the formulation of principles.

Even when Rawls says that the Kantian ideals are embedded in our culture, he sometimes makes this admission in guarded language: "One is to imagine that, for the most part, they [citizens of a democratic society] find on examination that they hold these ideals, that they have taken them *in part* from their society" (*KC* 568–69, emphasis added). He is saying that their society is only a partial, not the whole, source for their Kantian ideals. If their society is only a partial source, there must be some other source, namely, their transcendental source. In all fairness, I have to confess, Rawls does not maintain the same guarded language in most of his assertions about Kantian ideals.

In his Dewey Lectures, I should also point out, Rawls is preoccupied with the problem of consensus. He tries to give a stronger argument for the acceptance of the original position than in *A Theory of Justice*. In this book, he talked of the choice of principles, which depends on the choice of contract situations. Now he says that this chain of choices cannot go on indefinitely, and that all choices must be rooted in the ultimate ideals we do not choose but simply accept. These ultimate ideals are the ideals of persons and social cooperation that constitute the original position, and they are not the objects of choice because they are embedded in our culture (*KC* 568). At this point, Rawls sounds more like Hume than like Kant. If our political culture dictates the ultimate ideas for the principles of justice, it surely annuls the Kantian principle of autonomy. We no longer legislate for ourselves; our principles are prescribed by our political culture.

He is now maintaining that his ideal contract is based on factual consensus. This line of argument is not totally new. Even in *A Theory of Justice,* he tries to secure the factual basis of consensus for his theory of justice (*TJ* 581). He wants to accept it as a sociological fact that requires no metaphysical account. He admits that his contract argument is open to "the general complaint that it appeals to the mere fact of agreement" (*TJ* 580). In response to this criticism, he neither appeals to the timeless perspective of the original position nor gives any philosophical defense of his position. Instead he assumes that any theory of justice is justified as long as it is based on the premises we all share (*TJ* 581).

As Rawls says, no doubt the chain of our choices cannot go on indefinitely. We have to come to a point where we must accept certain ideals for our normative discourse. But the point of ultimate acceptance should not be dictated by our culture any more than by a dictator. We should endorse our ultimate ideals because they are transcendent. This is the Platonic position, and Rawls often takes this position, too. Let us now consider some of the statements he made from a Platonic perspective. He compares his program to Chomsky's theory of universal grammar (*TJ* 47). This comparison has drawn much criticism. It has been said that Rawls's analogy is faulty because the linguistic intuitions of native speakers are authoritative in deciding the grammatical character of any linguistic expression.[27] Linguistics is no more than an empirical science, which determines the grammar of a language by a sociological investigation of speech conventions in a given community. Linguistics follows the natural rather than the constructive model.

In defense of Rawls, it should be said that there are two kinds of linguistics: normative and empirical. This distinction is similar to Kant's distinction between two features of ethics: the empirical and the rational part.[28] The empirical

---

27. For example, R. M. Hare, "Rawls' Theory of Justice," in *Reading Rawls*, 86.
28. Kant, *Groundwork of the Metaphysics of Morals, KGS* 4:388–89. *KGS* stands for the Prussian Academy Edition of Kant's Collected Works.

part is the sociological or psychological observation of people's moral behavior. It belongs not to ethics proper, but to anthropology and psychology. Ethics proper is the rational part; it has nothing to do with empirical investigations. Likewise, normative linguistics can be distinguished from positive linguistics. Even the sense of grammar can have normative and empirical sides. The linguistic intuitions of native speakers are authoritative in deciding the questions belonging to the empirical side of grammatical sense. Whether a verb should come before or after a subject in a sentence is a question of empirical grammar. But empirical grammar presupposes normative grammar. A sentence that obeys the rules of empirical grammar can still fail to make sense if it violates normative grammar.

Rawls compares his Kantian constructivism not to any and all linguistics, but especially to Chomsky's theory of universal syntax. He describes Chomsky's theory as an attempt to characterize "the ability to recognize well-formed sentences by formulating clearly expressed principles" (TJ 47). Chomsky calls such an ability linguistic competence, and his theory of universal grammar describes linguistic competence. His universal grammar is the normative grammar that underlies all empirical grammars of natural languages. Analogously, Rawls's theory of justice is derived from the moral capacity, or rather his two principles describe the moral capacity. His theory of justice gives the norms that shape the moral sense, just as the universal grammar gives the norms that shape the grammatical sense.

Linguistics on such a normative level may be none other than logic; etymologically *logic* means the science of speech. Chomsky's theory of universal grammar may be no more than a theory of formal syntax. His theory of deep linguistic structure appears to be only a theory of the logical structure of predication.[29] If Rawls's analogy of Kantian constructivism to linguistics is taken on the normative level, it can dissolve another dispute about reflective equilibrium. This one concerns the following question: Whose considered judgments are to be matched against the principles of justice? The considered judgments may belong to an individual or to a society as a whole, and the scope of reflective equilibrium can change accordingly. The only thing Rawls says to clear up this important question is his cryptic statement "So for the purposes of this book, the views of the reader and the author are the only ones that count. The opinions of others are used only to clear our own minds" (TJ 50).

This appears to be a cavalier statement. Why should the views of the reader and the author count more than those of others? What prerogatives do they have over other people? Moreover, this cavalier attitude appears to be incompatible with Rawls's ever-present concern for consensus. As Peter Singer says, Rawls

29. Chomsky, *Lectures on Government and Binding* (Dordrecht, 1981).

always writes of "our" judgments, never "mine" or "yours." [30] Surely he cannot attain consensus by ignoring the opinions of the multitude. But consensus plays different roles in normative and empirical linguistics. Empirical linguistics has to begin with consensus. It is impossible to determine whether a certain expression (for example, "like I said") is grammatical or ungrammatical without empirically finding out whether its usage is widely shared in the speech community. But normative linguistics does not depend on such an empirical survey because it defines the universal conditions for making meaningful assertions. It prescribes the normative ground for consensus, whereas empirical linguistics discovers consensus by empirical observations.

The cavalier statement by Rawls comes after the following analogy to linguistics (*TJ* 50):

Here too there is likely to be a similarity with linguistics: if we can describe one person's grammar we shall surely know many things about the general structure of language. Similarly, if we should be able to characterize one (educated) person's sense of justice, we would have a good beginning toward a theory of justice. We may suppose that everyone has in himself the whole form of a moral conception. So for the purposes of this book, the views of the reader and the author are the only ones that count. The opinions of others are used only to clear our own heads.

Read in context, the last sentence does not sound cavalier at all. Rawls is assuming the distinction between the empirical grammar of a particular natural language and the normative grammar of all languages. Though the former cannot be known without an empirical survey of a relevant community, the latter can be described with one person's sense of grammar. The reader and the author are more than enough for Chomsky's or Rawls's enterprise.

Rawls also compares his Kantian constructivism to a normative enterprise in logic and mathematics (*TJ* 51–52): "Note, for example, the extraordinary deepening of our understanding of the meaning and justification of statements in logic and mathematics made possible by developments since Frege and Cantor. A knowledge of the fundamental structures of logic and set theory and their relation to mathematics has transformed the philosophy of these subjects in a way that conceptual analysis and linguistic investigations never could."

Rawls evidently regards conceptual analysis and linguistic investigations as empirical approaches that explore and clarify the ideas and conventions embedded in our culture. The normative approach of Frege and Cantor is quite different; it appeals to transcendent norms. It can give us a deeper understanding of logic and mathematics by providing the basic principles for constructing

---

30. Peter Singer, "Sidgwick and Reflective Equilibrium," *The Monist* 58 (1974): 495.

these normative sciences. Every normative science requires a set of normative ideals that transcend all cultures. Likewise, Rawls's Kantian constructivism can be a normative enterprise only if it is securely based on some transcendental ideals. For they alone can provide eternal standards for normative construction. Without such a transcendental basis, his Kantian constructivism turns into a Hobbesian project of seeking consensus and coherence in the world of positive norms.

CHAPTER FOUR

Formal Rationality

Rawls's Kantian constructivism is a great battle against intuitionism. It is a battle of distrust. He is too cautious to accept the metaphysical implications of rational intuitionism. He cannot believe in a mental telescope for locating Platonic entities (*KC* 558). Nor has he ever seen self-evident moral properties or propositions. In spite of this pervasive distrust, he cannot undertake his constructivist program without using some basic intuitive ideas about moral persons and social order. His battle of distrust against intuitionism cannot be conducted without his having trust in intuitionism. Here lies the paradox of his Kantian constructivism; it is a strange mix of trust and distrust of intuitionism.

The distrust of intuitionism is not new with Rawls; it is embedded in the scientific ethos of the modern world. Our scientific world view is physicalistic; it recognizes only the reality of physical objects and their properties and relations. This view, sometimes known as scientific materialism, leads to the demarcation of facts and values. Facts are elevated to the objective world of reality; values are relegated to the subjective world of desires and feelings. Normative entities have no objective existence. This picture of norms and values is known as moral (or normative) antirealism.

As we shall see in chapter 6, the rise of modern natural science has encouraged the development of antirealism, which usually turns into normative positivism and subjectivism. This tendency has been accentuated in our century by the development of logical positivism, which has celebrated the power of natural science. In the normative world, logical positivism has produced emotivism and noncognitivism. According to emotivism, moral statements have only emotive meanings; they express our feelings.[1] They are like "Hurrah!" or "Ouch!" They are neither true or false. At best, they are instruments of emotive persuasion. Emotivism is the height of normative skepticism.

Emotivism and skepticism undercut the rational basis of nor-

---

1. The theory of emotive meaning is given by A. J. Ayer, *Language, Truth, and Logic*, 2d ed. (London, 1948), and Charles Stevenson, *Ethics and Language* (New Haven, 1944).

mative discourse. There are two kinds of rationality: formal and material (or substantive). The requirement of formal rationality is different from that of material or substantive rationality. It is a question of substantive rationality whether drug addiction is rational or irrational. It cannot be settled by the logical principle of formal rationality. The requirement of formal rationality is to avoid logical contradictions; it is the minimal requirement for all judgments and inferences. If emotivism and noncognitivism are correct, they discredit the very idea of substantive rationality. Hence the idea of formal rationality becomes a last resort for saving the rationality of normative discourse.

Many have tried to convert the requirement of formal rationality into a formal decision procedure for settling normative issues. Such a procedure is purely formal. As I noted in the last chapter, John Rawls once tried his own version of a purely formal procedure only to recognize its futility. His notion of the original position contains too many substantive ideas to qualify as a purely formal procedure. But it may be instructive to understand the nature of a purely formal procedure in order to reach a fuller appreciation of Rawlsian proceduralism, because it has grown out of the notion of a purely formal procedure.

Prescriptivism

The best example of a purely formal procedure can be found in R. M. Hare's prescriptivism. Hare agrees with emotivists in admitting the semantic gap between descriptive and evaluative terms but does not accept the emotive account of evaluative terms. In his view, the function of evaluative statements is not to express emotions but to commend and prescribe (*LM* 1–16).[2] If I say, "This is a good strawberry," I am commending this strawberry. The word *good* neither describes a property of the strawberry nor expresses my emotion. It constitutes my speech act of commendation.

The performative acts of commending and prescribing can be given as imperatives because they are meant to serve the function of guiding choices and actions (*LM* 127). This leads to his prescriptivism: all moral judgments are prescriptive. Moral prescriptives are not pure commands; they are supported by reasons. He tries to anchor those reasons in the connection between description and evaluation (*LM* 111). What is the connection between the descriptive statement "This strawberry is large, red, and juicy," and the evaluative statement "This strawberry is good"? He says that their connection is not logical or one of entailment. The evaluative statement can be derived from the descriptive statement only if the two statements presuppose a major premise that specifies the standard for good strawberries.

2. *LM* refers to R. M. Hare, *The Language of Morals* (Oxford, 1952).

Hare does not distinguish standards from principles. For him, standards are principles; to make decisions by following standards is to make them on principles (*LM* 70). To make a moral judgment is to make it on principle. How do we find right moral principles? They are neither self-evident nor to be found anywhere. They have to be made. Hare maintains that principles are created by our actions and decisions. And they do not stay the same after being created and adopted. Our decisions and principles constantly interact with each other; they mutually revise each other (*LM* 65). He says that moral judgments "can only be verified by reference to a standard or set of principles which we have by our own decision accepted and made our own" (*LM* 78).

At this point, Hare sounds like an existentialist. His voluntarism is equal to Sartre's. In fact, he invokes the renowned existentialist's authority in his denial of the view that general moral principles exist antecedently to the making of any moral judgments (*FR* 37–38).[3] He also follows Sartre's lead in accepting the Kantian requirement of universalizability: a prescription is not moral unless it can be universalized. A moral prescription is valid only if it can be derived from a principle that can be universally accepted. Universalizable principles give the reasons or rational support to moral prescriptions. This is his thesis of universal prescriptivism (*FR* 89).

How can one tell whether a principle can be universalized? Hare offers the hypothetical or imaginary test of thought-experiment. For example, he considers the law that creditors may exact the payment of debts by putting debtors into prison (*FR* 90–91). You may be inclined to accept the rule, if you imagine yourself in the position of a creditor. You would gladly put your debtors into prison if they do not pay. To this point, you are considering the law without universalizing it. Once it is universalized, you will, as a debtor, be subject to the same punishment. As it happens, you have an unpaid debt to someone, and you would not assent to the law as a universal prescription. Hence the law cannot be universalized. Hare calls it the golden rule argument. He acknowledges its affinity to the method of an impartially sympathetic spectator (*FR* 94).

Hare recognizes four elements in his imaginary test of universalizability: logic, facts, inclinations, and imagination (*FR* 93–98). The first of them is the universal prescriptivity, which is derived from the logical properties of moral language. Facts and inclinations can be empirically ascertained. From these three factors, Hare maintains, we can always derive right moral prescriptions as long as we have sound imagination. This is his proceduralism; it is a formal procedure for finding right solutions to moral problems.

Hare maintains that his prescriptive method can give a universally valid judgment on any moral issue. Moreover, his method employs no substantive moral

3. *FR* refers to R. M. Hare, *Freedom and Reason* (Oxford, 1963).

ideas. His decision procedure relies solely on the logical property of moral language, prescriptivity and universalizability. In this regard, his method is different from naturalism or intuitionism, which have to presuppose substantive moral concepts. To be sure, prescriptivity and universalizability alone cannot make moral judgments; they have to presuppose empirical content, that is, the speaker's aims and situation. But empirical content is likely to generate the diversity and multiplicity of prescriptions, thereby making it impossible for Hare's method to produce universal prescriptions that can be accepted by everybody. How does his prescriptive method control the diversity of empirical content and maintain the universality of its prescriptions? This is the most critical question for Hare's theory.

To return to Hare's example of the debtor-imprisonment law, Hare assumed that you would not assent to the law if you were to consider it from the position of a prospective debtor. Therefore you would not accept its universalization. We can apply the same method to the law that puts murderers into jail. Surely you would not assent to this law if you considered it from the position of a murderer. Therefore you would not accept its universalization. If we are to use this method, I wonder how many laws can be universalized. Hare must have something else in mind. He may be asking you to consider the law from both positions, debtor and creditor, and then tell him whether you would universalize it. That is quite different from considering it only from one of the two positions. If his method takes into account both positions, it can use the golden rule argument.

The golden rule argument requires bilateral considerations or the reversal of positions. If you take a bilateral perspective and reject a rule, you are objecting to its universalization. If you accept it from a bilateral perspective, you are endorsing its universalization. When you take a bilateral perspective, Hare assumes, you are taking the perspective of everybody affected by that rule. Yours is a universal perspective; it will be adopted by everybody else who impartially considers the interests of both parties affected by the rule. To endorse a rule from a universal perspective is to universalize it; it is to endorse it as a universal prescription for everybody concerned. The idea of a universal perspective is essential to Hare's universal prescriptivism.

Let us now suppose that your bilateral perspective is not universal; it is in fact different from my bilateral perspective. Hare considers the possibility that firm believers in the rights of property and the sanctity of contracts may roundly endorse the law for imprisoning debtors for their failure to discharge their obligations, even if they have to be subject to the same law (*FR* 103). From their perspective, the law can be universalized. But their perspective is not universal; it is different from yours or mine. And our perspective is no more universal than theirs. Hare's prescriptivism turns out to be perspective-dependent and perspective-relative. Universal prescriptions can vary from agent to agent if they have different perspectives.

Hare's program of universal prescriptivism has turned out to be perspective-relative. His program can succeed only if we can find a way to overcome the relativity of perspectives. How can we amend his program and achieve his goal? Hare has assumed that the question of universal prescription can be settled by appealing to the basic desires and aversions we all share. He says that most people have basically similar inclinations about important matters in life. Few people would like to be starved or run over by cars (*FR* 97). The people with normal desires will universalize the same laws (*FR* 173). But there are abnormal people, and their universalization will be different from the universalization of normal people. In that case, we may attain some uniformity of moral prescriptions by restricting the procedure of universalization to those with normal desires.

For such a restriction, Hare has to find a criterion for discriminating normal from abnormal desires. But that would be an impossible burden on his program. The demarcation of normal from abnormal desires is a substantive issue, and Hare's program is meant to be a purely formal procedure. Even if he can find a way to settle the question of demarcation, that is not enough to save his program. The diversity of desires is not the only factor for producing the multiplicity of prescriptions. As Hare notes, different moral and social ideals can lead to different universalizations. One may support the universalization of the debtor-imprisonment law because one is committed to the moral and social ideals of property rights and the sanctity of contract. One may reject the universalization of the same law from utilitarian considerations (*FR* 101).

Moral ideals are much like aesthetic ideals, Hare notes; the golden rule argument does not easily apply to them (*FR* 138–39). The golden rule arguments are effective in the domain of conflicting interests, but moral and aesthetic ideals often transcend the prosaic world of interests. If truly committed to an ideal, one is prepared to sacrifice even one's ultimate interest for the glory of the ideal. When people become fervently committed to their ideals and immune to the golden rule argument, Hare calls them fanatics. A good example is a Nazi committed to the ideal of producing a super Aryan race by exterminating all Jews and other inferior races (*FR* 160–62). Would a Nazi be prepared to accept this ideal as a universal law even if he were a Jew? We may tell him that he was born of two pure Jews, though he did not know of it. He may change his view and disapprove of Nazism. Or he may uphold the Nazi ideal even at the cost of losing his life. Hare maintains that his universalization decision depends on the nature of his commitment to the Nazi ideal.

Hare considers an imaginary debate in which a liberal tries to demonstrate to a Nazi that the latter's ideal cannot be universalized. Though ideals are preeminently important, the liberal tells the Nazi, they should not be allowed to override other people's important interests. Moreover, it is crazy to ignore or sacrifice one's vital interests for the sake of one's ideals, as in the case of a Nazi willing to be exterminated if he turns out to be a Jew. Hare says that the Nazi can respond to the liberal with disdain and contempt. He will say that to be deterred by one's or others' interests is to betray one's lofty ideal. If one is truly dedicated to an ideal, the Nazi maintains, his dedication should override everything else.

The imaginary debate between the liberal and the Nazi is a battle between two ideals. The liberal is advocating his ideal against the ideal of the Nazi. Hare says they simply have different ideals as to what constitutes a good man and a good society. The liberal would like to universalize his ideal, and the Nazi would like to do the same thing for his ideal. A conflict of ideals means a conflict of perspectives. We cannot have universal prescriptions without having universal perspective. The multiplicity of perspectives means the multiplicity of prescriptions. Hare talks as though this problem of multiple prescriptions and their relativity were restricted to the domain of ideals. But there is no way to erect a wall between interests and ideals. Ideals inevitably affect our interests because they often define human interests. That is the power of ideals. Insofar as our ideals shape our interests, there can be no universal perspective for making prescriptions for the domain of interests. In the absence of a universal perspective, Hare's prescriptivism can be nothing more than a private decision procedure.

Formal and Substantive Principles

It is time we locate the source of Hare's problem. He has maintained that his universal prescriptivism is derived from the logical property of moral language. He says, "Offenses against the thesis of universalizability are logical, not moral" (*FR* 32). Those offenses consist in making logically inconsistent judgments. If the thesis of universalizability is only logical and no substantive principles follow from it, you may assume that it is useless for moral reasoning because moral reasoning requires substantive principles. Although the formal principle is useless by itself, Hare insists, "it is capable of very powerful employment in moral argument when combined with other premises" (*FR* 35). By "powerful employment" he is referring to the substantive results he has produced by his method of universal prescriptivism.

How can Hare produce substantive prescriptions from the formal property of moral language? This question is quite complicated by the fact that, in Hare's hand, the logical requirement of universality takes on many shapes. We can clarify this semantic feature of Hare's program by using J. L. Mackie's distinction of three levels in universalization.[4] On the first level, universalization requires only that similar cases be decided similarly; hence proper names should not be admitted as relevant factors. On the second level, universalization requires role reversal; it asks you to put yourself in the position of the other person. This, the golden rule argument, rules out generic differences as irrelevant to moral considerations. The difference between creditors and debtors is a generic one and should be ignored by giving equal consideration to both parties. On the third level, universalization has to take into account differing ideals and perspectives. The conflict between a liberal and a Nazi cannot be handled by the first or second level of universalization: its resolution requires the third level of universalization.

All three levels of universalization express the idea of impartiality; they can be called the three levels of impartiality. The first level is the impartiality over differing cases. One cannot maintain impartiality by deciding two similar cases differently. The second level of universalization is the impartiality over different persons or parties, for example, the impartiality between a creditor and a debtor. The impartiality over different cases is independent of the impartiality over different parties. If a judge treats creditors more favorably than debtors in every case, he maintains the impartiality over different cases but not over creditors and debtors. The third level of universalization expresses the impartiality over different ideals and perspectives.

These three levels of impartiality are all substantive; they become increasingly richer in substantive content. The first level is the easiest; it has been regarded as merely formal by many. But the question of which two cases should be treated as similar is not a formal one, though it is a formal principle to treat like cases alike. There are no two cases exactly alike in every respect. The principle of formal impartiality requires that two cases be treated alike if they are similar in relevant respects. What are relevant respects? This question cannot be settled by a formal principle; it requires substantive criteria.

The second level of impartiality is even more substantive and difficult than the first. It is hard to spell out what it means to be impartial between creditors and debtors because their positions are not identical. In Hare's view, they are in identical positions: both of them hate to be imprisoned. But it is absurd to settle the rightness of the debtor-imprisonment law on such a flimsy basis. On such a flimsy basis, we should endorse the law that eliminates all prisons. What sorts of things should be taken into consideration in treating the creditor and the debtor impartially? This is again the all-important question of relevance for normative decisions. The question cannot be settled by the principle of impartiality. On the contrary, the principle presupposes the criteria of relevance.

4. J. L. Mackie, *Ethics* (Harmondsworth, 1977), 83–104.

What kind of things should be taken into our impartial consideration? Should we limit our consideration to the fact that the debtor has failed to repay the loan? Should we not also consider the fact, for example, that he has been sick and incapacitated? Or the fact that the creditor has been a ruthless crook and made the loan at an exorbitant interest rate? In our impartial consideration, we have to demarcate relevant and irrelevant factors, and we cannot make this demarcation without using some moral ideas. And those ideas constitute the substantive basis for making impartial decisions between the two parties.

The third level of impartiality is not only the hardest, but often impossible. When two parties align themselves with competing ideals, we may try to be impartial to both of them by adopting a morally neutral perspective. But such a neutral perspective is irrelevant to settling moral disputes. If the impartial perspective cannot be morally neutral, it must operate with its own moral ideals. These ideals constitute the substantive basis for the third level of impartiality.

Every level of impartiality presupposes its own substantive basis. Because the substantive basis can take many different forms, the principle of impartiality can also be given many different interpretations. The important question for the principle of impartiality is not whether it should be dependent or independent of a substantive basis, but whether it should be spelled out formally or used informally. This important recognition is what guides John Rawls's theory of justice. He spells out the substantive basis for his principles of impartiality or fairness in terms of Kantian ideals.

An impartial perspective is not formal but substantive, insofar as it stands on a set of substantive moral ideas. Likewise, the idea of impartiality is a substantive principle. But Hare has regarded it as a formal principle on the ground that it is derived from the logical property of moral language. What is really the logical form of moral language? It is only a linguistic device for expressing a substantive moral idea. Only because the logical form of moral language embodies the substantive idea of impartiality can Hare derive substantive moral principles from the supposed purely logical property of moral language. Our natural language of morals incarnates our commonsense moral intuitions. Hence to appeal to moral language is to appeal to our moral intuitions, even when our appeal is restricted to its logical property.

Hare's formal procedure often appears to convert a formal principle into a substantive one. His appears to be a program of transubstantiation. In this mystical process, many critics have charged, Hare smuggles in substantive principles in the guise of formal principle. He has rightly denied the charge of indecent traffic. He does not have to smuggle in anything because substantive moral ideas are already there in the guise of a formal principle. The difficult problem with those hidden ideas is their multiplicity; there are so many of them that he does not know which one to pick. This embarrassment of riches shows up best in his exposition of the relation between his formal principle and utilitarianism.

Hare often identifies the formal principle of universalizability with the golden rule. He also says that when it is extended from bilateral to multilateral cases it functions like the principle of utility (*FR* 117–123). It requires us to consider the interests of all the affected parties equally and maximize their satisfactions. Hence the formal principle of equal consideration is equivalent to the substantive principle of utility. But he is not always quite sure of their equivalence. When it comes to the question of distribution, he says, his formal principle will favor equal distribution rather than the maximization of total happiness (*FR* 121). He says that at this point if his formal method is extended to multilateral situations he cannot tell "what kind of utilitarianism if any will emerge" (*FR* 122–23). He can be certain only that his formal procedure is "the formal foundation of any such theory." He identifies his formal principle with the utilitarian maxim "Everybody to count for one, nobody for more than one" (*FR* 118).

The utilitarian maxim is a computation procedure that counts every person equally. It does not allow attaching a greater importance to one person than to another. This highly egalitarian principle is quite different from the principle of maximization, which is a principle of aggregation. The latter can operate with a nonegalitarian counting rule, for example, by assigning a greater importance to the preferences of educated people than to the preferences of uneducated people. The counting rule is procedural; the rule of maximization is substantive. The two rules are independent; either of them can be adopted without the other.

How can Hare's formal principle be equivalent to these two different principles unless he is using the notion of equivalence in a dubious manner? In his later writings, he tries to eliminate this anomaly by establishing the equivalence of his formal principle with the principle of utility. This is his project of synthesizing Kant and utilitarians: a clearheaded Kantian and a clearheaded utilitarian would find themselves in agreement (*MT* 43, 50).[5] In making this attempt, he assumes the equivalence of his formal principle with the utilitarian counting principle. Then he assumes that the counting principle leads to the principle of maximization.

In the name of equivalence, Hare exchanges his formal principle for the counting principle, which he sometimes regards as equivalent to the Kantian principle. Then he claims the equivalence of the latter to the principle of utility on the ground that both of them can be regarded as applications of the principle of impartiality. He overlooks an important difference between the Kantian and the utilitarian approach. The principle of maximization is essential for the

5. *MT* refers to Hare, *Moral Thinking* (Oxford, 1981).

utilitarian, but not for the Kantian approach. The problem of maximization concerns numbers, among other things: how many people are going to be affected by the adoption of any rule. Let us take the case of debtors and creditors. If we consider their relation as a bilateral case, we do not have to know how many debtors and creditors there are. But if we want to maximize their utility we have to know their number.

Let us imagine a community consisting of nine Nazis and one Jew. The utility functions of these ten persons are such that this community can have a greater utility by exterminating the lone Jew than leaving him alone. On the counting level, we can give equal weight to the interests of the lone Jew and all others. On the adding level, however, we can achieve greater utility for the community by sacrificing his interests. If so, the principle of utility will be vetoed by the lone Jew, and a Kantian will support his veto. Contrary to Hare's claim, no clearheaded Kantian is likely to endorse the principle of utility as his ultimate principle.

Kantians and utilitarians have differing ideals of impartiality, and neither of them is derivable from Hare's formal principle. The idea of impartiality is really an incomplete and indeterminate idea. The idea of impartiality between creditors and debtors is one thing, and the idea of impartiality between murderers and their victims is another matter. The idea of impartiality for liberals is different from the idea of impartiality for Nazis. The ideal of impartiality does not mean much until it is placed in a specified context. Hence it can be accepted by a Kantian, a utilitarian, or even a Nazi. This explains the embarrassment of riches Hares encounters under his formal principle. It hides an idea indeterminate enough to be framed in any shape he desires. It can be indiscriminately used for the justification of utilitarianism, Nazism, and Kantianism.

Moral Intuition and Moral Criticism

Let us compare the basic difference between Hare's proceduralism and the intuitionism of commonsense morality. Both of them accept the principle of impartiality but offer divergent arguments for it. Hare's proceduralism says that the principle of impartiality is morally right because it can be universalized. To say that it can be universalized means that someone can accept it as a universal law. Its rightness is supposedly certified by the formal procedure of universalization. Contrary to Hare's formal approach, commonsense intuitionism endorses the principle of impartiality on the substantive ground. It is absurd to prove its rightness by the argument of acceptability. That is putting the cart before the horse. Commonsense morality says that it should be accepted as a universal law because it is a substantively correct principle.

In *Moral Thinking*, Hare tries to provide a proper place for commonsense moral intuitions. He has been accused of neglecting the important role of moral intuitions and of not appreciating the stability of general standards and principles upheld by our intuitions. He has often talked as though our moral standards and principles were perpetually revised in every moral judgment. In Urmson's words, he is overlooking the difference between standard-setting and standard-using.[6] In this regard, he is again like an existentialist. I have already noted his sympathy with the existentialist ideal of freedom in the adoption and rejection of moral principles.

Hare has tried to meet this charge of excessive volatility by recognizing two levels of moral thinking. In the first level, moral thinking is intuitive; in the second, it is critical (*MT* 25–43). Under normal circumstances, Hare states, our moral thought is intuitive. We follow general standards and principles that are inculcated in us. Our moral intuitions are formed by those general standards and principles. But our intuitions often conflict or clearly fail to be adequate to particular situations. Then we have to reflect critically on our intuitions and revise or reject some of them. In this critical process, we rely on the principle of utility. Hence the principle of utility is the ultimate moral principle. Those who can conduct moral thought at this lofty critical level are called the archangels, and those who are stuck on the intuitive level are called the proles. The archangel is a utilitarian; the prole is an intuitionist.

These two levels, intuitive and critical moral thought, roughly correspond to the well-known distinction between positive and critical moralities. Positive morality is conventional morality; it operates within a framework of established conventions or standards and principles. Critical morality takes a critical stand on the norms of positive morality. In Hare's view, moral intuition is the intuition of positive norms, and all positive norms are established by the procedure of universal prescriptivism.

The principle of utility is the ultimate principle for the procedure of universal prescriptivism because it is the principle we would all accept as our ultimate universal law. Hence all positive norms and our intuition of them should be subject to this ultimate principle. When our intuitions get out of line, they can be realigned by readjusting their coordination under the guidance of this highest principle. When our intuitions come into conflict or fail to be adequate to any particular situations, we have to revise them by subjecting them to the ultimate test of utility-maximization. To consider and dispose moral issues from the perspective of this highest principle is to ascend to the critical level of moral thinking.

Hare's view of moral intuitions is unacceptable to commonsense morality. In addition to positive intuitions, commonsense morality recognizes critical intuitions. The function of positive intuition is to accept and follow positive norms

6. This is the criticism Urmson makes against Stevenson's emotive theory of moral judgments, in his *Emotive Theory of Ethics* (London, 1968), 64–71, 77–80.

and standards, but the function of critical intuition is to subject those positive norms and standards to criticism. Even the principle of utility can be subject to criticism, and its moral inadequacy can be exposed. But this discredit cannot be done by appealing to the principle of utility itself. Even if the principle of utitility is endorsed as the highest moral principle, its endorsement is not made by the principle of utility itself. It requires the service of higher critical intuitions.

The Principle of Generic Consistency

Alan Gewirth believes that the first principle of morality should be formal, that is, that its denial should be self-contradictory. But he has learned the Rawlsian lesson; he knows that a formal principle cannot produce moral precepts without presupposing some material concepts. He locates his material basis in the idea of a rational agent. For every rational agent, he says, freedom and well-being are two necessary goods. Every agent claims generic rights to these necessary goods (*RM* 64).[7] They are called generic rights because they are rights to the general goods of freedom and well-being. These rights impose on others the duty of noninterference. Now an agent recognizes that any other agent has the same rights to her freedom and well-being and that she has to respect the rights of others if she wants them to respect hers. Thus she comes to accept the following precept: Act in accord with the generic rights of your recipients as well as with those of yourself (*RM* 135). This precept is called the Principle of Generic Consistency (PGC).

Gewirth stresses that the PGC is the principle of logical consistency. The PGC is not only formal, but also generative; it is a formal principle for generating all moral precepts and duties. This formal program contains two doubtful ideas: the concept of generic rights and the concept of generic consistency. Let us grant that every agent values her freedom and well-being as her two necessary goods. Gewirth takes this fact as the basis for his assertion that every agent has generic rights to freedom and well-being. But the fact that I value something does not automatically give me the right to it. By Gewirth's logic, I can have the right to the whole world. Even if someone gives me that sort of right, what kind of right is it? Gewirth says that generic rights are not moral but prudential (*RM* 69, 71, 89). The idea of prudential rights seems to elude our normal intelligence. Moreover, he insists that generic rights are deontic, though not moral. How can a right be deontic and yet not be moral? That idea is not any easier to grasp. For these reasons, R. M. Hare maintains that the concept of generic rights is based on a series of equivocations.[8]

7. *RM* refers to Alan Gewirth, *Reason and Morality* (Chicago, 1978).
8. R. M. Hare, "Do Agents Have to Be Moralists?" in Edward Regis, ed., *Gewirth's Ethical Rationalism* (Chicago, 1984), 52–58.

Gewirth is trying to derive the concept of rights from the concept of an agent. Such a derivation need not be mysterious. If the agent is conceived in terms of rights, then the concept of rights can be derived from the concept of the agent. On the other hand, if the agent is conceived without reference to rights, then there is no way to derive the concept of rights from the concept of the agent. Gewirth constructs his concept of an agent solely in terms of freedom and well-being and then tries to derive the concept of generic rights from the concept of an agent. That appears to be impossible; there is a logical gap between the concept of generic rights and the concept of a rightless agent. Gewirth tries to fill this gap with the principle of consistency.

Gewirth maintains that it is logically inconsistent to claim generic rights for oneself without recognizing the same rights for others. E. J. Bond has expressed his difficulty in recognizing this alleged logical inconsistency.[9] This difficulty has been shared by most of Gewirth's readers. Logical inconsistencies should not be elusive; they can be located in a pair of propositions because logical consistency is the incompatibility of two or more propositions. Here are two propositions on generic rights:

1. I claim my generic rights.
2. I deny the same generic rights to others.

These two propositions can be true at the same time; there is no logical inconsistency.

These two propositions are incompatible with the proposition that no one should claim more rights for oneself than for others or that one can claim only equal rights for everyone. This is the principle of equality, and Gewirth seems to presuppose this principle in his argument of self-consistency. In that case, his formal generative program produces generic rights from three premises: (1) the concept of an agent, (2) the principle of self-consistency, and (3) the principle of equality. He acknowledges only (1) and (2) and uses (3) without mentioning it. When all three of these premises are spelled out, his program no longer appears to be only formal. It is empowered by the substantive principle of equality.

Gewirth's principle of generic consistency operates roughly with the same logic as Hare's principle of universalization. The important difference between the two lies in the presence and absence of constraints. Hare's formal program has placed no constraints whatsoever on the ideals and preferences of an agent. Hence it is acceptable to moderates and fanatics alike. Gewirth's program controls the contingency of ideals and preferences by restricting them to freedom and well-being. So he says that his PGC should be distinguished from two other versions of consistency: simple consistency and appetitive-reciprocal consis-

---

9. E. J. Bond, "Gewirth on Reason and Morality," *Metaphilosophy* 11 (1980): 36–53.

tency (*RM* 162). Appetitive-reciprocal consistency is the requirement of the golden rule; simple consistency is the requirement of treating the same cases in the same way. Unlike these two formal rules of consistency, Gewirth says, his PGC has determinate contents: freedom and well-being. Hence it is well equipped to cope with the problem of fanatics and secure substantive equality for all.

The problem of fanatics is the problem of relativity in universalization. By packing substantive contents into his formal program, Gewirth tries to avoid the problem of relativity. But he does not really succeed insofar as his concepts of freedom and well-being are only generic and indeterminate. He considers a Christian Scientist who refuses, on religious grounds, to consent to a blood transfusion, at the risk of his life (*RM* 262). He regards this case as a conflict between freedom and well-being. He says that the PGC is caught in a dilemma: "If a blood transfusion is forced on the Christian Scientist, then the requirement of freedom is violated; but if a blood transfusion is not forced on him, then he is allowed to bleed to death so that the requirement of well-being is violated (*RM* 262)."

Gewirth now says that there is no real dilemma in this case. The freedom requirement is inapplicable to this case because the Christian Scientist lacks the relevant knowledge to give his informed consent. The PGC requires that the Christian Scientist should be given a blood transfusion against his will and over his freedom. Marcus Singer has registered a passionate objection on behalf of the Christian Scientist.[10] In his view, the PGC cannot endorse Gewirth's pronouncement. Instead, it should dictate exactly the opposite conclusion. The Christian Scientist does not merely lack the relevant knowledge for his well-being, as Gewirth says, but is acting from his deep religious commitment. His religious belief is so important to his existence that his freedom of conscience should be respected even at the cost of his life. The concept of well-being that does not include the sanctity of religious commitment and conscience should not be allowed to interfere with ethical deliberation.

Singer firmly believes that the value of autonomy should be protected at any cost, even at the cost of total well-being. Singer's position is not any more or any less logically consistent than Gewirth's. But that does not prove that they are equally right. Logical consistency alone never settles critical moral issues because it is no more than the minimum requirement for all our thought. If the principle of logical consistency cannot settle the question of a blood transfusion for the Christian Scientist, it surely cannot settle the question of generic rights.

The notion of generic rights is basically indeterminate because it stands on the indeterminate concepts of well-being and freedom, which are in turn derived from the even more indeterminate concept of a rational agent. Since this

10. Marcus Singer, "Gewirth's Ethical Monism," in *Gewirth's Ethical Rationalism*, 23–38.

indeterminate idea is the substantive basis for Gewirth's formalist program, its indeterminacy infects every assertion that can be derived in that program.

The Ideal Dialogue

Jürgen Habermas conceives rationality in terms of formal requirements for communication. When we communicate with one another, he holds, we make validity claims. They fall into four categories: the intelligibility of what is said, its truth, the correctness or appropriateness of speaking, and the veracity of the speaker.[11] Under normal circumstances, these four validity claims are not questioned. But any one of them can be questioned and challenged at any moment. The communicative act before such a challenge is called action; it is called discourse after such a challenge. When a validity claim is challenged, it must be justified. The problem of justification arises on the level of discourse.

The distinction between action and discourse obtains for both descriptive and normative communication. If the intelligibility of your descriptive statement is questioned, you have to make it intelligible. If its truth is questioned, you have to justify it. If the correctness of your normative assertion is challenged, you have to justify it in terms of accepted norms. If the validity of those norms is challenged, you have to justify those norms. The exchange of these questions and answers, challenges and responses constitutes a dialogue. Habermas recognizes a set of formal conditions for such a dialogue. The participants should be free and rational and earnestly engage themselves in a cooperative enterprise of finding out what is true or correct. The exchange of their ideas should not be distorted by deception, coercion, or any other impediments. A dialogue that can meet those formal conditions is called an ideal speech situation.[12]

On Habermas's theory, consensus is the test of descriptive truth and normative correctness. A proposition is true if and only if it can be accepted by all the participants in an ideal speech situation. A norm is correct if and only if it can be accepted by all the participants in an ideal speech situation. When a norm is accepted by such a consensus, it is called, in Habermas's terms, "a rational will," and it expresses "generalizable interests."[13] The idea of generalized interests is the idea of "what all can want." In an ideal speech situation, Habermas says, all participants should have the freedom to find out what each of them wants. How does Habermas move from what each of them wants to what all of them want? He says that this move is made by the principle of universalization or the generalization argument. He does not seem to recog-

11. Habermas, *Theory and Practice,* trans. John Viertel (Boston, 1973), 18.
12. Habermas, "Wahrheitstheorien," in H. Fahrenbach, ed., *Wirklichkeit und Reflexion* (Pfullingen, 1973), 211–65.
13. Habermas, *Legitimation Crisis,* trans. Thomas McCarthy (Boston, 1973), 108.

nize any significant difference between the two, and he lumps them together by referring them jointly to Grice, Baier, Singer, and the Erlangen School.[14]

Habermas assumes that the method of universalization or generalization can always deliver the right norms for securing generalized interests. He is concerned only with the suppression of generalized interests by the illegitimate exercise of power. How can we detect such a suppression? He offers the method of counterfactual reconstruction. For any social norm of any given society, we can always ask whether it would have been accepted as an expression of their generalized interests by all the members of that society if they had deliberated in an ideal speech situation. This method is counterfactual, first, because most social norms are established without the benefit of an ideal speech situation and, second, because most societies are manipulated by deception and coercion.

Habermas has adopted this counterfactual method from Paul Lorenzen and Oswald Schwemmer of the Erlangen School, who have tried to develop a method of evaluating social norms. Since social norms are embedded in the historical context of a society, they have to be reconstructed before they can be critically evaluated. This reconstructive method consists of two stages: the factual and the critical genesis of a culture.[15] The factual genesis is a historical reconstruction of a normative system. The critical genesis is a critical assessment of the normative system, and its method is the test of ideal or rational deliberation. It is to see whether the social norms are in accord with the requirement of rational deliberation.[16] Rational deliberation requires two principles: the principle of practical rationality and the principle of morality. The former is the same as the principle of universalization, and the latter remains unexplained and unspecified.

Lorenzen and Schwemmer recognize two problems in the principle of universalization: its context-relativity and its indeterminacy. They are fully aware of the problem of indeterminacy Hare has encountered in his universal prescriptivism; incompatible norms can be endorsed by the principle of universalization. They are forthright in recognizing this problem and in accepting the principle of morality for resolving it.[17] If both the liberal and the Nazi ideals can be endorsed by the principle of universalization, the choice between the two can be made by the principle of morality. Their theory of practical reason demands the cooperation of these two principles. By the time they accept the principle of morality, their program is no longer formal or morally neutral.

The problem of context-relativity is equally troublesome. The test of univer-

14. Ibid., 108–09.
15. Lorenzen and Schwemmer, *Konstructive Logik, Ethik und Wissenschaftstheorie* (Mannheim, 1973).
16. Ibid., 209–10.
17. Ibid., 118–20.

salization for a norm can be made only in the context of public speech and action, and such a context is always determined by our history and culture.[18] In such a context, Lorenzen and Schwemmer say, our original desires are culturally transformed, and on the basis of such transformed desires we will be deciding what each of us wants and what all of us want. In that case, the method of universalization becomes circular; it tries to validate some cultural norms by presupposing some other cultural norms. If the presupposed cultural norms are invalid or incorrect, whatever is prescribed by the method of universalization will be equally invalid or incorrect. If the method of universalization is used as a method of critical genesis, it can give only an internal critique of cultural norms.

Habermas tries to meet the charge of cultural relativity by claiming the transcendental validity of an ideal speech situation. As long as people can talk under the formal conditions of an ideal dialogue, they can recognize their undistorted needs and desires. This is the counterfactual knowledge that can be used for the critique of social norms. But the idea of undistorted needs and desires may be only a phantom, one that cannot be located in any cultural context. As Karl Marx says, every culture may suppress and distort people's needs and desires. If so, undistorted needs and desires can be found only beyond and outside culture, that is, in the world of nature before the arrival of culture.

Habermas does not believe that human needs and desires are predetermined in nature. In that case, the undistorted needs and desires can be located only in an unoppressive social order. If the idea of undistorted needs and desires presupposes the idea of an unoppressive social order, Habermas's counterfactual method becomes circular. He has been seeking undistorted needs and desires as the base point for determining legitimate social norms, but those needs and desires cannot be located except under an unoppressive social order. But an unoppressive social order is none other than a set of legitimate social norms.

So far I have taken Habermas's project as a special version of universalization/generalization. That may not be quite accurate; his project may be more like the method of consensus than of universalization/generalization. He stresses consensus and agreement as the goal of an ideal speech. But the idea of consensus is ambiguous, as Steven Luke points out. When a norm is acceptable to everyone, it meets the test of consensus. The word *everyone* may, however, refer to three different types of agent: an actual agent, a representative agent, and an ideal agent.[19]

If *everyone* means an actual agent, Luke says, it is highly unlikely to achieve

18. Habermas, *Legitimation Crisis*, 109–10.
19. Steven Luke gives a similar critique of Habermas's program of universalization in his "Of Gods and Demons: Habermas and Practical Reason," in John Thompson and David Held, ed., *Habermas: Critical Debates* (Cambridge, 1982), 134–48.

a consensus on any norms. It is possible to reach a consensus for representative or ideal agents. But the consensus for representative individuals runs into the problem of how to determine the character of representative individuals. Luke says that the representative actors are not real people but only constructs of a social theory.[20] A counterfactual reconstruction based on such a theory can be rational only to the extent that the theory is itself rational. He seems to feel the difficulty of deciding the rationality of a social theory, though he does not say so.

What really counts for the program of consensus is the rationality of representative individuals rather than that of a social theory for constructing them. The rationality of those individuals is not merely formal, but substantive. They are rational only if they have undistorted interests. Habermas's idea of undistorted interests presupposes the normative standard of substantive rationality. This is why he cannot give an independent characterization of undistorted interests. He can give no guideline for discriminating undistorted from distorted interests. The idea of undistorted interests remains an empty ideal in Habermas's program of ideal speech.

We have no way of deciding whether the representative individuals of any society have distorted or undistorted interests. If most societies are organs of suppression and distortion, as Habermas says, their representative individuals are most likely to have distorted interests. A consensus of those individuals is normatively worthless. The program of consensus can take on normative significance only on the level of ideal agents. But who are ideal agents for Habermas? They are those whose interests are undistorted. So we come back to the idea of undistorted interests.

The idea of undistorted interests underlies Habermas's program of ideal speech. He talks as though an ideal speech required no more than a set of formal conditions and as though those formal conditions were sufficient for resolving all normative issues. But no ideal speech can gain normative significance without appealing to the idea of undistorted interests. And this idea is not formal but substantive.

The Neutral Process

The idea of an ideal speech is very much like the method of neutral dialogue that has been the ideal of adjudication in the common law tradition. Before an impartial judge, the litigants should be given the equal right to state their charges freely against each other and the equal opportunity to reply to those charges. By this method of rational discourse, the judge must be able to reach a rational judgment on the dispute. This is the ideal of neutral process for adjudi-

20. Ibid., 140.

cation. The Legal Process School has tried to use this ideal for overcoming the normative chaos that has been unleashed in the world of law by legal realists.

Henry Hart and Albert Sacks open their monumental *Legal Process* by distinguishing substantive and procedural understandings in law.[21] For social cooperation, they hold, every modern society has to develop a system of institutionalized procedures for settling disputes. Disputes and conflicts are inevitable in a society, whose members try to satisfy their respective wants under the conditions of interdependence. There are two ways of settling disputes and conflicts. One of them is to resort to raw force and violence, and the other is to follow established peaceful procedures. The latter is the principle of institutional settlement: "Decisions which are the duly arrived at result of duly established procedures of this kind ought to be binding upon the whole society unless and until they are duly changed." [22]

Hart and Sacks apply their idea of duly established procedure to the three branches of government. Legislatures are better equipped than the other two branches to deal with substantive issues in making laws. The executive is better equipped for implementing the laws. Courts are best equipped for resolving disputes on the interpretation of the laws. In this division of power, substantive issues are given over to the legislative and the executive branches, and the judiciary is left only with the procedural function of resolving disputes. Since substantive issues are political, the first two branches of government cannot be politically neutral. But the third branch can maintain political neutrality because its institutional obligation is limited to ensuring procedural fairness.

The institutional obligation of courts is to maintain their procedural neutrality, or fidelity to neutral procedures. Hart and Sacks express their high confidence in such a procedural impartiality: "There are no disputes of any kind which cannot be effectually settled by establishing an impartial and sufficiently prestigeful tribunal to hear them, giving both sides or all sides of the dispute an opportunity to present their evidence and argument, and then having the tribunal make its decision." [23]

This idea of a neutral tribunal was given concrete expression in Henry Hart and Herbert Wechsler's joint work, *The Federal Courts and the Federal System*.[24] This casebook shows the way to decide legal disputes by a neutral method; a series of searching questions and answers is supposed to deliver a correct solution to every dispute. This method is presented as a neutral dialogue. But the neutral method applies differently to statutory and to constitutional in-

---

21. Hart and Sacks, "The Legal Process" (manuscript), 3.
22. Ibid., 4
23. Ibid., 666.
24. Hart and Wechsler, *The Federal Courts and the Federal System*, 1st ed. (Mineola, N.Y., 1953). This book has been revised and reissued twice (1973, 1988).

terpretations. When judges interpret a statute, they function as agents of the legislature. They do not have to go beyond what is provided for by the statute. But the interpretation of the Constitution is not so simple as that of a statute. The Constitution is stated in such abstract language that judges cannot interpret it without appealing to substantive standards and principles. These standards and principles must be neutral if the constitutional cases are to be decided by the neutral method. But what is a neutral principle on substantive grounds? Are there substantively neutral principles? These questions of substantive neutrality became critical for the Legal Process School.

Herbert Wechsler raised the question of neutral principle in his Holmes Lectures.[25] He begins with a simple notion of neutrality; it is no more than the formal principle of deciding like cases alike. But he does not stay with this simple notion. He shifts to a substantive notion of neutrality: a neutral principle equally favors the interests of all parties concerned. By this substantive standard, he holds that the Supreme Court's decision in *Brown v. Board of Education* violates the principle of neutrality. The desegregation order unequally affects the freedom of association for the white and for the black. Some white and some black students do not want to go to the same school, while others want to attend desegregated schools. The Court's decision clearly favors the interests of the latter over the interests of the former. Therefore, Wechsler concludes, it is not neutral.

A few years later, Henry Hart took up the same problem in his own Holmes Lectures of 1963. As if he had been reopening Wechsler's question, he proposed to consider the principle of equal opportunity as a basic commitment in the constitutional law. The Brown case surely concerns the principle of equal opportunity as much as the freedom of association. Though the Supreme Court decision may not be neutral in regard to freedom of association, it may be neutral in regard to equal opportunity. Admitting that equal opportunity was an important value, Hart asked on what neutral principle this value could be justified. Then he confessed that he had realized on the very eve of the lecture that he could find no neutral principles for its justification. Having announced this, he sat down before a hushed audience in the crowded Ames courtroom.[26]

By their rigorous scrutiny, two eminent architects of the Legal Process School have driven themselves to the same sad conclusion: the neutral method of legal dialogue can never reach any decisions on substantive issues without appealing to substantive principles. They had hoped to find a value-free method of settling legal disputes, but every substantive principle is value-laden. The real-

25. Wechsler, "Toward Neutral Principles of Constitutional Law," *Harvard Law Review* 73 (1957): 1–35.

26. This account is from Philip Bobbitt, *Constitutional Fate* (Oxford, 1982), 56–57.

ization that formal procedures apart from substantive principles are vacuous has undermined the high hopes of the Legal Process School. But the idea of neutral procedures always presents an irresistible appeal to lawyers, especially the resourceful ones. One of them, Bruce Ackerman in his theory of Neutral Dialogue, has tried to reinstate the method of neutral dialogue as a universal decision procedure for all normative questions.

Neutral Dialogue is designed as an ambitious method of resolving all problems of social justice. Ackerman tries to illustrate its use by setting up an imaginary scenario in which a group of people about to colonize a new planet are traveling on a spaceship. For Ackerman, the problems of social justice are the problems of power relations among the different members of a society. He divides those problems into five phases of human life: birth, education, wealth (distribution of material resources), exchange (transaction of material resources), and trusteeship (disposal of material resources). He identifies many problems with these five phases, and stages neutral dialogues in order to resolve them. It appears as though these engaging conversations had been hatched out of the dialogical eggs laid by Hart and Wechsler in their *Federal Courts and the Federal System*.

Neutral Dialogue is a method of questioning and justifying the claims of power and right. It is governed by three formal principles: Rationality, Consistency, and Neutrality. The principle of Rationality requires the participants to explain their positions by giving reasons whenever anybody questions the legitimacy of their powers (*SJ* 4).[27] The principle of Consistency requires that those reasons be consistent with one another, even if they are given on different occasions (*SJ* 7). The principle of Neutrality consists of two rules of exclusion: no reason can be supported by either the claim that one's conception of the good is better than another's or the claim that one is superior to another (*SJ* 11).

Ackerman's imaginary spaceship is about to land on a new planet, and its commander calls a plenary meeting to decide on an equitable rule for the distribution of manna. The members of the assembly are about to propose the rules of distribution and select the best one. The selection procedure consists of two tests: Rationality and Neutrality. The proposals that fail the rationality test are not worthy of being considered for adoption (*SJ* 34–36). For example, an infeasible proposal fails to meet the rationality requirement; it is irrational to propose a rule that cannot be implemented. The requirements of the rationality test are quite different from the principle of Rationality he has introduced. The latter concerns the right and duty to participate in the justificatory arguments; the former concerns the logical requirements for considering any proposal as

27. *SJ* refers to Ackerman, *Social Justice in the Liberal State* (New Haven, 1980).

worthy of being taken seriously. It is quite confusing because both of them are called the requirements of rationality.

The most important feature of the new rationality requirements is that of relevance: the reasons given in support of proposals must be relevant. Suppose a member of the spaceship asserts that his proposed rule of distribution is better than others on the ground that the sky is blue. This is an example of an irrelevant argument (*SJ* 39–40). There is no connection between the proposed rule and the fact that the sky is blue. This fact can be equally connected or unconnected to any other proposed rules; it fails to meet the differentiation test (*SJ* 40). Now suppose the speaker comes back with a new reason: the blue sky is an indication of God's will that his proposal be accepted. Ackerman's reply is his refusal to accept any reasons that cannot be verified by standard empirical techniques (*SJ* 41). The speaker, however, does not give up and now appeals to his intuition: he has an overwhelming moral sense that the blueness of the sky favors his proposal. This appeal to moral intuitions can be matched by appealing to counterintuitions. Nothing can be settled by appealing to intuitions.

The test of relevance concerns the distinction between a bad reason and no reason (*SJ* 41). The test of rationality rules out all irrelevant reasons as being no reasons. This process of elimination, however, leaves intact many worthy proposals, and the test of neutrality will determine which of them is to be adopted. Hence the test of neutrality is the second and final stage of selection, while the test of rationality is the initial, preliminary stage. What sorts of reasons and considerations, then, can pass the test of relevance? Ackerman recognizes two: the superiority and inferiority of persons and their conceptions of the good (*SJ* 43–44). Although these pass the test of relevance, he holds, they will fail the test of neutrality. This brings up a controversial point: How can we tell whether something can pass the test of relevance?

Some of us may feel that the superiority or inferiority of persons and their conceptions of the good cannot pass the test of relevance because they are not any more relevant to the distribution of manna than the color of the sky. We may even insist on their irrelevance as an essential feature of our liberal credo. It is our liberal faith that the distribution of free goods like manna should never be influenced by the superiority and inferiority of persons or by their conceptions of the good. On what ground can Ackerman regard those things as relevant, while regarding the blueness of the sky as irrelevant? Ackerman has no answer to this question, and his distinction between relevance and irrelevance appears to be totally arbitrary. This is the first strike against his Neutral Dialogue. For the distinction between relevance and irrelevance is essential to any form of rational dialogue.

Our distinction between relevance and irrelevance is usually based on our commonsense intuitions. But Ackerman cannot use commonsense intuitions for his demarcation of relevant and irrelevant reasons in his Neutral Dialogue because commonsense distinctions are not morally neutral. The Neutral Dialogue must be able to offer a neutral distinction between relevance and irrelevance; lacking such a neutral distinction, it cannot even get off the ground.

Now we come to the test of neutrality. The two rules of exclusion do not allow you to say that you are better than others or that your conception of the good is better than that of others. But they allow you to say that you are as good as others and that your conception of the good is as good as others'. Suppose I claim an equal share to yours on the ground that I am as good as you are or that my conception of the good is as good as yours. You can dispute my claim for two different reasons. First, you may tell me that my premises are false: I am not anywhere as good as you are, and my conception of the good is vastly inferior to yours. You may be right in this. What counsel can I expect from Ackerman for the defense of my claim?

Ackerman says, "It is downright easy to think of several weighty arguments in support of Neutrality. The first one is a skeptical argument: While everybody has an opinion about the good life, none can be known to be superior to any other" (*SJ* 11). This skeptical argument appears to be excessive. Although some life-styles may be hard to rank, many of them are clearly inferior to others. For example, who would say that the life of a thief or a hit man is not inferior to the life of an honest farmer or a carpenter? Ackerman's next argument is that all conceptions of the good are equal because everyone has the right to experiment in life without interference from others. That is another strange argument. It appears impossible that the right to experiment in life can make the life of a thief as good as the life of an honest farmer.

These two arguments are the only ones Ackerman gives in support of his claim that any conception of the good life is as good as any other. But he does not extend the same arguments in support of the other claim permitted by the principle of neutrality: "I am as good as you are." Later in a sample dialogue, he seems to indicate that "I am as good as you are" is an expression of moral equality (*SJ* 16). But he does not explain the idea of moral equality. As an expression of moral equality, "I am as good as you are" may mean either that I am morally as good as you are or that I have a moral right equal to yours. The former assertion is implausible; it asserts the universal equality of moral merit. The latter is indeed plausible, but it is the expression of equal moral right. In that case, the principle of neutrality amounts to no more than the assertion of equal moral right.

So we have two different arguments in support of the principle of neutrality: the skeptical argument and the equality argument. How do these two arguments work in Neutral Dialogue? Richard Flathman accepts the skeptical argument for his interpretation of Neutral Dialogue. He distinguishes two senses of neutrality: Neutrality₁ and Neutrality₂. The former is the social ideal of equality, and the latter is a conversational constraint. He characterizes the aim of Neutral

Dialogue as the derivation of Neutrality$_1$ from Neutrality$_2$. He maintains that this derivation cannot be made as long as Neutrality$_2$ is supported by nothing better than skepticism.[28] He is quite right on this point. As long as Neutral Dialogue runs on a skeptical ground, I have the right to say, "I am not sure that I am as good as you are" or "I do not know whether my conception of the good is as good as yours." But I have no right to tell you, "I am as good as you are" or "My conception of the good is as good as yours." These statements are positive assertions that cannot be sustained by skepticism.

Let us now take the constraint of neutrality as an expression of moral equality. Then the function of Neutral Dialogue is to translate moral equality into social equality. Neutral Dialogue allows you to assert that you and I should be equal in the division of manna because you and I are morally equal ("I am as good as you are"). Ackerman admits that this assertion can be challenged. But he says that the challenge can be defeated by showing the intelligibility of the assertion: "Even if you disagree with A when he says, 'Since I'm at least as good as you are, I should have an X that is at least as good as yours is,' there is something intelligible here with which to disagree. The only thing, then, that I want to say on behalf of my script is that it can be said" (SJ 16).

If intelligibility means making sense, I am questioning the intelligibility of your assertion. Your assertion has three parts: it asserts moral equality, equal right to manna, and the logical link between the two. Even if the first two are intelligible, the last one is not. It is unintelligible how equal rights to manna follow from equal moral rights. The link between the two can be made by postulating that moral equality means equal social rights. In that case, the derivation of social equality from moral equality is not any different from the derivation of social equality from social equality.

This is only one-half of the neutrality requirement. I have talked only about the two statements it permits. There are two statements it does not permit: "I am better than you are" and "My conception of the good is better than yours." Ackerman does not explain why these statements should be excluded. But we can assume that they are excluded because they assert moral inequality, that is, unequal moral rights for individuals. We can also assume that the rejection of moral inequality means the rejection of social inequality. This again shows that the convertibility of moral and social equality is the basic premise for Neutral Dialogue.

This account of the neutrality principle reveals its true character. It is not simply a formal constraint on Neutral Dialogue, but an alternative statement of the principle of equality. Although Neutral Dialogue purports to derive substantive equality from formal equality, it really derives social equality from

28. Richard Flathman, "Egalitarian Blood and Skeptical Turnips," Ethics 93 (1983):357–366.

moral equality. Neither of them is any more formal than the other; both are substantive. Moreover, the derivation can be made only because moral equality is taken to be equivalent to social equality.

Here lies the secret of Ackerman's program. The substantive equality of a liberal society is supposed to be delivered as an outcome of Neutral Dialogue. But we now find that Neutral Dialogue cannot get off the ground without presupposing the liberal ideal of equality. Ackerman has claimed to derive the social ideal of equality from Neutral Dialogue. Instead, he has constructed Neutral Dialogue on the basis of the social ideal. At best, Neutral Dialogue may be taken as a way of interpreting and applying the general principle of equality to particular situations. In that case, it is not an independent, but a subservient procedure.

CHAPTER FIVE

Instrumental Rationality

In normative discourse, the idea of formal rationality has been used in many different senses. It may mean the logical principle of consistency in the universalization of moral prescriptions or the formal conditions of communication in the discourse of moral justification. Whatever guise it may take, it is not strong enough to generate universal prescriptions. Moral prescriptions made by formal procedures are incurably agent-relative; different agents favor different prescriptions. But their differences may be negotiable; they can perhaps be resolved by agreement. This is the hope that has inspired David Gauthier's theory of morals by agreement.

For his contractual approach, Gauthier stipulates two conditions. First, the agents are nontuistic; they take no interest in each other. They are not affected by mutual feelings of love or hatred. Second, they are equally rational, but their rationality is restricted to the maximization of individual utilities. Such rationality may be called nontuistic rationality; it is purely instrumental and morally neutral. The agents of nontuistic rationality look like the rational maximizers in John Rawls's theory of justice. But they are not placed behind a veil of ignorance. Instead they negotiate with one another in full knowledge of who they are and what they have.

Gauthier recognizes two types of rational choice: straightforward maximization and constrained maximization (*MA* 167).[1] Straightforward maximization is the maximization of individual utility with no constraint whatsoever. It is the principle of rational choice in the world of perfect competition; there is no need to place constraints on rational behavior in a free market. The unconstrained operation of free markets produces optimal results for everybody concerned. But when markets fail, the individually rational choices produce collectively suboptimal results. Such a situation is characterized as the Prisoner's Dilemma. Rational choices have to be constrained; straightforward maximization has to be replaced by constrained maximization.

1. *MA* refers to David Gauthier, *Morals by Agreement* (Oxford, 1986).

Hobbes's state of nature is one big Prisoner's Dilemma. Predation is an instance of straightfoward maximization. Although it is rational from the perspective of each individual, it leads to collective disaster, a war of all against all. Such suboptimal consequences can be avoided by a cooperative strategy that places constraints on the rationality of individual choices. Hobbes translates these constraints into a system of natural laws.[2] Gauthier's project is similar to Hobbes's; he proposes to identify those constraints as morals. To understand Gauthier's derivation project, we have to be clear about his idea of morality. By *morality* he means not any particular moral code or convention, but any set of impartial constraints on the pursuit of individual interest (*MA* 6–7). For him, the idea of fairness or impartiality is the essence of morality. To derive morality from rationality is to demonstrate that the constraints of impartiality are dictated by the instrumental rationality of nontuism.

Gauthier's project consists of two stages. The first is concerned with the rationality of bargains: what kind of principles would be accepted by rational agents for governing their interactions, and what sort of dispositions would be developed by them to ensure their compliance? The rationality of bargains consists of three elements: initial bargaining condition, bargaining procedure, and compliance. In the second stage, Gauthier tries to demonstrate that the principles and dispositions rational agents adopt and develop in the first stage coincide with the principles and dispositions of morality. The first stage is presented in nonmoral terms, and the idea of morality enters only in the second stage.

Minimax Relative Concession

The bargaining procedure is the formula for dividing the cooperative surplus between the participants. The cooperative surplus is the fruit of cooperation above and beyond the costs of cooperation, and its distribution will be governed by the terms of cooperation. It is Gauthier's thesis that rational people would agree on the principle of minimax relative concession for the distribution of their cooperative surplus. In most cases, Gauthier says, this principle demands that all participants make the same proportionate concession if a rational compromise is to be reached.

One of Gauthier's examples of the principle of minimax relative concession (*MA* 137–39) involves Adelaide and Ernest, who have to divide the return from their cooperative venture. First, they have to cover their costs. What is left over is their cooperative surplus. If Adelaide is to receive all of it, she will get $500. If Ernest is to receive all of it, he will get only $50. The sum of their coopera-

---

2. Gregory Kavka gives an excellent account of moral constraints embodied in Hobbes's theory of natural laws. *Hobbesian Moral and Political Theory* (Princeton, 1986), 338–68.

tive surplus changes, depending on who gets all of it. The two sums are the maximum gains the two people can make, respectively. They can reach a compromise by making concessions. Five hundred dollars is the biggest concession Adelaide can make; $50 is the biggest concession Ernest can make. They can agree on making the same proportionate concession. Adelaide concedes $147, and Ernest concedes $15. She settles for a payoff of $353, and he for one of $35. Their relative concessions are proportionately equal; $15/$50 is equal to $147/$500.

We can imagine a simpler case. April and Eric have to divide their cooperate surplus of $500, which remains the same regardless of who gets it. The maximum concession April can make is $500, which is the same as the maximum concession Eric can make. The principle of minimax relative concession dictates an equal division of $250 each. By accepting this compromise, they are making the same proportionate concession, namely, one-half of their respective maximum concessions.

The relative concession can be expressed by the formula: $(u\# - u)/(u\# - u^*)$. The utility the agent commands at the initial bargaining position is represented by u^*, and the maximum utility she can claim is represented by $u\#$. The maximum concession she can make is represented by $(u\# - u^*)$. The utility she gains through the bargain is represented by u, and the actual concession she makes at the bargain is represented by $(u\# - u)$. The relative concession is the ratio of the actual concession $(u\# - u)$ and the maximum possible concession $(u\# - u^*)$.

Gauthier has to prove that the principle of minimax relative concession is the principle rational people would use for making bargains. He can make this proof by showing that it will be accepted under the condition of equal rationality. To make this point, he distinguishes between narrow and broad compliance. A person is said to be narrowly compliant if she is disposed to cooperate only on the terms that come close to the ones endorsed by the principle of minimax relative concession. A person is said to be broadly compliant if she is disposed to cooperate on any terms that can yield less than the principle of minimax relative concession prescribes, but more than she can get without cooperation.

If you are broadly compliant, you are willing to work for a share much smaller than your partner's. You give him the lion's share of the cooperative surplus, leaving only the squirrel's share for yourself. That is irrational; it is incompatible with the condition of equal rationality. You can do better for yourself if you are as rational as your partner. Let us now suppose you have the opposite disposition to broad compliance; you are disposed to cooperate only if you can get more than the principle of minimax relative concession allows. Now you are demanding the lion's share for yourself in all your bargains. If other people are as rational as you are, they will abandon you and turn to someone else for cooperation. If they are as rational as you are, they will find someone else to bargain with. Then you are left with nobody to cooperate with and you will fail to maximize your utility. That too is an irrational outcome. In the world of equally rationally beings, to be more than narrowly compliant is as irrational as to be less than narrowly compliant. Gauthier says that equal rationality demands equal compliance (*MA* 226). Equal compliance means accepting the principle of minimax relative concession.

Thus Gauthier establishes the principle of minimax relative concession as the principle of rational concession in a bargain. Jody Kraus and Jules Coleman have questioned his premise of narrow compliance. They say that rational people need not be always narrowly compliant, that is, they can sometimes be broadly compliant.[3] If all the members of a community are equally rational, they can all be broadly compliant. In fact, universal broad compliance can give them a much greater scope of cooperation than universal narrow compliance. Universal broad compliance is as consistent with the condition of equal rationality as universal narrow compliance.

Kraus and Coleman's next objection concerns the importance of opportunity cost in making a rational bargain. They maintain that whether you demand a lion's share or settle for a squirrel's share depends on your advantage and opportunities.[4] If your prospective partner demands a lion's share, it is still rational for you to accept his bid if nobody else can provide the goods and services you desire from him. The principle of minimax relative concession can set rational terms of agreement only when the two parties have equal opportunities as well as equal rationality. Gilbert Harman has voiced a similar objection: equal rationality is insufficient to yield the principle of minimax relative concession.[5] If one party commands a much greater bargaining power than the other party, it is not rational for the first party to follow the principle of minimax relative concession. The principle of minimax relative concession can be rational only under the condition not only of equal rationality, but also of equal bargaining power.

Harman does not explain what he means by "equal bargaining power." Perhaps we can link it to the notion of opportunity cost. Let us consider a simple case of two persons, Jason and Justin, who can jointly earn $200 for a day's work. Since their abilities and contributions are equivalent and they are equally rational, they agree to split their joint earning into two equal halves. Their co-

3. Jody Kraus and Jules Coleman, "Morality and the Theory of Rational Choice," *Ethics* 97 (1987): 740–45.

4. Ibid., 744.

5. Gilbert Harman, "Rationality in Agreement," *Social Philosophy and Policy* 5 (1988): 7.

operative surplus is $200; neither of them can make any money except through this partnership. Since each of them can make the maximum concession of $200, the principle of minimax relative concession requires each of them to concede $100. They make a bargain to work for $100 each for a day.

We can now assign unequal bargaining powers to Jason and Justin. One day after Jason and Justin's agreement, Jason receives an offer of $70 for a day's work from a third party. But Justin gets no offer from a third party; he can make nothing without renewing the contract with Jason. Under these conditions, their cooperative surplus is only $130 ($200 − $70), and the maximum concession each of them can make is $130. The principle of minimax relative concession divides the surplus equally between them: $65 for each. Justin and Jason have to divide their total earning of $200 into two unequal shares: $135 for Jason and $65 for Justin. By the principle of minimax relative concession, Justin's share is one-half of the cooperative surplus. But Jason's is one-half of the cooperative surplus and his cost of $70, which he could have made by taking the outside offer.

The following day, Justin receives an offer from a third party to work for $50 a day. Their cooperative surplus changes again. It is now only $80 ($200 − $50 − $70), and each of them can make the maximum concession of $40. By the principle of minimax relative concession, Jason should get $110 ($40 + $70), and Justin should get $90 ($40 + $50). Surely bargaining powers have changed and dictated different terms of contract, but none of their bargains violates the principle of minimax relative concession. When their bargaining powers change, their cooperative surplus changes. Consequently the principle of minimax relative concession exacts different concessions in different bargains, although Jason and Justin are doing the same job with the same skills. But the same principle holds for all their bargains; it surely does not ignore bargaining powers.

The importance of bargaining powers for relative concessions is even more dramatic in James Fishkin's illustration, which exploits Gauthier's own example.[6] Suppose a person Q is drowning and another person P happens to be nearby. P has nothing to do with Q's drowning; he is an innocent bystander. Q has gotten himself into this dilemma all on his own. P, the would-be Rescuer, wants to make a rational bargain with Q for the rescue job. Fishkin says, the Rescuer can demand one-half of Q's future earnings. This is a rational demand by the principle of minimax relative concession, on the assumption that the utility of his future earnings is linear. It should be equally rational for Q to concede to P's demand. So P agrees to rescue Q on these terms. This is what the principle of minimax relative concession dictates.

---

6. James Fishkin, "Bargaining, Justice, and Justification: Towards Reconstruction," *Social Philosophy and Policy* 5 (1988): 46–64.

Let us assume that rational agents accept the principle of minimax relative concession, though its acceptance stands on the questionable premise of narrow compliance. Let us see how close the principle comes to reflecting our intuitive sense of fairness. This consideration belongs to the second stage of Gauthier's derivation project. He maintains that the principle of minimax relative concession is the same as the principle of maximin relative benefit, and that the latter principle is the principle of impartiality (*MA* 155). It is the principle that impartially distributes mutual benefit in a cooperative enterprise. These two principles describe the division of a cooperative surplus from two opposite perspectives, concession and benefit. When the concessions are rational, the division of benefits is impartial and fair, and vice versa. Gauthier writes, "Impartiality and rationality coincide in bargaining" (*MA* 155).

In Fishkin's view, the agreement between P and Q is obviously inequitable and iniquitous. But Gauthier sees nothing wrong in the hypothetical deal: "It would seem that the second party could have no reason to refrain from accepting benefits in return for what enables the first party to avoid disaster. It may be pure good luck on her part that she is able to provide the needed aid, and pure bad luck on the other party's part that he needs the aid that she can provide. But why is this morally objectionable?" [7]

On Gauthier's theory, whatever is dictated by the principle of minimax relative concession is fair; it accords with the principle of maximin relative benefit. In Fishkin's view, however, the terms of agreement between P and Q are unfair because they are imposed on a helpless party under "coercively structured bargaining situations." [8] In support of his view, Fishkin can cite the authority of Roman law, which recognized the iniquity of contracts made under such coercive conditions.[9] Q (the Rescuee) is under coercive condition because P (the Rescuer) holds a monopoly power over Q. P is the only one who can provide the needed help for Q. To exercise monopoly over someone is to take advantage of another person. Gauthier repeatedly says that the basic idea of fairness or impartiality is not to take advantage of others. Since P is taking advantage of Q's helpless situation, P's extortion is unfair by Gauthier's own standard of fairness.

There are many forms of coercion. When someone takes advantage of another's helpless situation, let us call it situational coercion. The tactic of situational coercion also operates in the negotiation and renegotiation between Jason and Justin. Their rational bargain changes its terms in response to the offers

---

7. David Gauthier, "Morality, Rational Choice, and Semantic Representation: A Reply to My Critics," *Social Philosophy and Policy* 5 (1988): 201. This is Gauthier's reply to Fishkin's criticism.
8. Fishkin, "Bargaining, Justice, and Justification: Towards Reconstruction," 48.
9. This is also true of American and most European laws.

they can get from a third party, although they are doing the same work with the same skills. Operating under the principle of minimax relative concession, Jason and Justin should keep looking for more and more outside offers and seeking better and better bargains from each other, though they have no intention of terminating their cooperation and are doing the same work with the same skills. They appear to be bent on exploiting each other's situation to the hilt. Mutual cooperation is no more than mutual exploitation.

By Gauthier's principle, however, neither of these two cases involves exploitation. They are only matters of rational negotiation, and any outcome of a rational bargain is fair and impartial. This is the discrepancy between Gauthier's and the commonsense standard of fairness and impartiality. If Fishkin is right, rational bargains can be fair only if they satisfy one further condition: they should be made under noncoercive bargaining situations or avoid situational exploitation. To be sure, situational exploitation need not be one-sided; two parties can exploit each other's situation. Under the principle of minimax relative concession, a scheme of cooperation is always a scheme of mutual exploitation. To that extent, it may be impartial, but it still offends our sense of fairness.

Our sense of fairness demands that situational exploitation be avoided, but this condition is not morally neutral. It can be defined only in moral terms. If Gauthier has to use this condition along with the condition of equal rationality for defining fair bargains, he cannot define fair bargains in morally neutral terms. This is one of the formidable obstacles to his project of deriving morality from rationality.

The Initial Bargaining Position

Let us now turn to the first phase of rational bargain, the initial bargaining positions. What sorts of initial positions are required for making a rational bargain? Gauthier says that the rationality of initial positions can be secured by two conditions: the noncoercive bargaining position and the Lockean proviso. That is, a rational bargain cannot be made if any of the parties to the bargain has to negotiate from a coercive position or has violated the Lockean proviso.

Gauthier explains the rationality of noncoercive bargaining positions by the example of a bargain between slaves and masters (*MA* 190–92). Since slavery is a costly system, the masters offer to abolish it if the slaves continue to provide the same services without coercion. So they reach the Bargain of Mutual Benefit. But the slaves are in a coercive bargaining position when they make this bargain. After the slaves are freed, they realize that they can sell their services for a better price. So they will revoke the Bargain of Mutual Benefit and sell their services elsewhere or renegotiate their agreement with their former masters. It is not rational for the slaves to keep the bargain. This is Gauthier's proof that the Bargain of Mutual Benefit is not a rational bargain. But Gauthier does not seem to recognize the difficulty of distinguishing this case from the bargain between P (the Rescuer) and Q (the Rescuee). Let us assume that P has imposed on Q exactly the same terms the masters imposed on the slaves in the Bargain of Mutual Benefit. After his rescue, Q will take exactly the same course of action that the slaves have taken. Q will refuse to keep the bargain and demand renegotiation. The two cases are structurally identical.

In spite of their structural identity, Gauthier treats these two bargains differently. In his view, one is made under coercion, and the other is not. One is rational to keep, and the other is not. Gauthier seems to draw this distinction from the fact that one case involves slaves, while the other does not. But this distinction can make no difference to the rationality of respective bargains, as long as both cases involve rational people. If one of them is rational to keep, the other must be equally so. Gauthier may feel on moral grounds that it is more reprehensible to exact enormous concessions from helpless slaves than from helpless free individuals. But to be influenced by such a feeling is to contaminate his theory of rational bargain with moral considerations, which are irrelevant at this point.

Jody Kraus and Jules Coleman have contested Gauthier's claim that it is not rational for the slaves to keep the Bargain of Mutual Benefit.[10] The former slaves may have no place to go or no other means of livelihood if they sever their relation with their former masters. Whether the former slaves will or will not keep the agreement with their former masters largely depends on their opportunity costs. What is truly decisive is not the question of rationality, but that of opportunity; or rather they are inseparable. But Gauthier appears to consider the rationality of the freed slaves as being separate from their available alternatives.

The idea of a noncoercive bargaining position clearly belongs to our commonsense morality, but it cannot be derived from the rationality of the individual maximizer. This is an important discrepancy between morality and rationality, if rationality is taken in Gauthier's sense. To this extent, the second stage of his derivation project is again defective.

The Lockean Proviso

The Lockean proviso is the prebargain rule of appropriation. It prescribes a set of natural rights in the state of nature: the rights of individuals against one another in their use of natural resources.[11] Consequently it determines what

---

10. Kraus and Coleman, "Morality and the Theory of Rational Choice," 725–28.
11. Gauthier's conception of natural rights is quite different from the traditional conception. It is what Christopher Morris calls seminatural rights in his "Natural Rights and Pub-

each party can legitimately bring to the bargaining table. Gauthier recognizes the difficulty of interpreting the proviso. The most stringent version allows one to appropriate natural resources only if one can leave "enough, and as good" for others. Gauthier regards this reading as too stringent (*MA* 202–03). He considers Robert Nozick's interpretation: the Lockean proviso is meant to ensure that "the situation of others is not worsened." He regards even this interpretation as too strong because there are situations in which one could avoid this only by worsening one's own position. So he qualifies the Lockean proviso: "It prohibits worsening the situation of others except where this is necessary to avoid worsening one's own position" (*MA* 203).

Gauthier tries to explain how the proviso works. Let us suppose, he says, you and I are fisherfolk. If you seize the fish I catch against my will, you violate the Lockean proviso. That is clear and easy. Now you live upstream and use the river for the disposal of your wastes. Your polluting behavior kills the fish in my part of the river. Gauthier says that you do not violate the proviso! This is not easy to understand. Although you worsen my position, he explains, you do not improve your situation by the disposal. "The cost you impose on me is not necessary to the benefit you receive; it is not a *displaced cost*" (*MA* 212).

The question of whether you are improving your position or not should have reference to a base point. Gauthier says that the base point is the absence of the other party (*MA* 211–12). If the downstreamer had not been there, the upstreamer could have dumped his waste without imposing any cost on anyone. If this is the base point for comparing his positions, the upstreamer does not improve his position by polluting the river. When the cost is occasioned solely by the presence of *A*, it is not a displaced cost if the position of *B* is not better than it would have been in the absence of *A*. This is Gauthier's presence/absence test for displaced costs. Gauthier applies this test to our earlier story of *P* (the Rescuer) and *Q* (the Rescuee): *P* does not violate the proviso by refusing to rescue *Q* because *Q* would not be any worse off even if *P* were not there (*MA* 204).

Gauthier does not say why the same presence/absence test cannot be used by the downstreamer. He can take the absence of the upstreamer as the base point for evaluating his position. In comparison with this base point, his position has been worsened by the upstreamer's polluting. Therefore the upstreamer has violated the proviso. This argument by the downstreamer is in accord with Gauthier's interpretation of the proviso: "It prohibits worsening the situation of others except where this is necessary to avoid worsening one's own position" (*MA* 203).

Gauthier's argument against the complaint of the downstreamer is based on

---

lic Goods," in *The Restraint of Liberty: Bowling Green Studies in Applied Philosophy* 7 (1985): 102–17.

the premise that the upstreamer has not really gained anything by dumping his waste in the river. This premise is doubtful for two reasons. First, you may be gaining something by dumping your waste into the river. If you do not dump them into the river, you may have to leave them around your house or haul them away to some other place, both of which are costly and unpleasant. Second, whether you are gaining anything or nothing appears to be totally irrelevant to the question of whether you are hurting me or not. Suppose you throw a cinder block out your window, and it lands on my head. You are not gaining anything; you are not displacing any cost. You are not taking advantage of me. Nevertheless, you are killing me. Would Gauthier say that you do not violate the Lockean proviso?[12]

Gauthier complicates the fisherfolk story. Now suppose you and I begin to trade, he says. Viewed from this vantage point of social interaction, he says, your polluting activity worsens my position against yours because you are improving your position by worsening mine. Hence you are violating the Lockean proviso (MA 212). But there is no guarantee that your polluting behavior will always improve your position. In fact, if I catch polluted fish or little fish, you will suffer in trade, too. Your position will be worsened by your own acts of pollution. In that case, you cannot violate the proviso. Only when you improve your position do you violate the proviso. Whether you violate the proviso or not depends on whether you are bettering or worsening your situation by polluting the river. It is likely that your polluting may violate the proviso one day and not the next because the pollution of the river may affect your position differently from day to day.

Gauthier uses another example to illustrate the proviso. Several people inhabit an island, whose land and resources compose a commons for all. One of the inhabitants, Eve, decides to appropriate a plot of land for her exclusive use. She grows marvelous fruits and sells them to others. Her cultivation of the private plot hurts no one but benefits many. Under these circumstances, Gauthier says, she does not violate the proviso (MA 215). The example set by the first appropriator is followed by many, and all the available land has been appropriated. There is no more land for the countless people to be born in later generations. Does not the act of appropriation, which does not violate the proviso in its own day, violate it against the dispossessed of later generations? Gauthier

12. Gauthier assumes that to hurt someone without the prospect of gaining something for oneself is morally innocent, whereas to hurt someone in order to gain advantage for oneself is morally wrong. But injury to others cannot be morally justified on the ground that it is not motivated by the desire for selfish gains. Injury to others carries its own moral weight. For this reason, it is wrong to inflict gratuitous suffering on anybody, though nobody else gains from it. By the utilitarian standard, injuries to others without the motive for selfish gains is worse than injuries caused by such a motive because the former is more likely to decrease the total utility of all concerned.

holds that appropriation does not violate the proviso if it produces favorable consequences for the society as a whole in terms of four criteria: density of population, duration of life, material well-being, and breadth of opportunity (*MA* 288).

In the face of these four criteria, the justification of appropriation requires a completely different interpretation of the Lockean proviso. In his initial interpretation, Gauthier took the proviso as a rule governing the relation of individuals: one person cannot improve his position by displacing the cost onto another. This is a deontic theory of rights. But this deontic context of individual rights is replaced by a collective context of general consequences in his later interpretation of the proviso.[13] The four criteria are the consequences of the proviso on the general conditions of life and culture over a long period of time. Though such a consequentialist consideration is important to utilitarians, it is irrelevant to self-interested rational agents, who are seeking the maximization of their individual utilities.

No doubt, some general consequences affect the self-interested individuals, but Gauthier makes no distinction between those consequences that affect the interests of rational agents engaged in a rational bargain and those that do not. He is appealing to a broad notion of general consequences that cuts across even the boundary of generations. Such a long-range collective consideration dictates a radically different reading of the proviso than the individualistic consideration of the Prisoner's Dilemma. The difference between these two considerations is especially important to the property right of the dispossessed. The collective consideration can justify the property rights of the rich against the dispossessed, but the individual consideration cannot. It is not rational for anyone to abide by the proviso and end up with no property of her own, if she is solely concerned with her own well-being.

The presence/absence test is purely individualistic; it has nothing to do with collective considerations. This test says that one party cannot be said to worsen the position of another party, if the former's absence could not have affected the position of the latter any differently than his presence would have done. By this test, the proviso can secure the property right of the dispossessed against the property owners. If the latter had not been there first and appropriated all the usable land, the former would not have been dispossessed. On the other hand, as Gauthier believes, the same proviso can justify the right of property owners against the dispossessed on consequentialist grounds.

The shift from individual to collective considerations is the most serious weakness in Gauthier's argument for the Lockean proviso. By the time this

13. A similar shift takes place in Robert Nozick's justification of the Lockean proviso in *Anarchy, State, and Utopia* (New York, 1974), 174–82.

shift is made, his idea of rationality is utilitarian. To be sure, utilitarians are rational in their own way, but their rationality is clearly incompatible with non-tuistic rationality. Gauthier appears to have shifted to the idea of collective rationality and general consequences because the proviso cannot be justified by the rationality of individual maximizers.

Gauthier links the proviso to the question of predation. Assuming that rational people appropriate natural resources under the proviso, he wants to prove that they will not raid others' appropriations. Predation is a violation of the proviso and is irrational because the violators will be excluded from profitable cooperation between equally rational people. If people agree to bargain and cooperate with those who violate the proviso, Gauthier says, they will encourage more predatory activities. Hence it is irrational to cooperate with those who break the proviso (*MA* 195). It is rational to exclude from bargaining those with unfair initial entitlements because their exclusion will discourage future predatory behavior.

Kraus and Coleman argue that the rationality of excluding predators from bargaining depends on a threshold population of narrow compliers.[14] If there are already enough narrow compliers to discourage future predators, it is irrational for you to turn down a profitable bargain with a predator. Your refusal would make no difference to the deterrence of future predators. If there are not enough narrow compliers to discourage future predators, it is again irrational for you to turn down a profitable bargain with a predator. Again, your refusal would make no difference. Your refusal would make a difference only when you are at the critical point of pushing the number of narrow compliers over the threshold. Only then is it rational for you to reject a profitable proposal from a predator. Except for this rare occasion, the rule against predation cannot be endorsed by the principle of rationality.

There is one more objection to the proviso; this is the problem of information cost. Suppose you are determined not to negotiate with anyone who has violated the proviso; you have to find out how your prospective partner has acquired her present possessions. Obtaining that sort of information may be costly. If she has inherited some of her possessions, you have to find out how her ancestors acquired that part of her possessions. That may be even more costly. It may be irrational to incur such information costs; it cannot help your cause of utility maximization. In this regard, the application of the proviso is completely different from the application of the minimax relative concession rule. The information required for the latter is not so extensive and so costly as the one required for the former. Gauthier can eliminate the problem of information cost by postulating costless information. In fact, his entire theory may

14. Kraus and Coleman, "Morality and the Theory of Rational Choice," 737.

stand on the assumption of costless bargaining. But this assumption renders his contractarian project too implausible for the real world, as Kraus and Coleman suggest.[15]

In Gauthier's theory, the function of the Lockean proviso is twofold. On one hand, it is meant to serve as the principle for the appropriation of natural resources. On the other hand, it is meant to keep predators, social parasites, and free riders away from the bargaining table. The second of these two functions can be endorsed by morality; it is in accord with our sense of fairness. But it cannot be endorsed by the rationality of individual maximizers. This is another discrepancy between morality and rationality. The problem with the other function of the proviso is even more serious. For if the proviso cannot protect the right of the dispossessed, it is incompatible with the requirement not only of rationality, but of morality.

Rationality and Morality

I have not discussed the difficult problem of compliance: why rational agents should comply with the rational bargains they make. Although this is an important problem for Gauthier's project, it is not so important for my purposes. Instead, I will reconsider how the dictates of rationality match up with the dictates of morality. Though nontuistic rationality has turned out to be ineffectual in endorsing the general principles Gauthier wants to uphold, let us now suppose that he has given a theory of morals defined in terms of those principles. Can we accept it as a convincing account of morality? Annette Baier says that the rationality of nontuism excludes many such areas of traditional morality as the parental care of children and aid for the poor.[16] Children and the poor have nothing to bring to the bargaining table. Though benevolence has long been regarded as an important moral virtue, Christopher Morris says, it cannot be accommodated within Gauthier's theory of rationality.[17]

These criticisms are correct. There is an obvious extensional discrepancy between traditional morality and the morals that "arise in and from the rational agreement of equals" (*MA* 232). By *morality,* however, Gauthier means nothing more than justice between nontuistic individuals; for that reason, he locates the essence of morality in the idea of impartiality. Only in the last two chapters of his book does he clearly state the equivalence of morality and justice. The title of his book, *Morals by Agreement,* is misleading. It should have been called *Justice by Agreement.* Hence the right question is not whether he has

15. Ibid., 747.
16. Annette Baier, "Pilgrim's Progress," *Canadian Journal of Philosophy* 18 (1988): 315–30.
17. Christopher Morris, "Relation between Self-interest and Justice," *Social Philosophy and Policy* 5 (1988): 145.

given a correct account of morality, but whether he has given a correct account of justice.

On Gauthier's theory, justice is impartiality, and impartiality is whatever can be accepted by equally rational beings. I have already considered the discrepancy between the impartiality dictated by the principle of minimax relative concession and the sense of fairness commended by commonsense morality. From the commonsense perspective, Gauthier's principle appears to be a principle of mutual exploitation. It encourages all nontuistic individuals to take advantage of others' bargaining positions, as we have seen in the cases of Jason and Justin and the Rescuer and the Rescued. This problem arises under the condition of equal rationality. When this condition does not obtain, Gauthier's principle generates another serious problem.

In a world of equally rational beings, it may be rational to accept the impartiality of nontuism. But the real world is seldom peopled by equally rational human beings. If Justin is far more rational and intelligent than Jason, it is irrational for him to follow the principle of minimax relative concession. Justin can get Jason to work for $20 instead of $100, if Jason does not know any alternative. Even if Jason is as intelligent as Justin, Justin may not have to pay anything to Jason if Justin has the power to force Jason to do his bidding. Justin tries to negotiate with Jason only insofar as Jason has the power of refusal. This is in line with Gauthier's endorsement of Hume's assertion that we should not feel "any restraint of justice" in dealing with creatures vastly inferior in intelligence and power to us (*MA* 308).

In Gauthier's theory, the circumstances of justice are Prisoner's Dilemmas, which require social cooperation. If people have equal powers over one another, they can drive themselves into Prisoner's Dilemmas. But if some of them are intelligent or powerful enough to coerce or control others, they can avert Prisoner's Dilemmas without making any rational bargains. It is irrational for the powerful to reach an agreement to cooperate with the multitude because they can do better without such an agreement. They have no need of justice or impartiality. Morality is necessary only for those who cannot control others. Gauthier endorses this view: "We care for morality, not for its own sake, but because we lack the strength to dominate our fellows or the self-sufficiency to avoid interaction with them. The person who could secure her ends either independently of others or by subordinating them would never agree to the constraints of morality. She would be irrational—mad" (*MA* 307).

Such is the essence of instrumental morality, which has been hatched in the matrix of the Prisoner's Dilemma. It is about time to examine the appropriateness of the Prisoner's Dilemma as a model for questions of justice. To be sure, Gauthier is not the first to use this model; in fact, the practice has become quite fashionable among moral philosophers. The essential character of the Prisoner's Dilemma consists of two elements: the nontuism of two prisoners and their Hobbesian equality ("Even the weakest can kill the strongest"). The two prisoners do not care about what each of them can do to or for the other; each of them is solely concerned with what he can get for himself. They have equal power to confess their crime to the authority and gain special benefit at the expense of each other. Their power relation is the Hobbesian equality; neither of them can control the behavior of the other. If one of them were to have power enough to control the behavior of the other, he could prevent the Prisoner's Dilemma. Under these conditions, it is rational for both of them not to confess to the crime. This is their rational bargain, and it can give them the constrained maximization of their utilities.

Since the rationality of their bargain is equally beneficial to both of them, it may be regarded as impartial. But it is quite different from the commonsense notion of impartiality, which seeks fairness and justice apart from the conditions of equal rationality and of Hobbesian equality. In questions of justice, we do not normally consider how rational the parties involved are, how powerful they are, or whether they satisfy the condition of Hobbesian equality. If there is any inequality of power or rationality between them, we regard the questions of justice as even more serious. We also assume that the weak deserve the consideration of justice more than the powerful. This is the basic divergence of Gauthier's conception from the commonsense conception of justice.

Gauthier recognizes that his nontuistic conception of justice is basically the same as Hume's. Justice is a compromise between our weakness and our strength. If we are strong, we do not need it; if we are weak, we cannot get it. Justice is a necessary evil for those living in the world of equal power and rationality, where none of them has the power to dominate the others. Gauthier concedes that justice has only instrumental value; no one wants to seek it for its own sake. In the real world, however, most people cannot have the benefit of justice. They are not equal enough to others, and most of them live under domination. To be sure, domination is often disguised through deception and ideology, and what passes for morality is usually no more than a massive ideological concealment of the exploitation of the weak. This is roughly Gauthier's picture of justice in the real world.

When moral constraints are used as instruments of domination and deception, Gauthier says, they disguise manipulation and exploitation. By the standard of instrumental justice, however, such manipulation and exploitation cannot be regarded as unjust because they are compatible with the principle of rationality. Those who are manipulated and exploited are not rational or powerful enough to look after their interests, and what they are getting is what they deserve by the principle of instrumental rationality. What they should get under the condition of equal rationality cannot be used as the criterion of justice for condemning what they do get, when and where the condition of equal rationality does not obtain. Gauthier admits that justice and reason part company when the equality of rationality does not obtain (*MA* 313). This is a misleading statement. He can say that justice and reason can part company only if he assigns them independent existence. On Gauthier's theory, however, justice has no independent existence; it is only an instrument of rationality. Instead, he should say that reason dissolves justice when the condition of equal rationality does not obtain.

Essential Justice v. Instrumental Justice

Gauthier finds this implication of his theory of justice quite disturbing. He admits that such a view of justice and morality can subvert moral order as a cooperative adventure for mutual advantage (*MA* 309). In one of his earlier papers, he passed an even more ominous verdict on the ideology of nontuism and individualism.[18] A society whose members all seek nothing but individual interests is destined to collapse into competitive chaos. Such a society has only centrifugal force and no centripetal force to counterbalance it. The unmitigated individualism of self-interest corrodes all social bonds. In the past few centuries, he said, the centrifugal force of individual interests in the West has been contained by the centripetal force of love and patriotism. It is these two rather than the myth of social contract that have been the real support of social order. But now that love and patriotism have been exposed as ideological myths, Gauthier concluded, "the triumph of radical contractarianism leads to the destruction, rather than the rationalization, of our society."[19]

This is Gauthier's fear of nontuism and its instrumental rationality. His fear can now be accentuated and amplified by the fact that he has converted instrumental rationality into instrumental justice. The force of evil is always frightening, but it becomes far more sinister when it assaults us under the cloak of justice. Gauthier tries to find a way to cope with the menace of nontuistic rationality and its instrumental justice through the astounding claim that it is not the justice of real people (*MA* 315–19). Instrumental justice is merely the justice of economic man, and the concept of economic man is but a fiction far removed from real people. Gauthier says that real justice is not only instrumental but essential and that essential justice is sought for its own sake rather than as an instrument. Finally he holds that essential justice truly flourishes with liberal individuals.

What then is the relation of essential to instrumental justice, and of liberal individuals to economic men? I have to clarify these two points before laying out a complete picture of Gauthier's theory. Gauthier holds that an economic man recognizes only instrumental value in his activities. Their ultimate end is

18. David Gauthier, "The Social Contract as Ideology," *Philosophy and Public Affairs* 6 (1977): 130–64.
19. Ibid., 163.

the satisfaction of his preferences. Hence his rationality is purely instrumental. He is asocial; his social interaction with others has only instrumental value. His lack of self-sufficiency is simply an evil; so is his need for participation in social activities (*MA* 325). For these reasons, morality has only instrumental value for economic man; its only function is to enable him to endure social cooperation without getting victimized by others. Morality does not engage his affections; he has no reason to love morality for its own sake. In fact, free affectivity is the prerogative of economic man; he never gets enchained by affections for anything other than the satisfaction of his preferences.

Gauthier insists that real human beings are different from economic man, although economic man constitutes a part of every human being. Real human beings love participation for its own sake, whereas economic man looks upon it as a necessary evil (*MA* 336). Consider an orchestra: even if you master every orchestral instrument, Gauthier points out, you alone cannot make an orchestra. An orchestra accomplishes something you can never do individually. He asks, "Have we reason to regret that some music requires an orchestra?" Social union is not a cause of regret, but a source of enrichment. Instead of lamenting over the need for social participation, Gauthier tells us, we should rejoice over it.

Gauthier is presenting two ways of looking at social order. From the perspective of economic man, it is a necessary evil; it reflects human deficiency. From the perspective of real human beings, it is a positive good; it enriches and enlarges human capacities and accomplishments. Gauthier holds that morality takes on different colors when it is viewed from these two perspectives. From the negative perspective of economic man, it appears as an unwelcome constraint. From the positive perspective of real human beings, it makes shared activities welcome and stable, ensuring the absence of coercion and deception. When people appreciate participation for its own sake, they will come to value their fellow participators and "place a new value on the moral framework within which participation flourishes. . . . Having first engaged their reason, morality now engages their affection" (*MA* 338). When morality is accepted for its own sake, it ceases to be instrumental justice and becomes essential justice. Essential justice comes about as the conversion of instrumental justice in the context of participation. Instrumental justice is the morality of nontuism; essential justice is the morality of tuism.

If the nontuism of economic man is so different from the tuism of real people, why does Gauthier accept the former as the premise for his theory of justice rather than the latter? Would it not be better to begin with a premise which is truer to reality? As he repeatedly claims, he wants to construct a theory of morality on a set of realistic assumptions. If he begins with an unrealistic picture of human beings, he is likely to produce an unrealistic theory of justice. If he does, then he has to replace it with a more realistic theory of justice.

Gauthier is seeking a more realistic theory of justice in his attempt to replace instrumental with essential justice. This maneuver appears to be an unnecessary detour that could have been avoided by beginning with a truer or more realistic picture of human beings.

Gauthier may be able to give the following defense of the detour. He has identified the Prisoner's Dilemma as the model for the circumstances of justice. He may now say that the Prisoner's Dilemma is a situation typical of economic man, whose nontuistic rationality inevitably leads to the Prisoner's Dilemma. Hence his nontuistic rationality should be taken as the premise for a theory of justice. Furthermore, the conversion of instrumental into essential justice does not change its content. The conversion is only a matter of perspective. As soon as instrumental justice is taken for its own sake rather than as a means, it becomes essential justice. Hence nothing is lost in the conversion, and there is really no detour in Gauthier's theory of justice.

On Gauthier's theory, the conversion of instrumental to essential justice is also the conversion of economic man into real people, or the nontuism of the former into the tuism of the latter. But his account of this conversion appears to be faulty. He begins with an unfair picture of economic man. There is no reason to assume that he cannot appreciate participation for its own sake. If he can find satisfaction in participation, he will look upon it as an end in itself. In this regard, he is no different from real human beings. They look upon participation as an end in itself because they find satisfaction in it. Economic man does not have to deny that social cooperation enriches his life. He knows that there are many things he cannot do alone; that is why he is seeking cooperation. An orchestra is indeed a good example of social cooperation any economic man would love to accept. He may find a greater pleasure in playing with an orchestra than in his solo performance. Economic man need not hate to be with others; in fact, he may be gregarious.

Gauthier assumes that the love of participation leads to the love of fellow participators. What sort of love is this? I may love to play with an orchestra whose members are all my slaves. I can love them for their parts in my orchestra. Since they are my slaves, they cannot demand even instrumental justice. Now suppose they are free and make a rational bargain with me. Our bargain is nevertheless dictated by instrumental justice, even though I value my participation in the orchestra and love its members. I still regard the other players as mere means for giving me a chance to play with an orchestra. My love for them continues to be nontuistic.

I can have essential justice with the members of the orchestra only when I recognize their intrinsic value, that is, by taking an interest in their well-being or treating them as more than merely a means to my own satisfaction. Such behavior is to adopt a tuistic attitude. To be sure, tuism does not coincide with altruism. Even when I take a negative interest in your well-being and take pleasure in your misfortune, my attitude is tuistic. Any interest whatsoever one takes in the well-being of others is bound to lie in the realm of tuism, whether the interest is positive or negative.

One special form of tuism is the basic premise for the commonsense notion of justice and impartiality. This is to regard all human beings as ends in themselves. It is possible to be impartial by treating everybody as a mere means. But that surely contravenes the idea of justice and fairness. The idea of impartial justice is to give equal consideration to all parties, and this is the idea of equal respect. This idea holds whether the parties are equally rational or not, whether equally powerful or not. The idea of equal rationality does not enter as a relevant consideration in the tuistic conception of justice. If tuism is the basic premise for essential justice, the conversion of instrumental into essential justice amounts to the rejection of nontuism, which Gauthier has taken as the premise for his definition of instrumental justice and morality.

Gauthier's conversion theory has two parts: psychological and definitional. The psychological part is his claim that one can begin with instrumental justice and turn it into essential justice by appreciating it for its own sake. This is an empirical assertion, and it may be true for some people and false for others. The definitional part is his thesis that instrumental and essential justice are identical in content. This is the questionable part; they cannot be identical.

The impartiality of tuism is different from the impartiality of nontuism. Whereas the latter is the impartiality in demanding relative concessions, the former is the impartiality of equal consideration. For an illustration of this point, let us go back to the rational bargain between P (the Rescuer) and Q (the Rescued) in our earlier story. P demands one-half of Q's future earnings, and that is impartial by the principle of minimax relative concession. But it is not impartial by the standard of equal consideration; P is taking advantage of Q's helpless condition. The measure of equal consideration can be determined by the veil of ignorance. Someone who can occupy either P's or Q's position would never say that P is entitled to one-half of Q's future earnings. This is not to say that different people will give exactly the same answer to what is Q's fair payment for P's rescue service. In spite of their different estimates, they can easily rule out P's exorbitant demands, which can still be permitted by the principle of minimax relative concession.

The same thing may hold for the bargain between Jason and Justin that we considered earlier. The impartiality of nontuism should permit unequal terms of contract when one of them receives an outside offer from a third party, although they perform identical functions in their present joint adventure. The commonsense notion of impartiality and fairness should permit no change in their bargain, as long as they do the same job with the same skills. In this case, the principle of equal consideration takes into account only what each of them truly contributes to their joint undertaking. If one of them gets a chance to make more money elsewhere, he can terminate their relation and accept the new offer. In the case of Justin and Jason, the outside offer ($70 a day) is considerably lower than the present payment ($100). But one of them uses the outside offer to alter the present contract, which gives equal shares to them. Though such a self-seeking maneuver is dictated by the instrumental justice of nontuism, it appears unfair and indecent by the commonsense notion of justice and fairness. This is clearly a difference of content between essential and instrumental justice.

If essential justice means the justice of tuism, it cannot be defined in terms of nontuistic rationality. Instrumental justice cannot turn into essential justice just because it is being appreciated for its own sake. The two can never coincide in content. At best, they can overlap somewhat. When two parties are equally rational and powerful, they can strike a bargain that can be fair by the standard not only of instrumental, but also of essential justice. This overlap is not accidental. Under the condition of equal rationality and power, two parties can prevent themselves from taking advantage of each other. Where there is no taking advantage, there is essential justice. Essential justice obtains as the consequence of equal rationality and power. As soon as equal rationality is separated from equal power, however, instrumental and essential justice part company. In the commonsense notion of justice, the problem of justice is inseparable from the problem of unequal powers; people need justice because of their unequal power.

Critical Rationality

Gauthier identifies one further important difference between economic man and real human beings. The rationality of economic man is not only instrumental, but lacks critical reflection. Economic man is nothing more than a maximization machine; he never critically evaluates his utility function. He does not care whether he is a satisfied pig or a disgruntled philosopher. But the rationality of real human beings is critical and reflective. Gauthier identifies the idea of reflective rationality with the traditional idea of autonomy (*MA* 343). Such an identification, however, is spurious. One does not have to be critical and reflective to be autonomous. Economic man is fully able to meet the traditional standard of autonomy as long as he is allowed the freedom to maximize his utility. He knows what he wants and how to get it. His autonomy can be assured as long as he is protected against coercion.

The idea of critical and reflective rationality is much richer than the idea of autonomy. Let us see what is required by such an idea. There are two ways of critically evaluating one's utility function: factually and evaluatively. Your utility function may be based on false information; you may have wrong beliefs about your preferences and your chance of fulfilling them. By acquiring better information, you can devise better ways of maximizing your utility. This is a factual criticism of your utility function; it is a critical inquiry into its factual bases. This type of criticism is only instrumental; it is only in the service of your utility function, which retains its essential identity unaffected by the critical inquiry.

Critically reflecting on the principle of straightforward maximization, let us suppose, you realize that your utility function can be better served by the principle of constrained maximization. This is a critical assessment of your principle, and Gauthier takes it as an example of critical reflection in one of his earlier papers.[20] But even this sort of criticism is only instrumental; its function is to deliver a greater utility. It does not affect the character of your utility function itself to know that constrained maximization is more profitable than straightforward maximization. Gauthier is now seeking critical reflection that goes beyond all levels of instrumental function. But he does not tell us much about this exalted function of critical rationality.

Let us now suppose you begin to question your preferences. You have long wished to be a good wife and mother; you have always looked upon domestic bliss as the ultimate end of your life. Now you begin to suspect that your preference has been shaped by the genderization of society. So you decide to reject your earlier wish and seek a professional career. Even this sort of critical reflection need not disturb your utility function. On comparing the utility of domestic life with that of a professional career, you find that the latter is clearly superior to the former. So you choose a professional career over domestic life, but you have not really altered your utility function. This type of critical reflection is still factual; you are only comparing two sources of utility.

These different forms of critical reflection are compatible with the concept of economic man. If critical reflection is understood in these forms, it is an important element in the notion of instrumental rationality. On what grounds then does Gauthier say that economic man lacks critical and reflective rationality? He says that economic man is not truly critical and reflective because his preferences are easily manipulated by others. In that regard, he is no different from the citizens of *Brave New World* (*MA* 323). What economic man lacks is not critical reflection, but autonomy; or rather, by *critical reflection* Gauthier really means autonomy.

If economic man and the citizens of *Brave New World* are not autonomous because their preferences are shaped by social forces, then autonomy can be attained only by shaping one's own preferences without getting influenced by others. But that sort of autonomy is not realizable in the real world. As Gauthier admits, no one can escape the pressure of socialization, and our preferences are

20. David Gauthier, "Reason and Maximization," *Canadian Journal of Philosophy* 4 (1975): 427–31.

constantly shaped by social pressures (*MA* 351). If autonomy cannot be defined as freedom from social causation, how should it be conceived? Gauthier says that it should be understood as the "capacity to alter given preferences by a rational, self-critical, reflective procedure" (*MA* 349).

Here we have Gauthier's circle of autonomy and reflection. When we ask him what critical reflection is, he says it is autonomy. When we ask him what autonomy is, he says it is critical reflection. His accounts of autonomy and critical reflection do not explain anything because they are circular. Moreover, the circular link is highly questionable. Critical reflection may very well be an autonomous activity, but not all autonomous activities need be critical or reflective. Since critical reflection is only one special form of autonomy, we cannot determine its essential character by simply linking it to autonomy. We have to determine its differentiae.

The critical reflection that lies beyond the power of economic man is critical evaluation. Let us distinguish critical from factual evaluation. We make a factual evaluation in making our choices by appealing to the facts of subjective preferences. For example, I may be confronted with the following questions:

1. How can I get a well-paying job?
2. Would a well-paying job make me happy?
3. Should I be the sort of person who is made happy by nothing other than a well-paying job?
4. How do I decide what sort of person I should be?

The first of these questions is a question of means for a given end; it can be settled by appealing to relevant facts. Question (2) can also be settled by consulting relevant facts. It depends on my preferences whether or not a well-paying job will make me happy; my preferences belong to the domain of facts. I may again appeal to facts in settling question (3). If I want to be the sort of person who can be made happy by a well-paying job, I may say, "I should be that sort of person." My preference is the ultimate court of appeal. In that case, question (4) can be handled in the same way. On all four questions, critical reflections remain within the domain of factual evaluation.

I may question the belief that all our choices are questions of subjective preferences. I may distrust or even despise my own preferences. But I can critically examine my own preferences only by appealing to objective values. Such an examination is truly critical. In that case, our ultimate choices are questions of objective value. Factual evaluation is factual judgment; it can be made within the domain of facts. Although factual evaluation is within the power of economic man, critical evaluation goes well beyond his power because it cannot be made within the domain of facts. Only if critical reflection is taken as critical evaluation is it something terribly missing in economic man. But the acceptance of critical reflection means the acceptance of objective standards and values, although Gauthier does not seem to be aware of this point. This is a long way from his starting point.

As Christopher Morris correctly notes, Gauthier begins with the subjectivity of values and preferences.[21] His acceptance of nontuism as his premise follows from the subjectivity of values and preferences. In the world of subjective values and nontuistic people, what kind of agreement can be accepted as fair and impartial? He has tried to answer this question with his theory of rational bargains. This is his derivation project, which has given the twin products of instrumental justice and instrumental rationality. These two are not easy even for Gauthier to swallow, and he tries to replace them with essential justice and essential rationality. Neither of them can be constructed from subjective preferences. They presuppose objective values and standards. There seems to be no way of dispensing with objective values and standards, which in turn cannot be accounted for without accepting the intuition of those values and standards.

21. Morris, "Relation between Self-interest and Justice," 144.

CHAPTER SIX

Aristotelian Revival

Formal rationality is too barren to provide normative standards; instrumental rationality is too servile to perform this lofty function. These two verdicts constitute the crisis of normative rationality. Since this crisis is a unique product of modernity, it is only natural that we should feel nostalgic for the classical conception of practical reason. In ancient Greek philosophy, human reason was never content to perform merely the servile instrumental function. Neither was it compelled to spin out formal procedures. It reigned over the kingdom of norms through its unchallenged power of intuition. Hence there has been a natural temptation to recover and revive the classical tradition in normative disciplines. At the center of this revival is the Aristotelian tradition.

In *After Virtue*, Alasdair MacIntyre tries to retrieve and reconstruct an Aristotelian theory of virtue for our age. His definition of virtue is given on three successive levels: social practice, individual existence, and tradition. On the first two levels, MacIntyre presents two sets of virtues. But the third level (tradition) does not define a third set of virtues. Tradition is the historical dimension of both social practices and individual existence: it gives a fuller understanding of the virtues defined on the first two levels (*AV*2d 204–25),[1] that is, virtues in the context of social practices and virtues in the context of individual life.

Virtues for Social Practices

MacIntyre defines a social virtue as "an acquired human quality" necessary for achieving the goods internal to a practice (*AV*2d 191). To understand this definition correctly, we have to be clear about two ideas: the notion of a practice and the notion of the goods internal to a practice. The game of chess, for example, is a practice. According to MacIntyre, there are goods internal and external to

1. *AV*2d refers to Alasdair MacIntyre, *After Virtue*, 2d ed. (Notre Dame, 1984).

playing a game of chess. Now suppose that you induce and encourage a child to play chess by rewarding him with candy. The reward is a good external to chess. The child may become good at chess and play it for its own sake. In that case, the child is recognizing and experiencing some goods internal to the game of chess.

External goods are contingently related to a practice, while internal goods are essentially related to it. Prestige, status, and money are external goods that can be associated with any practice; there are always alternative ways of obtaining these external goods. But the internal goods of chess can be found only in the practice of playing chess and in no other practices. Internal goods are always practice-specific. The internal goods of chess, according to MacIntyre, can be found "in the achievement of a certain highly particular kind of analytical skill, strategic imagination and competitive intensity" (AV2d 188). So described, the good internal to chess appears to be the achievement of technical skills or aptitude for chess.

In general, technical skills have only instrumental value. In that case, it is difficult to see how technical skills can constitute the internal good of a social practice, which is supposed to have some intrinsic value. Instrumental goods are used for the sake of achieving some intrinsic goods. The intrinsic good that is promoted by the technical skills of chess appears to be the satisfaction of playing chess. In that case, the internal good of a practice can be defined as the satisfaction of engaging in that practice.[2] This view of internal goods is too subjective for MacIntyre, as we shall see later. So he never describes his notion of internal good in psychological terms.

MacIntyre sometimes identifies the internal goods of a practice with the excellence of a product and the excellence in a performance (AV2d 187–90). If standards of excellence are the internal goods of a practice, virtues again appear to be the technical skills required for achieving those internal goods. But he emphatically dissociates the notion of virtues from that of technical skills (AV2d 193–94). If virtues are not technical skills, what are they? MacIntyre finally names three social virtues: justice, courage, and honesty (or truthfulness); all three are needed for achieving the internal goods of any practice (AV2d 191). The virtues "define our relationships to those other people with whom we share the kind of purposes and standards which inform practices" (AV2d 191). The true locus of MacIntyre's three virtues is the interpersonal relation for social cooperation as the common basis for all social practices.

MacIntyre's notion of a practice is restricted to the domain of social cooperation. Any human activity that requires no social cooperation is not a practice.

---

2. This is the interpretation Edmund Pincoffs places on MacIntyre's notion of goods internal to a practice in his *Quandaries and Virtues* (Lawrence, 1986), 97–98.

Mountain climbing is a practice if it is done in cooperation; it is not a practice if it is done individually. So are farming and fishing. Since whatever we do singly is not a practice, MacIntyre's practice-bound definition of virtue excludes all individual virtues, that is, such virtues required for individual activities as fortitude and temperance. Even the virtue of courage on his list is not an individual, but a social virtue. This virtue is the capacity to risk harm or danger to oneself for the sake of something or someone other than oneself (AV2d 192).

MacIntyre's list of three social virtues presents some problems. Why are all of them necessary for every social practice? Some of them may not be necessary for some practices. Conversely, some practices may require virtues other than these three. If virtues are practice-bound, different practices may require different virtues. Yet MacIntyre claims universality for his list of virtues, although he gives no reasons for making this claim. Let us consider the universality of truthfulness or honesty. It is clearly an important virtue for many practices, but there are practices whose viability can be endangered by it. Some practices, religious and secular, are founded on noble lies and hallowed myths. If truthfulness or honesty means the critical attempt to expose their falsity, it can destroy the foundations of those practices instead of achieving their internal goods.

By *justice* MacIntyre understands the requirement of treating all concerned in respect of merit or desert according to uniform and impersonal standards (AV2d 192). MacIntyre assumes that every practice requires treating people in respect of merit or desert. But there are many practices in which personal merit and desert are not important considerations. We do not haggle over the merit and demerit of our children in the practice of raising a family; we do not have to treat our friends with uniform, impersonal standards. Although some practices may need the impersonal virtue of justice, others—for example, maintaining a household—are powered by the personal force of love and loyalty. The virtue of impersonal justice can sometimes be detrimental and even corrosive to the success of practices such as these.

MacIntyre defines the virtue of courage as the capacity to take risk not for oneself, but because of one's care and concern for "some individual, community or cause" (AV2d 192). If the virtue of courage is for the sake of the care and concern of someone or something other than oneself, it should be better to claim the capacity or disposition for such care and concern as the ultimate virtue. Courage is only one of many subsidiary virtues that constitute the ultimate virtue of care and concern, which was called the virtue of charity in the medieval world and is the virtue of benevolence in the modern world. Care and concern for others require a multitude of virtues besides courage: circumspection, compassion, dedication, civility, self-sacrifice, and so forth. MacIntyre gives no reason for singling out courage from this multitude.

The surprising outcome of MacIntyre's practice-bound definition of social virtues is the universality he claims for them. If social virtues are defined in reference to social practices and their internal goods, they should be relative to practices. There is no reason to assume that one set of virtues can serve the multitude of practices equally well. Virtues should be practice-specific because each practice has its own internal goods and its own standards of excellence. Even the fact that many practices require social cooperation cannot assure that they require one and the same set of social virtues. The form of social cooperation can vary from practice to practice, and the multifarious forms of social cooperation may very well require different virtues. The practice-bound definition of virtue inevitably leads to the relativity of virtues.

MacIntyre himself stresses the relativity of virtues. Homeric virtues, he says, were different from Aristotelian virtues, which were in turn different from Christian virtues. All of these differed from the virtues of eighteenth- or nineteenth-century Europe (AV2d 181–82). MacIntyre may be seeking a way out of this bewildering variety and relativity of virtues when he appeals to the notion of practice as a common ground for his definition of virtue and presents one set of universal virtues. Without those three virtues, he maintains, no practices can be sustained, "whatever our private standpoint or our society's particular codes may be" (AV2d 192).

The universality of MacIntyre's three social virtues, however, is only nominal. Although the three social virtues obtain in every practice and in every society, MacIntyre acknowledges, the moral codes that specify those virtues vary from society to society. The code of truthfulness operating among Lutheran pietists, for example, is different from the one operating among traditional Bantu parents (AV2d 192–93). The virtue of justice may appear to be substantively universal because it is said to be the use of uniform, impersonal standards. But even its universality can be reduced to a nominal one if it is given a merely formal interpretation. In the medieval guilds, MacIntyre says, a master could favor his children over his other apprentices. Since this rule can be applied uniformly and impersonally, it qualifies as a formal rule of justice. So the code of justice of the Homeric warriors is different from the code of justice of libertarian capitalists. In fact, the virtue of justice necessary for achieving the goods internal to the Homeric practice of warfare may very well be detrimental to achieving the goods internal to the practice of libertarian capitalism. In that case, MacIntyre's three social virtues are relative to each practice and each society. Their nominal universality cannot help us overcome their relativity.

The universality and the relativity of virtues concern the question of their values: Do virtues have universal values or only relative ones, relative to each practice or society? MacIntyre, maintaining only that all virtues can be justified by the internal goods of social practices, never raises this question. The only important question of value for him is the distinction between the internal and the external goods of a social practice. The value of internal goods, he claims, has a certain degree of objectivity that is not available to the value of external goods. Whereas such external goods as power and fame characteristically belong to some individuals, the achievement of internal goods is always for the whole community (AV2d 190–91). It is the common good.

By this distinction, the satisfaction of engaging in any given practice derives not from its internal, but its external good because it belongs to some individual. Consequently MacIntyre never identifies internal goods with the satisfaction of participation. Because external goods belong to individuals, they are the source of conflict and competition. Because internal goods belong to the whole community, they are the foundation of love and harmony.

We should remind ourselves that MacIntyre's definition of virtue is an attempt to revive the Aristotelian tradition of virtues. What relevance does this practice-bound conception of virtue have to our social world? MacIntyre says flatly that it cannot be realized in our social world. In his view, the politics of liberal democracy is not a practice, although politics in the Aristotelian sense is (AV2d 188). He maintains that modern politics, far from being a form of social cooperation, is a civil war in disguise. Whereas a practice is a cooperative project for the sake of some common good, the politics of liberal democracy is a battle for the acquisition of individual goods.

The common good can never be on the agenda of liberal democracies. The politics of naked self-interest, MacIntyre maintains, is an inevitable outcome of modern individualism, which in turn dictates the need for altruism. Aristotelian politics did not need the service of altruism because it did not have the notion of individual goods: "There is no way of my pursuing my good which is necessarily antagonistic to you pursuing yours because the good is neither mine peculiarly nor yours peculiarly—goods are not private property" (AV2d 229).

MacIntyre's initial definition of social virtues had no reference to the common good; he simply identified it with the internal good of a social practice. Now he appears to define the common good as an additional requirement for the constitution of a social practice: a social practice is not really a social practice unless it is meant to achieve the common good. By this additional requirement, the idea of social practice is simply incompatible with the idea of modern individualism. Modern individuals do seek collective goods, but not common goods. For example, national defense or pollution control is a collective good, meant ultimately for the satisfaction of individual needs and desires. But it is not a common good that belongs to the community as a whole.

Social virtues as MacIntyre sees them are impossible to realize in the world of individualism. This is his chilling prognosis on the prospect of restoring Aristotelian virtues in the modern era. The age of virtue is irrevocably lost, a point highlighted by the title of his book, After Virtue.

Virtues for Individual Life

The life of an individual cannot be merely a collection of social roles in various practices. It must transcend the limited goods of social practices; it must have its own unity and integrity (*AV*2d 203, 218–19). It requires a conception of the final telos and of the good that will enable us to order other goods. MacIntyre proposes to define individual virtues in reference to such a telos or good. But his conception of the final telos and the ultimate good is highly ambiguous. It can be taken either as a formal or a material concept.

Taken as a formal concept, the final telos or the ultimate good is none other than the unity and order of all the goods that an individual achieves in various practices. It is the question of how to rank and combine one's practice-bound roles and activities. It is the matter of making one's life "one kind of unity rather than another" (*AV*2d 203). MacIntyre also describes the final telos and the ultimate good as some overriding good and telos which warrants "putting other goods in a subordinate place" (*AV*2d 203). Such a concept is not merely formal, but substantive. It is the concept of some goal or object that transcends all the internal goods of social practices and even their various combinations. It is impossible to tell which of these two conceptions is MacIntyre's view.

The ambiguity and uncertainty in MacIntyre's conception of the ultimate good and the final telos may not matter after all because he says we do not know what they really are. Our quest for the good life is supposedly not like a miner's search for gold because, unlike him, we have no clear conception of the object of our search. It is supposed to be more like a medieval quest for some unknown object. William Frankena thinks that by "the medieval quest" MacIntyre refers to the quest for the Holy Grail, "a kind of indefinite pursuit of a (holy?) Grail not definable in advance." [3] But the quest for the Holy Grail was not a quest for something unknown or undefinable because it is known to be the Holy Grail. The only thing uncertain about the grail quest was its location.

MacIntyre's agnostic mood is reflected in his circular definition of the good life for man "as the life spent in seeking for the good life for man," and the virtues for seeking such a life as "those which will enable us to understand what more and what else the good life for man is" (*AV*2d 219). His definition of a good life is circular; it defines a good life in terms of a good life. In this circular definition of a good life, the function of virtues is to find out what a good life is. The essence of individual virtue lies in the perpetual search for a good life. This search is called a narrative quest because every human life is a narrative.

What virtues are necessary for conducting this narrative quest? If it is im-

---

3. Frankena, "MacIntyre and Modern Morality," *Ethics* 93 (1983): 585.

possible to say anything definite about the final telos and the ultimate good, it is equally impossible to say anything definite about the virtues required for this quest. The only virtue MacIntyre cites in this connection is constancy or integrity, the singleness of purpose in a whole life (*AV*2d 203, 219). Even the singleness of purpose does not amount to anything definite, if we are unsure of what we are really seeking. Thus MacIntyre's definition of virtue for the life of an individual turns out to be quite vacuous. His vacuous conception of virtue only reflects his vacuous and uncertain conception of the good life. Alan Gewirth says that MacIntyre's conception of the ultimate good for an individual life is so indeterminate that it can fit a Hitler or a Stalin.[4] His conception of virtue is equally compatible with the virtues of a Hitler or a Stalin. Neither of them could have been faulted for deficiencies in singlemindedness.

In his agnostic posture, ironically, MacIntyre is in complete accord with liberalism, individualism, existentialism, and emotivism, that is, with all the villains of modernity under his relentless censure. In fact, even the medieval quest took on an air of uncertainty and indefinability of object when the medieval religious ethos became infected by the emergent secular ethos, which has bred individualism and liberalism. It has been the credo of individualism and liberalism that the ultimate good for each individual can be determined not by any objective order of values—because nobody can be sure of such an order—but by his or her own autonomous decision. It is this spirit of modernity that has rejected Aristotelian normative ethics and its objective claims.

MacIntyre embraces the same spirit of modernity and its agnosticism in his rejection of Aristotle's metaphysical biology (*AV*2d 163). Though he does not explain what he means by "metaphysical biology," he appears to refer to Aristotle's natural teleology, that is, the idea that every living being has its ultimate telos determined by its nature and that the fulfillment of this telos is the ultimate good. The Aristotelian virtues are defined in this framework of natural teleology, that is, as those character traits constitutive of excellence in self-realization. Virtues are noble and beautiful; they need not be justified by their instrumental values. Whoever possesses them is an excellent member of the human species. The excellence in being a human should be understood in the same way as the excellence in being a frog or a horse. Excellence is species-specific. In that regard, the Aristotelian notion of virtue may be based on metaphysical biology.

Because MacIntyre rejects Aristotle's natural teleology, he is forced to fall back on narrative unity as the ultimate telos and good for the individual life. As J. B. Schneewind points out, narrative unity is not something that can be achieved for the life of an individual, but rather a necessary form of existence

4. Gewirth, "Rights and Virtues," *The Review of Metaphysics* 38 (1985): 754.

that every life must have retrospectively. That is the sort of unity endorsed by every "bourgeois moralist from Butler to Rawls." [5] Is there any way to tell whether one narrative unity is better than another? Without appealing to natural teleology, there may be none. Severed from Aristotelian natural teleology, the notion of a narrative quest and its unity brings MacIntyre's theory of virtue into a state of normative anarchy.

In this normative anarchy, MacIntyre is in perfect harmony with the modern ethos of liberalism, individualism, existentialism, and emotivism—the Gang of Four in the cultural revolution of modern Europe. Moreover, he does not seem to realize that the downfall of Aristotelian virtues in modern Europe was dictated by the downfall of Aristotelian teleological ontology. He wants to revive and restore Aristotelian virtues without accepting Aristotelian natural teleology as their ontological basis. He claims to have replaced Aristotle's bio-logical teleology with his social teleology (*AV*2d 196). His social teleology is presumably the teleology of social practices. But he has already announced the demise of social practices in the modern world.

MacIntyre's second definition of virtue turns out to be not any more useful to us than his first definition. According to the first definition, the tradition of virtue has irrevocably lost its social matrix. According to the second definition, it can never recover its ontological basis. MacIntyre's book is a lamentation over the death of virtue; *After Virtue* means "after the death and burial of virtue." This is indeed a crushing blow to the Aristotelian revivalist movement.

Aristotelianism and Modernity

Though it is by no means an easy task to revive Aristotelianism in an age that goes so against its grain, not all Aristotelians have been so pessimistic as MacIntyre. William Galston is a stalwart Aristotelian who does not want to give up the idea of human nature and ventures to delineate its underlying unity:

Wherever we observe human beings, certain patterns emerge. Let me list the most obvious and important: a distinctive kind of consciousness, self-awareness, that produces both introspection and the knowledge of mortality; a distinctive kind of comprehension, rationality; a distinct kind of commu-nicative competence; complex and differentiated passions; the interpenetra-tion of reason, passion, and desire that constitutes the moral realm; unique kinds of activities, such as artistic expression; a distinctive form of associa-tion that we call "political," containing enormously complex conventions; and finally, what we may with Rousseau think of as instinctual underdeter-

5. Schneewind, "Virtue, Narrative, and Community: MacIntyre and Morality," *The Journal of Philosophy* 79 (1982): 659.

mination. It seems reasonable to assert something like this ensemble of fundamental characteristics is what we mean by human nature and that they constitute some very general limits on possibilities.[6]

As Galston admits, his list is only schematic; it sets only the general limits of human possibilities. These general possibilities are compatible not only with Aristotelian ethics and politics, but also with any modern moral and political theories. These possibilities have to be developed, and Galston assigns special significance to the worth of "developed existence."[7] How do we know what the right ways of developing these possibilities are? In the Aristotelian tradition, this question cannot be settled without reference to natural teleology. But Galston regretfully refuses to "embrace teleology, with all its attendant difficulties."[8] Hence his important idea of developed human existence looks like a blank check that can be cashed even by existentialists. It is noteworthy that he uses the word *existence* ("developed existence" rather than "developed nature"), which is more familiar among existentialists than among Aristotelians.

J. Budziszewski is another worthy Aristotelian who has tried to "resurrect" human nature. He divides human nature into three levels: nature as the innate, nature as the characteristic, and nature as the full and appropriate.[9] The first two levels are familiar and unproblematic, but they are only the supporting levels for the third level. How should we understand the third level? What does it mean to reach the fully realized level of human nature? Budziszewski readily recognizes the inadequacy of natural reason for answering these questions. If, he says, the destiny of human creation is linked to God, as Christianity teaches, we can never know the character of human nature at its highest level without divine revelation. In his view, natural teleology should be replaced by theistic teleology.

The idea of human nature is either too much or too little. This has been the stumbling block for the revival of the Aristotelian tradition.[10] The problematic dimension of human nature is its normative dimension; the descriptive or factual dimension still remains familiar and unproblematic, as in Budziszewski's schema. But the demarcation of these two dimensions belongs to modern science. In Aristotelian science, the normative and descriptive dimensions are inseparably linked to each other. To know the essence of a horse is not any

6. Galston, *Justice and the Human Good* (Chicago, 1980), 34.

7. Ibid., 61–69.

8. Ibid., 34.

9. J. Budziszewski, *The Resurrection of Nature* (Ithaca, 1986), 33–42.

10. The same problem appears in Germain Grisez's and John Finnis's attempt to revive natural law. For a good discussion of their problem, see Russell Hittinger, *A Critique of Natural Law Theory* (Notre Dame, 1987), 168–89.

different from what a good or a bad horse is. In Aristotelian science, the concept of a horse is not only descriptive, but normative. When biology excludes its normative dimension, it is only empirical and descriptive. When it includes the normative dimension, it is meta-physical because the normative dimension does not belong to the physical world.

Modern science was born by rejecting Aristotelian science and by establishing the independence of the physical world. But we have to be careful about the concept of the physical world because it is highly ambiguous. In modern science, the physical world is conceived in purely descriptive terms; it is assumed to be totally free of norms and values. In Aristotelian science, however, the physical world was assumed to include both the normative and the descriptive dimensions. The Aristotelian conception of the physical world was much richer than the modern conception. When MacIntyre labels Aristotle's biology as a metaphysical science, he is accepting the modern practice of relegating the normative dimension to the metaphysical domain.

The idea of a purely descriptive science is by no means the invention of modernity. It is in fact older than Aristotle; its founder was Democritus, who was born some seventy years before Aristotle. Democritean atomism is purely descriptive and physical; it describes the size, shape, and motion of atoms, making no mention of their good or evil. Democritean science is mechanistic; it is value-free. It ignores the normative dimension of the world. Aristotle was convinced that Democritean science could not account for the teleological dimension of the world, which is clearly manifested in biological phenomena. Aristotelian science refuses to dissociate norms and telos from the physical world.

The two scientific traditions had two different conceptions of human reason. Aristotelian science stands on the unity of normative and descriptive reason; Democritean science dictates their separation. The conception of reason is much richer for the former than the latter. In Aristotelian science, reason has the power of knowing not only the factual but also the normative world. This rich conception of reason is contained in the Aristotelian conception of intellectual intuition and practical reason. Such a conception of reason is incompatible with Democritean science, in which reason knows nothing about norms and values. Its power is limited to formal and instrumental functions.

The emergence of modern science marked the rejection of Aristotelian science and the revival of Democritean science. MacIntyre's rejection of metaphysical biology is a rejection of Aristotelian science, which goes together with his rejection of Aristotelian practical reason. This is why he never mentions practical reason in his definition of virtues. His rejection of practical reason is fully manifest in his agnosticism and skepticism about the ultimate good or telos. If practical reason knows anything, it should know the nature of the ultimate good or telos, which is the essence of human nature. Practical reason produces practical science, the study of ultimate human good and telos.

MacIntyre's rejection of metaphysical biology is his rejection of human nature; it is his rejection of practical reason and practical science. Whereas Aristotle always appeals to human nature in his discussion of virtues, MacIntyre never does. That is un-Aristotelian. Since he rejects human nature, he also rejects practical reason. He never appeals to practical reason, either, in his definition of virtues. That is again un-Aristotelian. His rejection of practical reason is the rejection of the epistemological basis for the revival of Aristotelian virtues, and this rejection goes hand in hand with his rejection of human nature as the ontological basis for their revival. Why does MacIntyre reject these two basic premises of Aristotelian ethics and yet yearn for the revival of Aristotelian virtues? This is the most baffling question of MacIntyre's enterprise. Before taking up this question, however, I want to consider a few more un-Aristotelian moves MacIntyre makes.

Though MacIntyre refers to metaphysical biology for his definition of individual virtues, he does not even mention it in his definition of social virtues. For the latter, he appeals to the internal goods of social practices, also an un-Aristotelian move. To be sure, Aristotle does appeal to social practices in his definition of virtues, but he never dissociates them from his metaphysical biology. In Aristotle's ethics, the nature of social practices can be understood only in the context of human nature. Politics is an extension of ethics, which is a practical science of human nature. Hence social practices are as "natural" as any other human endeavor. The only legitimate criterion for assessing the value of a social practice is whether it is natural or unnatural, that is, whether it is in accord with human nature.

The concept of the natural good—the good that fulfills nature—is the ultimate test of value in the Aristotelian world. This test is obviously effective on the biological level. There is no difficulty in recognizing the natural goodness of health and the natural badness of sickness. But as soon as we extend the test of the natural good beyond the biological level, we can easily lose our confidence in its efficacy. What form of social association is in accord with human nature? Aristotle thought that this question can be answered by appealing to human nature, just as we can answer the question "What kind of food is in accord with human nature?" So he accepted natural slavery as a good form of social order. This reveals the extent of his faith in the natural social order. Since social order is dictated by human nature, social virtues are extensions of human nature just as much as individual virtues are.

The moderns cannot accept the unity of social order and human nature any more than the natural goodness of slavery. In the modern era, the concept of human nature has drastically changed. It is not only divorced from the normative dimension; it is no longer copious enough to cover social order. Whereas the Aristotelian conception of human nature accounted for not only the character of individual human beings but also their social existence, the modern conception considers only the nature of individuals in exclusion from their social relations. Whereas Aristotle called human beings social animals, the moderns have stressed their asociality. For Aristotle, social relation is an essential feature of human nature; for the moderns, social relation goes against human nature. They accept social organizations only for their instrumental value.

In his discussion of social practices, MacIntyre recognizes the independence of their internal goods. This is again un-Aristotelian. A loyal Aristotelian should relate the internal goods to human nature, but MacIntyre cannot do that because he does not accept human nature as the normative basis. Even if one believes in human nature, it is hard to relate the internal goods of a social practice to human nature. How can we tell whether the practice of slavery or monarchy is in accord with human nature? Aristotle endorsed both of them in the conviction that they best express human nature. That leads us to suspect that there is no real link between human nature and social practices. Aristotle may have only endorsed prevailing practices in the name of human nature. If so, what he has done is equivalent to what MacIntyre is doing now. MacIntyre never questions the internal good of social practices; he seems to accept uncritically all social practices.

If practice-bound virtues derive their value from the value of social practices, they can have no independent value. Hence they can never be used as criteria for assessing the value of any given practice.[11] Every practice can be justified by its own internal goods, whether it is the practice of slavery or cannibalism. But such an internal justification is morally worthless. The moral criticism or justification of a practice requires a perspective that transcends the internal perspective contained in that practice. But the internal goods of a practice can give only an internal perspective; there is no external or objective criteria for evaluating social practices. This is the verdict of modernity, which is tacitly accepted by MacIntyre's acknowledgment that the internal goods of social practices require no justification. This is clearly an un-Aristotelian notion of social virtues and practices.

Individual and Community

MacIntyre has correctly stressed the intimate connection between individual and community in the Aristotelian tradition. In his definition of virtues, however, he makes the un-Aristotelian move of separating social from individual virtues. In Aristotle's ethics, the two sets of virtues are inseparable because the individual life is inseparable from the life of a community. Almost every

11. This is Alan Gewirth's criticism of MacIntyre's theory of virtue in "Rights and Virtues," *The Review of Metaphysics* 38 (1985): 739–62.

virtue in Aristotle's ethics is defined in the dual context of individual and social behavior. The virtue of moderation may be the sole exception to this rule. The inseparable connection between individual and social virtues only reflects the inseparable connection between individual and community. But this inseparable link has been dissolved by modern individualism, which recognizes the priority of individuals to their community. MacIntyre's separation of individual and social virtues reflects this ethos of modern individualism.

MacIntyre is correct in stressing the incompatibility of the common good and modern individualism. For the moderns, the common good is no more than the collective good, the good that can be achieved only by collective efforts, but must be consumed for individual satisfactions. For the ancients, the common good is the good of a community, whose identity is prior to the identity of its members. For the moderns, however, a community is neither more nor less than the sum of its members. Hence the community cannot be regarded as an independent possessor of the good. Aristotle recognizes the distinction and conflict of common goods and individual interests. But MacIntyre does not allow such a distinction and conflict; the conflict of all individual interests is supposed to dissolve in the common good: "There is no way of my pursuing my good which is necessarily antagonistic to you pursuing yours because *the* good is neither mine peculiarly nor yours peculiarly—goods are not private property" (*AV*2d 229).

By such a high standard of the common good and its identity with individual interests, MacIntyre has a right to brand a liberal society as a civil war in disguise. But he is grossly misreading Aristotle on this point. Aristotle never presents such a picture of total harmony of individual interests with the common good. To be sure, Aristotle accepts the ideal of common good as the political telos of a state. In book 3 of his *Politics*, he advances a strong requirement for the constitution of a state (1280b30–39). A state is not a mere society, established for the prevention of mutual crime and the benefit of exchange. It is a community of families, created through friendship. Since friends are extensions of each other, they hold all things in common (*NE* 1159b29–33, 1166a32, 1170b7). The ideal of common good follows from his definition of the state as a product of friendship.

In Aristotle's *Politics*, however, the ideal of common good is so brutally compromised with the reality of the harsh world that it can chill the heart of any sober reader. To be sure, the function of the state is to provide a good life, that is, the life of excellence (*aretē*) and happiness (*eudaimonia*). But this benefit is restricted to the fortunate minority of the governing class. The vast majority— slaves, metics, laborers, farmers, and artisans—are excluded from citizenship because they do not have the leisure and other facilities for participating in the life of excellence. They are not accepted as members of the state but treated as its necessary means because their roles are ignoble and inimical to the life of excellence (*Politics* 1328b40–1329a21).[12]

Because the Aristotelian state has to depend on the servile function of the laboring class without granting them citizenship, Aristotle is constantly aware of their discontent and of the danger of revolt and revolution. He devotes the whole of book 5 of his *Politics* to the investigation of revolutions. He regards the secret of managing the subject population as an important state function (*Politics* 1269b8–13). Aristotle refers so often to the strife and conflict between the rich and the poor in his *Politics* that the entire treatise appears to be woven around the mighty tug-of-war between these two camps. For more than two thousand years—until Karl Marx's theory of class struggle—no treatise dealt with the antagonism and hatred between the rich and the poor with such incisive candor.[13]

To appreciate Aristotle's critical awareness of class struggle, one has only to read book 4 of the *Politics,* which examines oligarchy and democracy as the two most prevalent forms of government (*Politics* 1290a14–1296b3). Oligarchy is the government of the poor people by a few rich, and democracy is the government of the rich by the many poor. The word *demos* (people) means the poor, common people; it is equivalent to the Roman term *plebeians. Demos* does not refer to the collectivity of all human beings in the state, but only to the lowly and the ugly, the common people, who are excluded from the privileged class.[14] Because democracy is government by the lowest class, Aristotle follows Plato in ranking it as one of the lowest forms of government. The sense of disdain associated with the word *demos* in ancient Greece is diametrically opposed to the special aura of prestige and authority that the word *people* has gained in modern democracies.

Because the rich and the poor never trust each other, Aristotle says, neither party will ever consent to be governed by the other (*Politics* 1297a4–5). So both oligarchy and democracy have to resort to coercion and deception (*Politics* 1296a25–1296b2, 1297a14–1297b8). Consequently, neither of them turns out to be an honest, legitimate government. And yet they are the most prevalent forms of government because the conflict of the rich (*euporoi*) and the poor (*aporoi*) is the most divisive issue everywhere (*Politics* 1296a22–23).[15] So Aris-

12. For a good discussion of this point, see Martha Nussbaum, "Nature, Function, and Capacity: Aristotle on Political Distribution," in Julia Anna and Robert H. Grimm, eds., *Oxford Studies in Ancient Philosophy,* suppl. vol. (Oxford, 1988), 145–84.
13. G. E. M. de Ste. Croix tries to establish "a remarkable resemblance" of Aristotle's analysis of the state politics to Marx's economic approach in *The Class Struggle in the Ancient Greek World* (Ithaca, 1981), 71–80.
14. This is Ste. Croix's claim, ibid., 72–74.
15. Plato is equally concerned with the divisive conflict between the rich and the poor (*Republic* 550–52). He is so concerned with this problem that Alexander Fuks calls it Plato's

totle takes the opposition of oligarchy and democracy as the primary theme of investigation in the central books (4, 5, and 6) of his *Politics*.[16]

Aristotle never underestimates the difficulty of reconciling the rich and the poor. Whereas different functions can be combined in the same individual (a soldier can be a farmer or an artisan), he points out, the same person cannot be rich and poor at the same time (*Politics* 1291b2–10). This exclusionary relation of the rich and the poor is the cause of their perpetual antagonism. The only way to moderate and control this antagonism is to establish a large middle class. The middle class (*mesoi, hoi en mesoi*) is the political counterpart of the ethical golden (*meson, mesotes*) mean (*Politics* 1295a35–1296a21). For the same reason, he advocates the polity—the true union or fusion of oligarchy and democracy—as the best form of government for all practical purposes (*Politics* 1293b23–1194b40). The art of *real* politics for Aristotle is above all the art of keeping the rich and the poor from falling into a brutal battle of naked self-interests via the mediating service of the middle class.

The alluring ideal of common goods in Aristotelian politics only hides the ugly conflict of class interests. For that reason, political science cannot be a simple extension of Aristotelian biology. The science of biology need not be concerned with the wide discrepancy between its normative and factual dimensions, as long as it is restricted to the study of plants and animals. But the behavior of rational animals is quite different; it often diverges from its normative standard. But all the normative talk about the common good and social virtues may be but an ideological veneer over the harsh political reality. Tearing off this ideological veneer and exposing the true character of politics was a task left to Machiavelli. Such at least is the conventional understanding of Machiavelli, the political theorist. But we cannot fully appreciate his political theory until we understand the nature of Machiavellian individuals and their world.

Sovereign Individuals and Civil Society

Machiavellian individuals are a new breed of human beings that emerge by the end of the Middle Ages and reshape European culture during the Renaissance.

---

obsession in his "Plato and the Social Question: The Problem of Poverty and Riches in the *Laws*," *Ancient Society* 10 (1979): 33–78, and *Social Conflict in Ancient Greece* (Jerusalem, 1984), 80–171. That Plato and Aristotle share this concern indicates that the conflict between the rich and the poor was a pervasive and well-recognized issue in ancient Greece.

16. These three central books of *Politics* are generally regarded as empirical or realistic by Aristotle scholars in contrast to the other books, which are regarded as idealistic. According to Werner Jaeger, the idealistic books retain the trace of Platonic approach, while the realistic books fully display Aristotle's own empirical approach. See Jaeger, *Aristotle: Fundamentals of the History of His Development*, trans. Richard Robinson (Oxford, 1934), 263–75.

Obsessed with freedom and power, they are bent on controlling and conquering others by fraud and force. They are bold and brutal, cunning and cruel, resilient and resourceful. The prototype of the Machiavellian individual is portrayed in Boccaccio's *Decameron*. The heroes and heroines, whose exploits are described in one hundred stories over ten days, distinguish themselves by their ingenuity and audacity in coping with their adversaries. In my *Cultural Thematics*, I called them sovereign individuals to stress their determination to preserve liberty and autonomy at any cost.[17]

Let us consider some Machiavellian traits. The first is the idea of *animo* (soul).[18] Its meaning is completely dissociated from the Christian idea of the soul. It is the center of force and energy, from which all human actions emanate. It is the source of political ambition and militant spirit. That brings us to the next Machiavellian trait, *ambizione* (ambition), which is the drive for glory and power, the power to dominate others and to avoid domination by others. Power alone is not enough to sustain ambition; it should be supplemented by *ragione* (reason). Machiavelli's conception of rationality is instrumental rationality par excellence. The combination of reason and power is expressed by the Machiavellian tactics of fraud and force and by the Machiavellian metaphor of the fox and the lion in his description of an ideal prince.

The first manifestation of Machiavellian rationality is *inganno* (deception). The power to plot and deceive is essential to success; one should have the appearance of being honest and generous rather than the real virtues of honesty and generosity. *Ingegno* (ingenuity) is even better than inganno. A man of ingenuity does not have to resort to the lowly trick of deceiving others; he can openly outwit and outmaneuver his opponents. These and other virtues of instrumental rationality can be summed up under the general virtue of *prudenza* (prudence), and this is Machiavellian practical reason. The virtues of reason and the virtues of power together constitute *virtu*, the all-comprehensive Machiavellian virtue.

Machiavellian virtues, as John Geerken points out, are very much like Homeric virtues. They are the powers and skills needed to deal with hostile forces, as displayed in ambush, treachery, and conspiracy.[19] This is a surprising statement. Since Machiavellian virtues are meant for the citizens of a polis, they should resemble Aristotelian virtues rather than Homeric virtues, which

17. T. K. Seung, *Cultural Thematics: The Formation of the Faustian Ethos* (New Haven, 1976), 207–16.
18. This account roughly follows Martin Fleisher, "A Passion for Politics: The Vital Core of the World of Machiavelli," in Martin Fleisher, ed., *Machiavelli and the Nature of Political Thought* (New York, 1972), 114–47.
19. Geerken, "Homer's Image of the Hero in Machiavelli: A Comparison of Arete and Virtu," *Italian Quarterly* 14 (1970): 45–90.

were meant for warriors in combat. Perhaps MacIntyre was right after all in calling civil society a civil war in disguise. I can perhaps clarify the nature of Machiavellian virtues by distinguishing two different contexts of social interaction: the context of mutual care and trust and the context of mutual fear and distrust. Let us designate these two social contexts as the friendly and the hostile contexts.

By the context of friendly relations, I do not necessarily mean the relation of devoted friends. I am using the Aristotelian notion of friends: one's parents, children, and close relatives and neighbors, who can be regarded as extensions of oneself. They should be contrasted to strangers and enemies, all those who have no intimate ties with one another. In general, conventional morality assumes the friendly context as the basis for its conception of duties and virtues; it disregards our duty to strangers and enemies. Aristotle's ethics is no exception to this rule. Courage is the only Aristotelian virtue to be called on in dealing with enemies; all the other virtues are for dealing with friends and relatives. Hence his theory of virtue naturally leads to his theory of friendly relations in books 8 and 9 of *Nicomachean Ethics,* in which Aristotle tells us that virtues are best exercised among friends and relatives.

The Machiavellian virtues are conceived in the hostile context. But the hostile context can assume two different forms: the context of open hostility and the context of hidden hostility. The Homeric virtues are for the context of open hostility; they are necessary for waging a war between two armed camps. The Machiavellian context is not the context of open hostility; friends and enemies are not clearly divided between two armed camps or cities. Instead they live and work in the same city. This is the context of hidden hostility. Machiavelli recognizes these two types of hostile context. When he advocates violence and cruelty as legitimate tactics, he is talking in the context of open hostility. When he exalts the art of deceit and confidence game, he is operating in the context of hidden hostility.

Given these two contexts of hostility, open and hidden, the context of open hostility is nothing new. Machiavelli himself illustrates it with examples from antiquity. What is new is his recognition of the context of hidden hostility as a most pervasive matrix for human behavior. In the context of open hostility, we shut out our enemies from our city. We meet them only when we are ready to kill them. In the context of hidden hostility, however, we share our living space with our enemies within the wall of our own city. We have to conduct our daily business with them in fear and distrust. The Machiavellian world is the context of domesticated hostility. It is this context of domesticated hostility that constitutes the foundation of modern civil or liberal society. For this reason, one astute historian has said that the federation of American states was founded on mutual fear.

It is this context of hidden or domesticated hostility that produces what Wayne Rebhorn calls the fundamental moral ambiguity.[20] Whereas the context of open hostility usually marks out a clear boundary between friends and enemies, the context of domesticated hostility does not do so. The latter must operate within a hazy boundary between friends and enemies. Even one and the same person may be a friend on one occasion and an enemy on another. Even on the same occasion, he may be a friend in one regard and an enemy in another regard. Hence the context of domesticated hostility is not clearly demarcated from the context of friendly neighbors. Whatever a Machiavellian individual does can be taken in the context of either friendly or hostile relations. There is nothing wrong or morally ambiguous about killing or deceiving enemies; violence and cruelty are essential features of martial virtue. But the act of killing or deceiving does become morally ambiguous as soon as it becomes difficult to identify the victims as friends or enemies. The context of domesticated hostility inevitably intermingles with the context of friendly relations. This is a perpetual source of moral ambiguity in the Machiavellian world.

It is to Machiavelli's enduring credit that he recognized the context of domesticated hostility as the basic framework of political discourse. This recognition is much more important than his proposed solutions for dealing with political problems. Even those who cannot accept his proposed solutions will find it to hard to ignore the context of domesticated hostility as the premise for political discourse. The context of domesticated hostility is the world of sovereign individuals. If these individuals have to have their ways against each other and share the same living space in one city, they automatically constitute the context of domesticated hostility. This is the synchronic relation between Machiavellian individuals and the Machiavellian world. But the Machiavellian world also has a diachronic relation with the medieval ethos.

In the *City of God,* Augustine portrays two cities, the City of God, a city of friends, and the City of the Devil, a city of enemies. Although the devil is the archenemy, his hostility to human beings is not open but hidden. He lives with us, among us, and in us. There is no way of chasing him out of our city. We coexist and connive with him day and night. The devil is fully domesticated, and his domestication makes all of us his cohorts. Thus we constitute a city of domesticated hostility. This is the human city in sin, dramatically elaborated in Dante's *Inferno*. Time and again in his portrayal of Hell, Dante makes pointed allusions to contemporary scenes and events in Italy and Europe.

The Machiavellian city of domesticated hostility is a secular version of the city of devils. To that extent, secularization can partly account for Machiavelli's ideas. But there is another secular dimension that contributes to the emergence of the Machiavellian world. That is the rise of capitalism and the free market.

---

20. Rebhorn, *Foxes and Lions: Machiavelli's Confidence Men* (Ithaca, 1988), 15–21.

James Burnham describes the emergent market economy of Machiavelli's day: "The market was becoming world-wide. The volume of goods was multiplying; gold and silver were pouring in; serfs were leaving the land to make the commodities; manufacturing plants were becoming larger." [21]

The market relation emerged as the antithesis of medieval feudalism, which was a system of friendly relations in the Aristotelian sense. In contrast to the personal relations of lords and vassals, masters and serfs, the market established the impersonal relations of buyers and sellers. The market relation can easily become a relation of enemies if buyers and sellers have to compete for their customers. But the market introduces a completely new idea about outsiders. In traditional society, outsiders are automatically the target of hostility because they are a source of danger and damage. In a market, however, strangers can become the source of benefit as well as harm. Thus the market introduces the same sort of ambiguity and complexity into our relation with strangers that I have described in the Machiavellian context of domesticated hostility.

I began this consideration of the Machiavellian world with the concept of sovereign individuals. They have no natural ties with one another; they are strangers to each other. This is the final trait of Machiavellian individuals. The idea of sovereign individuals is not restricted to Machiavelli's political writings; they populate his literary writings too, especially his play the *Mandragola*. They are not confined to Machiavelli's works but rather are spread over the entire corpus of Renaissance literature from Boccaccio to Shakespeare. What kind of social order can they have without giving up their individual sovereignty? This is the political problem of sovereign individuals.

In my *Cultural Thematics,* I considered two resolutions to the problem: Boccaccian and Caesarian. The Boccaccian resolution is the system of government the seven ladies and three men adopt for telling one hundred stories in ten days in the *Decameron*. It is democratic and egalitarian. The Caesarian resolution is portrayed by Shakespeare in *Antony and Cleopatra*: one of the sovereign individuals, Octavius Caesar, subdues all others and identifies himself with the whole political order. This ideal has been personified in Elizabeth I as Gloriana, a virgin queen married to the whole country, in Louis XIV ("L'état, c'est moi"), Frederick the Great as the greatest servant of Prussia, Napoleon Bonaparte, and down to the totalitarian dictators of our century.

Machiavelli is torn between these two models. In the *Discorsi*, he endorses the republican ideal. The idea of a republic or commonwealth is to preserve the liberty of citizens, and their liberty cannot be preserved without equality and parity (*Discorsi* 1.55). You cannot find a better champion of liberty and equality. But Machiavelli knows that the ideal of a commonwealth or republic

---

21. Burnham, *The Machiavellians: Defenders of Freedom* (New York, 1943), 41.

is useless unless it can be realized. So he recognizes the need for a powerful political leader to establish a political order:

> But we must assume, as a general rule, that it never or rarely happens that a republic or monarchy is well constituted, or its old institutions entirely reformed, unless it is done by only one individual; it is even necessary that he whose mind has conceived such a constitution should be alone in carrying it into effect. A sagacious legislator of a republic, therefore, whose object is to promote the public good, and not his private interests, and who prefers his country to his own successors, should concentrate all authority in himself; and a wise mind will never censure any one for having employed any extraordinary means for the purpose of establishing a kingdom or constituting a republic. [*Discorsi* 1.9][22]

Machiavelli is convinced that such a concentration of power is justified by the sheer necessity of establishing a republic. But he also fears the abuse of power. After establishing a republic, he says, the founder should not leave his power and authority to his successors because most likely they will be abused (*Discorsi* 1.9). His argument for a powerful leader has a strong conditional premise: such a leader should be dedicated enough to the republican cause to sacrifice his private interests. This premise is surely questionable and probably impossible in the world of Machiavellian individuals, whose sole purpose is to protect and promote their individual interests. In the *Prince*, he describes the powers and virtues of a great political leader who makes no pretense of supporting a republican cause. The politics of his principality is an affair not of a republican cause, but of a sovereign individual.

Natural Order and Natural Intuition

Machiavelli's republican ideal is a legacy of the classical tradition. A republic is a natural community; it is a natural relation of mutual care among brothers and relatives. Machiavelli finds his model in the Roman Republic, founded by Aeneas and nurtured by his descendants. Such a natural community is not available to sovereign individuals because they are all strangers to one another. A natural community is ontologically prior to its members; its members have their existence only within its social framework. On the other hand, sovereign individuals are ontologically prior to any social organization they may join. Their social organization is artificial; it can be formed and dissolved by the exercise of their will.

In the classical and medieval worlds, the family had been the prototype of a

---

22. Translation by Luigi Ricci in Max Lerner, ed., *The Prince and the Discourses* by Niccolò Machiavelli (New York, 1940), 138–39.

natural community. Its existence spans successive generations; its members are born, live, and die under its nurture and protection. In our world, the family is becoming the prototype of an artificial social organization; it is formed and dissolved by the mutual consent of individuals. The medieval church was understood as an extended natural family with its Father, Son, and Mother. But the modern Protestant churches are much more like business associations; they can be formed and dissolved by the mutual consent of congregations.

The *Prince* is a treatise on an artificial social order; the *Discorsi* is a reflection on a natural social order. In that regard, Machiavelli is a great transitional figure, like Petrarch and Luther, who have been characterized as more medieval than the medievals and more modern than the moderns. Like these two transitional figures, Machiavelli is caught between two worlds. He can neither free himself of the classical idea of natural social order nor stifle the burgeoning new idea of artificial social order.

Let us reconsider Aristotle's idea of natural order and natural relation. We can detect two different notions in his descriptions of natural order and natural relation: descriptive and normative. His descriptive conception has two parts, biological and psychological. On the biological level, natural order is not confined to the human species. He notes that different species of animals have, by nature, different social relations (*Historia Animalium* 487b33–488a14).[23] Some animals live singly, while others live in a herd. The herding animals are the pigeon, the crane, the swan, and many kinds of fish. There are two kinds of herding animals: political and nonpolitical. Political animals are those that have as their function some single thing that they all do together: the human being, the bee, the wasp, the ant, and the crane. Some of these political animals have leaders; others do not.

By this biological standard, human beings are not the only political animals, and political orders are all biologically determined. Like the political orders of bees and ants, the human political order is natural because it is determined by the biological nature of the human species. The family is the beginning of the natural political order, but it is too small to provide all its needs adequately. A few families get together and form a village (*Politics* 1252b15–17). When several villages are united in a single, complete community, a state comes into existence (*Politics* 1252b27–31). The natural political order begins at the level of bare subsistence and expands to the level of higher existence. If earlier forms of human life (family and village) are natural, Aristotle says, so is the state (*Politics* 1252b32).

The idea of mutual care and trust is central in Aristotle's psychological con-

---

23. John Cooper has pointed out the importance of this passage for the interpretation of Aristotle's political theory in his "Political Animals and Civic Friendship," in Günther Patzig, ed., *Aristoteles' "Politik"* (Göttingen, 1990), 220–41.

ception of natural order. The members of a family do care for each other; theirs is not simply a relation of mutual convenience. The people involved in a relation of mutual convenience or advantage do not have to care for each other. In David Gauthier's terminology, their relation is nontuistic, whereas the members of a family have a tuistic relation. Aristotle regards the commercial relation as nontuistic; as noted earlier, the relation of sellers and buyers in a market is the relation of strangers.

Aristotle says that the two trading cities Corinth and Megara cannot make one city even if they are brought together geographically (*Politics* 1280b14–15). By the same logic, it is impossible to make a state by bringing together farmers, carpenters, shoemakers, and other people of different trades if their union is meant only to bring about mutual benefit to those people (*Politics* 1280b20–23). Aristotle says that their relation is limited to the exchange of benefits, and that is not a bond strong enough for making a state. People can make an association to protect themselves against crime, but their association is again only a relation of convenience. A state is a community of families, and such a social order can be established only among friends and relatives who live in mutual care and trust of natural bonds (*Politics* 1280b34–39).

The biological and the psychological conceptions of natural order may go together. A natural community that develops biologically is likely to be composed of members who do care for each other. But there is one problem with the idea of natural community: it can be perverted. Aristotle recognizes three forms of good government: monarchy, aristocracy, and constitutional government. When these three forms are perverted, they become tyranny, oligarchy, and democracy, respectively (*Politics* 1279b3–10). These perversions are "unnatural"; they deviate from natural order. These unnatural forms are unjust. Aristotle defines justice as a proper regard for the common interest or good (*Politics* 1279a17). In perverted governments, public interests are sacrificed for the sake of private interests. Once that happens, the state ceases to be a true community and becomes like a commercial relation or alliance between two states (*Politics* 1280b10). And its laws become mere conventions rather than a bond of justice. In Aristotle's normative conception of justice, the natural order is the order of justice, and it is concerned with the common good and the common interest.

Aristotle's three conceptions of natural order are biological, psychological, and political. He evidently assumes that they are interconnected in a sequence. A natural community that develops biologically will give its members their psychological bonds. When they have psychological bonds, they should sacrifice their private interests for their common interests. Then they will have justice. Justice is a natural product of natural order; hence it can be known by natural intuition. By *natural intuition* I mean an intellectual intuition of the nature of things. Earlier I noted that the nature of things is the object of Aristotelian intellectual intuition. Aristotle maintains that we have an essential intuition of the *nature* of things, that is, of their essences. In the Aristotelian world, essential intuition is the same as *natural* intuition.

In Aristotle's theory, whatever develops by the power of nature belongs to the natural order, and political order is a part of the natural order that can be known by natural intuition. Natural intuition is immanent because the nature of things is immanent. Having four legs and hoofed feet are properties of a horse, and those properties are immanently present in the nature of a horse. The intuition of those properties is immanent and natural. If natural intuition can recognize the nature of a human being, it can also recognize the essence of its social order. As long as human social orders are taken as natural orders, it is quite plausible to make a case for the natural intuition of those orders.

The Aristotelian thesis that the state is a natural order, however, is questionable on two grounds. There is a glaring difference between the political order of the human species and that of other species. The normative and the descriptive conceptions of natural order apply differently to human and non-human political relations. The normative conception of political order does not apply to nonhuman political orders; beehives and anthills do not face the danger of perversion and injustice. The descriptive conception is sufficient for the characterization of nonhuman political orders.

The descriptive conception, however, is not sufficient for understanding human political orders. On the level of family, the community of interests and the sense of mutual care are strong enough to assure the common good. In terms of biological and psychological bonds, human families may be as solid as beehives and anthills. But such stable and solid psychological bonds are clearly lacking on the level of state. For this reason, a state produces conflict between common and private interests. This is the deficiency of the state as a natural order. In the *Republic,* Plato tries to remedy this deficiency by strengthening the psychological bonds of the citizens in his ideal state. His remedy is to abolish and replace private families with one big family composed of the two governing classes (*Republic* 457c–464b). Plato believes that this is the only way to achieve a true unity of interests in a state.

Aristotle objects to Plato's remedy; it is worse than the disease. The community of wives, children, and properties places an impossible psychological demand on normal human beings (*Politics* 1262a16–31). It is impossible for any normal human being to treat all children as his or her own. The Platonic state ignores natural human bonds and replaces them with artificial bonds. But the natural bonds of families do not fully extend to form a durable community of interests on the level of state. The deficiency of natural bonds in the state can be made up only by the normative constraint of justice. Thus the normative conception of political order is necessary only for the state because it is woefully deficient in natural bonds.

These considerations are lurking in Aristotle's conception of the state as a natural order. But the state is clearly different from the natural order of beehives and anthills. It is plausible to call the family a natural institution; it is firmly held together by natural bonds of love and care. It is also plausible to regard the village as a natural extension of the family. It is plausible even to regard a tribal state as a natural social order. But when the state becomes big enough to accommodate thousands and thousands of strangers for their mutual benefit and convenience, it can hardly fit the Aristotelian conception of the state as the natural relation of mutual care and trust. Such a state is much more like a marketplace than like a family; it is much more artificial than natural. The state in the Machiavellian world was just such an artificial entity.

The demise of Aristotelianism marked the demise of natural intuition. With the emergence of sovereign individuals, artificial social orders have replaced natural social orders, leaving no room for natural intuition. Even in the world of physics, the emergent modern science rejected Aristotelian natural intuition. Aristotle thought that our natural intuition could tell why sublunary objects move up and down, while superlunary objects move in orbits. On earth, he said, light objects (fire and air) move upward, while heavy objects (water and earth) move downward. Light objects find their home in the upper region, and heavy objects find it in the lower region. It is in the nature of these objects that they seek their homes. The circular motion of celestial objects likewise reflects their nature; only circular motions are compatible with the eternal nature of celestial objects because they can be repeated for eternity.

The alleged natural intuition of terrestrial and celestial motions was refuted by Galileo's principle of inertia, which assumes that every thing either moves with a constant speed in a straight line or stays at rest unless disturbed by external forces. The same principle can account for both superlunary and sublunary motions. This principle is accepted not by intellectual intuition, but only as a postulate. Galilean science also denies the ontological distinction between the two worlds below and above the moon. In Aristotelian physics, the sublunary world was assumed to be mutable and corruptible, while the superlunary world was assumed to be eternal and incorruptible. Modern science affirms the identity and continuity of the two worlds; they are made of the same matter and governed by the same laws of motion. These assertions are based on observations rather than intuitions.

Now you can see why such a fervent Aristotelian as Alasdair MacIntyre cannot embrace Aristotelian biology and sociology. He has too clearly seen the demise of natural order and natural intuition, perpetrated by the rise of Galilean natural science and Machiavellian social science. Machiavellian sovereign individuals can no longer enjoy the security and comfort of the natural social order. In fact, they cannot have a social order until they construct one. Artificial orders require not intellectual intuition, but intellectual construction. Thus the emergence of sovereign individuals in the Renaissance prepares the ground for normative constructivism.

CHAPTER SEVEN

Kantian Reversal

The Machiavellian individual is a precursor of the Hobbesian individual, whose first attribute is natural liberty. The word *natural* in *natural liberty* is not normative as in the Aristotelian concept of natural order. It is purely descriptive. The world of natural liberty is the state of nature, "a war of every man against every man." It does not offer the prospect even of a Machiavellian resolution, a powerful, astute prince who can introduce order into chaos. In the state of nature, Hobbes says, all human beings are equal in strength and prudence. Even the weakest can kill the strongest, "either by secret machination, or by confederacy with others" (*Leviathan* 1.13). The state of nature is a state of natural equality. The conjunction of natural liberty and equality turns the state of nature into a state of perpetual hostility.

Since Hobbesian natural equality rules out Machiavellian resolution, the only way out of the state of nature is to seek peace by agreement. Hobbes says that this is dictated by the laws of nature. But those laws are radically different from natural law in the Aristotelian tradition, which is the law of natural order. His laws of nature are the dictates of prudential rather than moral reason; they are products of instrumental rationality. He defines a law of nature as "a precept, or general rule, found out by reason, by which a man is forbidden to do that which is destructive of his life or taketh away the means of preserving the same" (*Leviathan* 1.14).

Social order is created out of chaos by agreement in accordance with the laws of nature. This is the basic idea of Hobbes's theory of social contract in *Leviathan;* it is a theory of an artificial social order. The state of nature is not only a political chaos, but a moral anarchy. Nothing can be just or unjust before the making of a covenant (*Leviathan* 1.15). Justice lies in keeping a covenant; injustice in breaking it. Even after a covenant is made, both parties fear nonperformance. This fear of uncertainty can be eliminated only by establishing a sovereign who can enforce all covenants by coercive power. Hence Hobbes recognizes the existence of a sovereign as essential a condition for achieving justice as the making of a covenant. Thus he produces a positivistic theory of justice and morality: what is just or unjust is determined by covenants and the sovereign. Beyond these social institutions, there are no criteria of justice and injustice. Justice and injustice are social facts of artifice. This is Hobbes's normative positivism.

Hobbes's moral and political philosophy produced two theoretical repercussions. In political philosophy, it initiated the grand tradition of social contract theory, which produced Locke's theory of natural rights and Rousseau's theory of general will. In moral philosophy, Hobbes's ethical egoism generated the long debate between rational intuitionists and the moral sense theorists. Moral sense theory was developed by the Earl of Shaftesbury, Francis Hutcheson, David Hume, and Adam Smith. Rational intuitionism was championed by Richard Cumberland, Ralph Cudworth, Samuel Clarke, John Balguy, and Richard Price. In their debate, the moral sense theorists and rational intuitionists take each other as their chief opponent. But their original target was Hobbes's egoism and subjectivism, and their common goal was to secure an objective ground for morality.

Moral and Spiritual Order

Kant grew up with the Wolffian ethics of perfectionism, and then became enthusiastically involved in moral sense theory. For some years, he even taught it in his classes. He made his first serious attempt to organize his ethical ideas in the *Prize Essay*.[1] He says that ethics contains formal and material principles. The formal principle contains two rules of Wolffian perfectionism: the rule of commission—Do the most perfect you can; and the rule of omission—Abstain from doing that which can hinder the greatest possible perfection. Kant points out that these formal rules alone cannot tell us what our obligations are. He locates the material principle of obligation in moral sense: what is good or perfect is sensed by moral sense or feeling (*Gefühl*).

In the meantime, Rousseau's *Emile* and *Social Contract* arrived in Königsberg and gripped Kant's attention much more intensely than moral sense theory ever did. In the *Observations on the Feeling of the Beautiful and the Sublime,*[2] he

1. Its full title is *Untersuchung über die Deutlichkeit der Grundsätze der natürlichen Theologie und der Moral*, written in 1762 as an entry in the Royal Academy of Sciences of Berlin and published in 1764. *KGS* 2:273–301. *KGS* stands for the Prussian Academy Edition of Kant's Collected Works. Translated as *Inquiry concerning the Clarity of the Principles of Natural Theology and Ethics* in *Kant: Selected Pre-Critical Writings and Correspondence with Beck*, trans. G. E. Kerferd and D. E. Walford (Manchester, 1968), 3–35.
2. The original text is in *KGS* 2:205–56, and it is translated by John T. Goldthwait in *Immanuel Kant, Observations on the Feeling of the Beautiful and the Sublime* (Berkeley, 1960). I will refer to it as *Observations*.

tried to sort out the ideas he had absorbed from these two sources. He stresses the difference between virtue and other moral qualities. Whereas other moral qualities are only sentiments, he says, virtue is a matter of principle. He says that even good moral sentiments degenerate into depravities unless they are controlled by higher principles (*KGS* 2:217). His final charge against passions is their instability. Because our sentiments are largely determined by contingent external conditions, they are always fickle. On the other hand, virtue is stable and constant because it is based on a principle (*KGS* 2:221).

Kant's comparison of virtue and moral sentiment is his comparison of Rousseau and Hutcheson. Rousseau exalts virtue as a matter of principle, while Hutcheson defines virtue as a matter of sentiment. To establish the subjectivity and instability of sentiments and the objectivity and stability of principles is Kant's objective in the *Observations*. This is to abandon Hutcheson's moral sense theory in favor of Rousseau's moral theory. He also adopts Rousseau's view that freedom is the most essential feature of every human being. But freedom is the source not only of human dignity, but also of all moral and political problems. Because human beings are free, Rousseau says, they are essentially willful creatures; they assert their wills against each other. Hence the most crucial problem for human beings is how to devise a social order that brings harmony to their conflicting wills.

Following Rousseau, Kant recognizes the difference between the material and the spiritual order (*KGS* 20:93). The world of matter is the domain of necessity; the world of spirit is the domain of freedom. He formally states his idea of moral order in the *Dreams of a Spirit-Seer Explained through Dreams of Metaphysics* (1766; *KGS* 2:315–73). This treatise was a critical and satirical inquiry into the popular works of a renowned visionary, Emanuel Swedenborg, and his alleged power of communication with the spirits of the other world. Although he ridicules Swedenborg's visionary power, he takes seriously the notion that there is a community of spiritual beings. He believes that the universe cannot be made of only dead, inert matter. It must contain immaterial substances, which contain the principles of life. These immaterial beings must constitute a spiritual order, just as material substances constitute a natural order (*KGS* 2:329–30).

The idea of a spiritual order marks a critical point in the development of Kant's moral theory. He has accepted the Newtonian view of the physical universe, which leaves no room for human freedom and moral values. This is another reason he cannot easily accept moral sense theory. If Newton's picture of the physical universe is correct, the physical universe has no place for moral properties. If there are no moral properties, moral sense cannot be similar to the external sense of physical properties, as Hutcheson holds. Moral sense should be no more than private internal sentiments. Only by affirming the existence of a spiritual order independent of the physical order did Kant come to feel that the integrity of human freedom and moral life could be maintained. Thus the demarcation of two orders, phenomena and noumena, became the basic framework for his entire philosophy.

The human soul, Kant holds, belongs simultaneously to both orders. Two opposing forces move the human soul: the self-love that refers everything to oneself and the public spirit that draws the soul toward others outside of itself (*KGS* 2:334). He says that there is a secret power that compels us to adapt our intentions to the welfare of others (*KGS* 2:334). This secret power first manifests itself as moral impulses and then becomes the strong law of duty and the weaker law of benevolence. These phenomena indicate the dependence of our innermost motives on the rule of general will. Moral feelings are the constraints on the individual will exercised by the general will (*KGS* 2:335). He is now redescribing the nature of moral feelings in terms of Rousseau's general will.

Kant imagines a moral order in an analogy to the physical order. Just as gravitational force holds physical beings together, so the general will brings spiritual beings into a universal harmony. The physical world is governed by physical laws; the spiritual world is governed by spiritual laws (*pneumatischer Gesetze*). The spiritual world is the intelligible world; the physical world is the sensible world. Kant believes that Rousseau has discovered the key for unlocking the workings of the intelligible world, just as Newton has discovered the key for opening up the mystery of the sensible world. So he calls Rousseau the Newton of the moral world (*KGS* 20:58–59).

In the *Inaugural Dissertation* (1770), Kant made his first attempt at reorganizing metaphysics as a new science.[3] He reaffirms his two-world view. The sensible world is composed of physical substances, and spiritual substances make up the intelligible world. One is known by sensibility, the other by intellect. Sensibility is passive; it represents the object as it appears to the subject. Hence the sensible world is the world of appearances. Intellect is not passive, but active. Instead of receiving representations, it represents the objects through its own pure concepts. Hence it knows the objects as they really are rather than as they appear to our sensibility. The intelligible world is the world of noumena; the sensible world is the world of phenomena (*ID* 2.3–6).[4]

For our knowledge of phenomena, intellect performs only the logical function because the concepts of objects and their relations are given by sensibility. For our knowledge of noumena, however, intellect performs the real function; it is equipped with a set of pure concepts for representing objects and their relations as they really are. It provides the general principles of pure understanding for

3. The official title of the *Inaugural Dissertation* is *De mundi sensibilis atque intelligibilis forma et principiis* (*KGS* 2:385–419).
4. *ID* refers to the *Inaugural Dissertation*, and the numbers that follow *ID* indicate the sections and subsections in the text.

ontology and rational psychology. By those principles, we form the concept of some exemplar or perfection, *Perfectio Noumenon*. It is the common measure of all other things as far as they are real and is conceivable only by pure intellect. In the theoretical domain, the exemplar is the supreme being, God; in the practical domain, it is moral perfection (*ID* 2.9). He identifies these ideas of perfection as Platonic Ideas.

Kant's acceptance of these eternal Ideas appears to be his way of coping with the metaphysical problem of moral standards. He has rejected moral sense theory because it cannot provide permanent moral standards, and he has accepted Rousseau's idea that virtue requires moral principles. As soon as he understands those principles as eternal normative standards, he cannot avoid the following question: Where do these standards and principles come from? Platonism is an answer to this question. He calls Platonic Ideas the common standards of all perfections.

The Copernican Revolution

Shortly after the publication of his *Inaugural Dissertation*, Kant became highly critical of his own position. Knowledge of phenomena was supposedly gained by intuitions and knowledge of noumena by concepts. How can we be sure that the pure concepts of understanding are related to their noumenal objects? More generally, how is a representation related to its object? In the *Dissertation*, he says, he had overlooked this critical question of representation (*KGS* 10:130). With the formulation of this question, he repudiates the *Dissertation* and initiates Critical Philosophy. In the *Critique of Pure Reason*, Kant drastically revises his conception of human knowledge. He now holds that the world of phenomena is the only legitimate domain of knowledge. The world of noumena cannot be known.

How are the pure concepts of understanding related to phenomena? This is the question of representation, the relation of concepts and objects. Kant recognizes two ways of establishing the relation of concepts to objects. Either our concepts conform to objects or objects conform to our concepts. The latter is the priority of concepts to objects ("the conformity of objects to concepts"), and the former is the priority of objects to concepts ("the conformity of concepts to objects"). According to Kant, traditional metaphysics had assumed the priority of objects, that is, their existence independent of our concepts. In that case, he says, there is no way to account for a priori knowledge of objects because independently existing objects can be known only a posteriori. In order to save a priori knowledge, Kant advocates the priority of concepts to objects. This is known as Kant's Copernican revolution.

In his ethical writings, Kant extends the Copernican revolution to practical philosophy.[5] The relation of the will and its objects is for practical philosophy what the relation of concepts and objects is for the theory of knowledge. The will is pure practical reason, the faculty of rational choice and action. It is the practical counterpart of pure theoretical reason. The object of the will is the good. There are two ways of accounting for the relation of the will to its object. Either the good determines the will or the will determines the good (*CPrR* 64; *KGS* 5:62).[6] One is the priority of the will over its object, and the other is the priority of the object over the will. These two views concern the following question: Which is the ultimate source of the good, the will or the object? According to one view, the will chooses the object because it is good. The object is the ultimate source of the good; the goodness of the will derives from the goodness of its object. According to the other view, the object is good because it is chosen by the will. The goodness of the object derives from the goodness of the will, which is independent of the objects of its choice.

These two views of the good express Kant's distinction between the formal and the material concepts of the good. A material concept of the good refers to an object lying outside the will, namely, the object of desire. But a formal concept makes no such reference; it is contained in the will itself. Kant's distinction of formal and material concepts of the good leads to his distinction between formal and material (or substantive) practical principles (*CPrR* 19–30; *KGS* 5:21–30). A formal practical principle is a priori; a material practical principle is a posteriori. Pure practical reason can preserve its freedom and autonomy only by adhering to its formal practical principle because its operation is independent of empirical conditions. Kant says that traditional ethics has been based on material practical principles, which entail the heteronomy of the will. The goodness of the will is dictated by the goodness of its objects.

The formal practical principle provides the procedure of constructing moral rules; it is the categorical imperative:

> So act that the maxim of your will could always hold at the same time as a principle establishing universal law" (*CPrR* 30; *KGS* 5:30).

This version of the categorical imperative has been known as the formula of universal law in distinction from other versions given in the *Groundwork of the Metaphysics of Morals*.

How can we tell whether a given maxim can be accepted as a universal law? This is the difficult question with the formula of universal law. In the

5. John R. Silber, "The Copernican Revolution in Ethics: The Good Reexamined," *Kant-Studien* (1959–60): 85–101.

6. *CPrR* stands for *Critique of Practical Reason*, trans. Lewis White Beck (New York, 1985).

Groundwork, Kant tries to answer this question with the famous four examples. The first example concerns the maxim of suicide: "From self-love, I make it my principle to shorten my life if its continuance threatens more evil than it promises pleasure" (*GMM* 89; *KGS* 4:422).[7] This principle of self-love cannot become a universal law of nature because it annihilates itself. Kant says, "It is then seen at once that a system of nature by whose law the very same feeling whose function is to stimulate the furtherance of life should actually destroy life would contradict itself and consequently could not subsist as a system of nature" (*GMM* 89; *KGS* 4:422). Kant is overstating his case. Let us compare two maxims:

M1: I love myself in such a way that I will spare myself the pain and misery whenever they become unbearable.

M2: I love myself in such a way that I will kill myself whenever I feel self-love.

M1 is a suicide rule; *M2* is a rule of universal self-destruction. The latter cannot exist as a law of nature; a system of nature containing such a law will destroy itself. But *M1* is perfectly acceptable as a law of nature. It may even be a constructive rule, one that can enhance the quality of life. In that case, Kant's argument applies not to the suicide rule, but only to the rule of universal self-destruction. As many critics have pointed out, the suicide rule cannot be invalidated by the categorical imperative.

Kant's second example concerns a maxim about promise-making. I have an urgent need to borrow money and try to secure a loan on a false promise to repay it. He describes the maxim as follows: "When I believe myself in need of money, I will borrow money and promise to repay it, although I know I shall never do so" (*GMM* 40: *KGS* 4:422). He says that the maxim contradicts itself. If it were to become a universal law, nobody would ever take a promise seriously, and the institution of promise-making would be destroyed. Here again the strength of Kant's argument depends on the way the maxim is framed. It can be formulated in two ways:

M3: I will break every promise I make.

M4: I will break my promise in case of difficulties.

The universalization of *M3* will destroy the entire institution of promise-making, that of *M4* will not.

The third example concerns natural talents: whether they should or should not be developed for their own sake. This question should be distinguished from the question whether natural talents should or should not be developed for their

---

7. *GMM* refers to Immanuel Kant, the *Groundwork of the Metaphysics of Morals,* trans. H. J. Paton (New York, 1964).

usefulness. The latter question belongs to a hypothetical imperative. So Kant invites us to suppose that we are living in a country like the South Sea Islands, whose rich natural resources make it possible to lead a comfortable life without cultivating any of our talents. Under those fortunate circumstances, we have to choose between two maxims:

M5: One ought to cultivate one's talents.
M6: One ought to neglect one's talents.

Kant admits that neither of them can be ruled out by the test of self-contradiction. A system of nature can exist in accordance with either of them as a universal law. But he says that a rational being should choose M5 and cultivate talents, "since they serve him, and are given him, for all sorts of possible ends" (GMM 90; KGS 4:423).

Kant's assertion is open to two interpretations. One of them is to take it in the context of natural teleology: our talents and faculties have their own natural ends. The other interpretation is to take his assertion in the context of consequentialism: the cultivation of our talents will be useful for our life. The second interpretation has been ruled out because it belongs to a hypothetical rather than to the categorical imperative. The first interpretation is equally unacceptable because it is based on the concept of natural teleology. Such a concept is a material concept of the good, which is incompatible with Kant's notion of formal practical principle. All ideas of ends and purposes are material concepts of the good. Hence it is illegitimate to employ any of those ideas in testing the universality of moral maxims.

We run into a similar problem in the fourth example. We are considering the choice between two maxims concerning the morality of helping others in need.

M7: I will neither bother to help others in need, nor expect any help from them.
M8: I will help others in need and expect similar help from them.

Although M7 can exist as a universal law of nature, Kant says, a rational being cannot will that it should become a universal law. Such a universal law would deprive the rational agent of the love and sympathy of others in those occasions in which he or she would need the help of others (GMM 91; KGS 4:423).

For the first time, Kant is appealing to our desires. Since there can be instances in which we want to have others' aid, he says, we cannot will that M7 be a universal law. He seems to say that M8 is a rational choice because it can satisfy my possible future desire for others' aid. On the other hand, M7 is not a rational choice because it can frustrate the same future desire. But this argument is not conclusive; it can be inverted. It can be said that M8 is not a rational choice because it can frustrate my future desire not to be bothered with others' need, and that M7 is a rational choice because it satisfies the same desire. This is a case of conflicting desires. Either of the two maxims satisfies one of the two desires and frustrates the other. At best, Kant can say that *M8* is better than *M7* because the desire to have others' help is stronger or better than the desire not to be bothered with others' needs. But this argument for *M8* appeals to the strength or quality of desires, which violates the formal practical principle. The worth and strength of desires belong to material concepts of the good.

Formal Practical Reason

The formula of universal law cannot resolve any of Kant's own four cases. This is no big surprise for us, who have gone through Hare's test of universalization in chapter 4. Though Hare's universal prescriptivism is basically the same as Kant's first formulation of the categorical imperative, there is one technical difference. Kant recognizes two different tests for the formula of universal law. He says that the maxims of the first two examples require the formal test of self-contradiction, while the maxims of the last two examples require a much stronger test. These two tests are known as the contradiction in conception and the contradiction in the will.[8]

Hegel rejects Kant's claim that the formal test of self-contradiction is sufficient for some maxims. As we have seen, the first two examples cannot be handled by the formal test of self-contradiction. A formal test can get nowhere without a substantive presupposition. Hegel makes this point by using the maxim of stealing.[9] The maxim of stealing presupposes the existence of property and would destroy the institution of property if it were made into a universal law. Hence Kant would say that the maxim of stealing contradicts itself. But a system of nature can survive under the universal law of stealing as well as the universal law of not stealing. The two universal laws will produce two different systems of nature: one with property and one without it.

Hegel says that neither of the two systems of nature contradicts itself. In terms of formal rationality, a social system with property and a social system without it are equally rational. There is no formal reason to prefer one to the other. However, there can be substantive reasons for choosing one over the other. If a social system with property is better than one without property, then we should not accept the maxim of stealing as a universal law because it will destroy not only itself but also the property system. On the other hand, if a social system without property is better than a social system with property, we should accept the maxim of stealing as a universal law. The important question is not whether a maxim can destroy or frustrate itself, but what kind of social system is dictated by its adoption as a universal law.

8. This distinction is well explained by Onora O'Neill, *Constructions of Reason* (Cambridge, 1989), 96–101.

9. Hegel, *Phenomenology of Spirit*, trans. A. V. Miller (Oxford, 1977), 257–58.

To elaborate Hegel's point, let us consider the maxim of helping the poor. If it is universalized, it will eradicate poverty. But the eradication of poverty will destroy the maxim. Hence the maxim of helping the poor should not be universalized.[10] But we would prefer to universalize it even at the cost of destroying it because we want to eliminate poverty. The question whether the maxim of helping the poor should or should not be universalized really amounts to the choice between two worlds: a world in which the poor will be helped and poverty eliminated and a world in which the poor will be neglected and poverty preserved. The choice between these two worlds or social systems cannot be made by the test of self-contradiction because it is a substantive choice. For that reason, Kant's first two examples are in essence no different from his last two examples. They all involve substantive choices.

Onora O'Neill has made perhaps the best and most sustained effort to save Kant's test of contradiction in conception against Hegel's charge.[11] She enumerates a series of maxims that can produce contradictions if they are universalized. For example, consider the maxim of universal deception. If everybody tries to lie to or deceive everybody else, nobody can do it. The same is true of the maxim of universal slavery. If everybody became a slave, there would be nobody who could be a slaveholder. Nobody can be a slave without a slaveholder. We cannot do any better with the maxim of everybody becoming a slaveholder. These are some of the maxims that can be rejected by the test of contradiction in conception.

We should not stop with these examples, but consider what the relevance of this test is to moral worth. The test only proves that the maxim of universal deception or slavery is impossible to be realized. Why should this fact make it morally wrong to act in accordance with such a maxim? This is the question of relevance that is seldom raised in the discussion of the categorical imperative. In most cases, the discussion is limited to the question of how well or how effectively this test works or whether there are really any maxims that cannot pass the test. These questions make sense only on the premise that the question of relevance is already settled or is not a problem at all.

For the question of relevance, let us consider the maxim that one must give help but receive none. This maxim cannot be universalized any better than the maxim of universal deception or slavery. But it is unlikely that anyone who acts on this maxim should be regarded as morally reprehensible. The idea of

10. This example is from F. H. Bradley, *Ethical Studies* (Oxford, 1970), 155. He gives another example: the maxim of loving one's enemies would contradict or destroy itself because its universal adoption will leave no enemies to love. Bradley makes up these examples to illustrate Hegel's objection to Kant's formal test of maxims.

11. O'Neill, *Constructions of Reason*, 96. This is only the last of her attempts. Her previous attempts have appeared in her many other publications on Kant.

contradiction in conception appears to have no relevance whatsoever to moral worth. The idea of practical contradiction can have practical relevance. What is contradictory is impossible, and what is impossible should never be sought as a goal of practical reason. The avoidance of the impossible is dictated by practical rationality. Though the discrimination of the possible from the impossible is practical, it is not always moral.

There is one more reason to question the relevance of the formal test. Numerous scholars have noted that there are many maxims that can be universalized but that carry no moral significance. Let us consider the maxim that everyone should have a pet. Though it can be universalized, we cannot say that everyone ought to have a pet. The universalization test fails on both ends. There are maxims that can be universalized and yet impose no moral duties on anyone. On the other hand, there are maxims that cannot be universalized and yet impose no moral prohibitions. The formal test is really irrelevant for moral maxims.

Why should we then accept the test of contradiction in conception for our maxims? Kant never raises this question. Perhaps his reasons are contained in his theory of formal practical reason. He repeatedly stresses the formal character of practical reason: it is concerned only with the form of maxims and never with their content. He may assume that the formal test of contradiction arises out of the formal character of practical reason. But the formal test is irrelevant because the question of relevance is always substantive.

Let us consider some standard arguments for the moral relevance and significance of the universalization test. As we saw in chapter 4, this test can secure the fairness between different but similar cases or between two different parties in the same case. Henry Sidgwick thought that the categorical imperative could be accepted only as a rule of equity.[12] This is to recognize the relevance of the formal test for the sake of fairness or impartiality. This is not a formal but a substantive consideration. There is also the utilitarian consideration for the universalization test; it is a way of selecting the rule that can produce the greatest utility. John Stuart Mill thought that a universal rule gains moral significance only by virtue of the consequence of its adoption.[13] Again, this is a substantive consideration that is not available to formal practical reason and its formal practical principle.

The Substantive Principle

Kant gives another formulation of the categorical imperative, which he calls the principle of humanity:

12. Sidgwick, *The Methods of Ethics*, 7th ed. (London, 1907), 209–10.
13. Mill, *Utilitarianism*, ed. Oskar Piest (New York, 1985), 6.

Act in such a way that you always treat humanity, whether in your own person or in the person of any other, never simply as a means, but always at the same time as an end (*GMM* 96; *KGS* 4:429).

This version is also known as the formula of respect and is clearly not formal but substantive. But Kant insists that it is a formal principle. He applies it to the same four examples. Suicide is morally wrong because it amounts to the use of oneself as a means for escaping from painful circumstances. A deceitful promise is wrong because it uses another person as a mere means for one's advantage. Kant says that these two cases violate the simple negative injunction against using a person as a mere means.

The negative injunction, however, is not strong enough for the third and fourth examples. Neither of them appears to involve the use of a person as a mere means. Someone who neglects her talents cannot be blamed for using herself as a mere means. Kant locates her fault in neglecting her natural end: "Now there are in humanity capacities for greater perfection which form part of nature's purpose for humanity in our person. To neglect these can admittedly be compatible with the *maintenance* of humanity as an end in itself, but not with the *promotion* of this end" (*GMM* 98; *KGS* 4:430). "Nature's purpose" belongs to natural teleology. Kant is assuming that human perfection is a part of natural teleology and that the development of talents is required for human perfection. The concept of human perfection is not a formal but a material concept of the good. If the second formula of the categorical imperative endorses this material concept, it is clearly not a formal but a material practical principle.

The fourth example presents a greater embarrassment for Kant's formalism. Happiness is the natural end of all human beings, Kant says, and there are positive and negative ways of contributing to the happiness of others (*GMM* 98; *KGS* 4:430). The negative way, which is not to harm others, is not enough because it achieves only negative harmony with others. Positive harmony can be achieved by positively furthering the subjective ends of others. The harmony of subjective ends is again not a formal but a material concept of the good, one that can be endorsed only by a substantive practical principle.

The principle of humanity forbids us to use others as mere means. But this abstract principle becomes practically meaningful only with our knowledge of the limit of individual freedom. Do I use someone as a mere means by asking for his help? Do I infringe upon someone's freedom by competing against him in a free market? We have to know what our rights are and how far our freedom extends before we can tell whether we are using someone as mere means. We have to determine an order of freedom before we can follow the principle of humanity. But an order of freedom is a system of rights, which is not a formal but a material concept. Again we come back to the necessity of having some material concept for the implementation of the principle of humanity. This is inevitable because the principle of humanity itself is not formal, but material.

The fact that the principle of humanity is not formal but substantive is perfectly consistent with Kant's idea that the first two formulas of the categorical imperative stand in the relation of form and matter (*GMM* 103–04; *KGS* 4:436). But what is absolutely baffling is his further claim that the two formulas are independent and equivalent. In the first *Critique*, Kant has shown form and matter as inseparable complements. If the two formulas stand in the relation of form and matter, they can be neither independent nor equivalent.[14] All these dubious assertions appear to indicate his serious confusion about the exact relation of the two formulas, and his failure to separate formal from material practical principle in the *Groundwork*.

In the *Critique of Practical Reason*, Kant succeeds in making a clean break between formal and material practical principles. Instead of talking about alternative formulas of the categorical imperative, he gives only the formula of universal law and stresses its formal character (*CPrR* 42; *KGS* 5:41). He does not even mention the second formulation. He introduces respect for persons in connection with respect for moral law (*CPrR* 79–81; *KGS* 5:76–78). By interrupting his discussion of respect for moral law, he says that respect always applies to persons only, never to things. He stresses its difference from such other emotions as love, fear, and admiration. Whereas these emotions all reflect our reactions to empirical conditions—social positions, talents, and achievements, for example—our respect for persons transcends all empirical conditions. He further claims that our respect for a person is none other than our respect for moral law (*CPrR* 81; *KGS* 5:78). Respect for persons is not in the categorical imperative but only reflects our recognition of it as the highest law.

In the second *Critique*, Kant appears to stick rigorously to the concept of formal practical reason. But he does so only in the Analytic. In the Dialectic, he introduces the concept of the highest good, which consists of three components: virtue (moral good), happiness (natural good), and their exact proportion. It is not a formal, but a material concept. In chapter 2 of the Dialectic, Kant talks about our duty to promote the highest good. After denying the necessary connection between morality and happiness, the two components of the highest good, he says, "Nevertheless, in the practical task of pure reason, i.e., in the necessary endeavor after the highest good, such a connection is postulated as necessary: we *should* seek to further the highest good" (*CPrR* 129;

14. Onora O'Neill tries hard to explain how the first two formulas of the categorical imperative can be independent and equivalent, though they are related as form and matter. But her explanation is far from convincing. See her "Universal Laws and Ends-In-Themselves," *The Monist* 72 (1989): 341–62.

KGS 5:124–25). He adds that to further the highest good is not a privilege, but a duty.[15]

To promote the highest good is not a formal but a material practical principle. In the second *Critique*, thus, Kant manages to give two moral principles: the categorical imperative and the principle of the highest good. One is a formal principle, the other is material. It appears that Kant cannot escape the duality of formal and material practical reason. In spite of his attempt to bring about a Copernican revolution in ethics, he is stuck to this duality in both the *Groundwork* and the second *Critique*.

Two Conceptions of Rationality

Kant's Copernican revolution in ethics turns out to be only a facade; he gives not only a formal but a material practical principle. Moreover, his formal principle is so vacuous that he surreptitiously introduces material content in its application to obtain whatever result he wants to have. Even today's practitioners of Kantian ethics seldom use his formal principle; they invariably appeal to the principle of humanity. Behind the facade of the Copernican revolution, Kant is still entangled with both formal and material principles of practical reason. This is because he has inherited two different conceptions of rationality.

The idea of formal rationality comes from Hume and British empiricism. Hume maintains that all of our ideas are copies of sense impressions and that the power of human reason is restricted to the relation of ideas. The relation of ideas is nothing more than their logical relation. To know nothing more than the logical relation of ideas is what Kant calls the logical or formal function of reason in the *Inaugural Dissertation* (*ID* 2.5). The formal function is to employ the logical principles of identity and contradiction. Restricted to logical function, pure practical reason has no way of apprehending material principles; its role is limited to inspecting the logical consistency of moral maxims.

The idea of substantive rationality comes from Leibniz and the rationalist tradition. According to this tradition, the ideas of human reason are not copies of sense impressions, but a priori concepts. With these a priori concepts, human reason can know much more than what is delivered by empirical sensations. It even has the power to know the supersensible world of noumena. In the *Inaugural Dissertation*, Kant had accepted this view of substantive rationality

15. There has been a dispute between Lewis White Beck and John Silber on the moral duty of promoting the highest good. Beck, *A Commentary on Kant's Critique of Practical Reason* (Chicago, 1960), 242–45. Silber, "The Importance of the Highest Good in Kant's Ethics," *Ethics* 73 (1963): 183.

along with the Humean view of formal rationality. As we have seen, he became highly skeptical of the substantive view and began his Critical Philosophy.

Critical Philosophy dictates two different maneuvers for the theoretical and practical domains. In the theoretical domain, Kant simply shifts the use of the pure concepts of understanding from the noumenal to the phenomenal world. But such a simple shift is not possible for the practical domain; practical reason does not have its own pure concepts, the counterparts of the pure concepts of understanding. In the *Dissertation*, Kant held that practical reason derives its moral laws from Platonic Ideas. But these Ideas cannot be relocated to the world of phenomena. As long as practical reason had access to Platonic Ideas, it could play its substantive role. But Critical Philosophy eliminates its access to Platonic Ideas, and practical reason becomes purely formal. Its power is restricted to the use of logical principles.

Because Hume knows that purely formal reason does not have the power to deliver substantive moral precepts, he never calls upon reason to be a moral guide. He accepts moral sense theory. But Kant cannot do the same; he had already repudiated moral sense theory in the *Observations*. So he engages in the impossible task of generating moral laws from purely formal reason and tries to give this impossible task an aura of plausibility by smuggling in substantive principles under the name of formal rationality. Thus he mixes up the two conceptions of formal and substantive rationality.

It is often said that Kant's ethics is rationalistic. But this assertion means little until we spell out which of the two views of rationality really underlies his ethics. Which of these two views governs the *Metaphysics of Morals?* This work is supposed to be the application of the practical principle laid out in the *Groundwork of the Metaphysics of Morals*. But the former work diverges radically from the latter. In the *Metaphysics of Morals*, Kant demarcates the duty of justice (juridical or political duties) from the duty of virtue (ethical duties). This demarcation was never intimated in the *Groundwork*. Now Kant assigns the duties of justice to external freedom and the duties of virtue to internal freedom. His distinction between virtue and justice roughly corresponds to the traditional distinction between ethics and politics. He gives his theory of justice in the first part of the *Metaphysics of Morals* and his theory of virtue in the second part.

Kant says that the difference between justice and virtue concerns their maxims (*MM* 382).[16] The theory of justice starts with private ends and then tries to determine whether their maxims can be universalized. If their maxims can be accepted as universal laws, those private ends are shown to be consistent with the freedom of everybody concerned. This is exactly the formal procedure

---

16. *MM* stands for the *Metaphysics of Morals*, and numbers following *MM* indicate the page numbers of the Prussian Academy Edition of Kant's Collected Works, vol. 6.

Kant had advocated for all moral questions in the *Groundwork*. But he now says that this formal procedure is suitable only for the determination of juridical duties. For the duties of virtue, Kant reverses the formal procedure. The theory of ethical duties cannot begin with private ends because they are empirical. It must begin with maxims and find the ends. What he really means turns out to be not a reversal of the formal procedure, but a different version of the same procedure.

Kant defines ethical duties as those ends that are at the same time duties. There are two duties of this kind: the perfection of oneself and the happiness of others. Because these ends are at the same time duties, they generate their own maxims. Hence the maxims of ethical duties are quite different from the maxims of juridical duties. The latter must meet only the formal requirement; the former must fulfill the material requirement. He says, "The former [juridical duties] can only concern the formal element of the maxims; the latter [ethical virtues], however, concerns their matter, namely an end which is at the same time conceived as a duty" (*MM* 394–95).[17]

Kant is now recognizing two distinctly different types of maxim: the formal and the material. The formal maxim has nothing to do with its matter or the end of action; the material maxim is solely concerned with its matter. A formal maxim is valid if and only if it can be accepted as a universal law for governing the domain of external freedom. A material maxim is valid if and only if it is linked to an obligatory end, an end which is at the same time a duty. The duties of justice are determined by formal maxims; the duties of virtue are determined by material maxims.

Because justice and virtue involve different types of maxim, the principle of justice is different from the principle of virtue. Kant states the principle of justice:

> Every action is just [right] that in itself or in its maxim is such that the freedom of the will of each can coexist together with the freedom of everyone in accordance with a universal law. (*MM* 230, trans. John Ladd)

He restates this principle as the universal law of justice:

> Act externally in such a way that the free use of your will is compatible with the freedom of everyone according to a universal law. (*MM* 231, trans. John Ladd).

The "maxim" in the first quotation is absorbed into "a universal law" in the second. If the maxim can be accepted as part of a universal law, it fulfills the requirement of the categorical imperative. The principle of justice seems to

---

17. This quotation is from *The Metaphysical Principles of Virtue: Part II of the Metaphysics of Morals,* trans. James Ellington (Indianapolis, 1964), 53.

follow from the first formulation of the categorical imperative. This is Onora O'Neill's view, endorsed by Roger Sullivan.[18]

The principle of justice, however, is too complex to be exhausted by the formula of universal law. It contains one important element that cannot be found in the formula of universal law, and that is the reference to freedom. To account for this difference, Mary Gregor says that the principle of justice is similar to the second formulation of the categorical imperative. Just as the formula of humanity fixes absolute limits to our freedom, so does the principle of justice.[19]

The truth of the matter is that both formulations apply equally to the principle of justice because the principle contains two different features.[20] The formula of universal law concerns the form of the principle of justice, and the formula of humanity concerns its content, namely, freedom. In that case, the two formulas are indeed in the complementary relation of form and content and cannot be equivalent, as Kant claims. This is a clear way of showing the relation of the two formulas.

Kant states the principle of virtue:

Act according to a maxim whose ends are such that there can be a universal law that everyone have these ends. (*MM* 395, trans. James Ellington)

In the principle of virtue, universal laws are end-dependent; in the principle of justice, universal laws are end-independent. To clarify this difference, I want to consider the following two formulas:

1. A maxim is valid if it can be universalized.
2. A maxim can be universalized if it is valid.

The principle of justice takes formula 1; the principle of virtue takes formula 2. Formula 1 first determines whether a maxim can or cannot be accepted as a universal law. If it can be so accepted, it is good enough to be a universal law. Formula 2 first determines whether a maxim is valid or not valid. It is valid only if it concerns an end whose fulfillment is a duty in itself. Such a maxim can be universalized because it is valid. Universalization is a test for formula 1 but is a result in formula 2. Both principles are categorical imperatives; they command categorically. But neither of them is a formal principle, as we shall see.

---

18. O'Neill, *Acting on Principle: An Essay on Kantian Ethics* (New York, 1975), 38–39, 72; Sullivan, *Immanuel Kant's Moral Theory* (Cambridge, 1989), 247.
19. Gregor, *Laws of Freedom* (New York, 1963), 39.
20. Bruce Aune tries to connect the principle of justice first to the formula of humanity as an end in itself and then says that this connection requires the formula of the universal law of nature. This is another way of applying two formulations of the categorical imperative to the principle of justice. See his *Kant's Theory of Morals* (Princeton, 1979), 137–40.

The duties of virtue are duties to pursue obligatory ends. How can we tell those ends from others? This is the same question we have encountered in our reading of the *Groundwork:* How can we tell the difference between good and bad subjective ends? Though Kant did not raise this question in the *Groundwork,* he now says that it is the function of pure practical reason to recognize and identify obligatory ends. He calls practical reason the faculty of ends. He writes, "For practical reason to be indifferent to ends, i.e., to take no interest in them, would be a contradiction; for then it would not determine the maxims of actions (and the actions always contain an end) and, consequently, would not be practical reason" (*MM* 395, trans. James Ellington).

This is a radically different view of practical reason from the one he had advocated in his Copernican revolution. In the second *Critique* and in the *Groundwork,* he had stressed the formal character of pure practical reason: it is independent of material concepts of the good. But the concept of ends is a material concept, and he is now making it an integral feature of practical reason. Kant defines ethics as "the system of the ends of practical reason" (*MM* 381). He is abandoning the formal conception of practical reason and reverting to the material conception. This is the reversal of his Copernican revolution in ethics. The material conception begins with the concept of ends and the good and then moves on to maxims and laws, whereas the formal conception begins with the formal principle and maxims and then determines the ends and objects.

In his discussion of individual virtues, Kant almost completely ignores his earlier formalism. He divides all ethical duties into duties to oneself and duties to others and subdivides the former into perfect duties to oneself and imperfect duties to oneself (*MM* 421–47). Perfect duties to oneself are further divided into those duties to oneself as an animal being and those duties to oneself as a moral being. The first perfect duty to oneself as an animal being is to preserve oneself in one's animal nature. Kant says that this duty forbids suicide, wanton self-abuse, and self-stupefaction through the immoderate use of food and drink. Suicide is the total destruction of oneself as an animal being, and the others are partial self-destructions. All of these are forbidden because they contravene the duty of preserving oneself as an animal being.

In his discussion of these perfect duties, Kant mentions neither the maxim nor its universal form. Suicide is wrong not because of its maxim, but because it goes against the duty of preserving one's natural being and because it destroys the natural basis of oneself as a moral being (*MM* 422–23). Following his discussion of suicide, he raises many casuistical questions. Is it self-murder to plunge oneself into certain death (like Curtius) in order to save one's country? Should we regard the sacrifice of oneself for the good of mankind as a heroic deed? If one is given (like Seneca) the choice between suicide and an unjust death sentence, is suicide permissible? Bitten by a mad dog, a man already feels hydrophobia coming upon him. Since he is convinced that there is no cure for this malady, he decides to terminate his life as the only way to avoid spreading his misfortune to other people. Is he doing something wrong? Kant answers none of these questions; he only presents them as questions to be considered.

There is no doubt about how he would answer those questions if he were still operating under the rigor of his formalism. In fact, there are some Kant scholars who take these casuistical questions to mean that he does not allow suicide even for a victim of rabies.[21] They assume that Kant is still rigidly holding on to his formalism. If he were, he would not even permit these questions to be raised because all of them concern the contingent circumstances for suicide. They are irrelevant under his formal practical principle. Why then does Kant raise these casuistical questions? The questions make sense only if we assume that he is reorienting himself from formal to material considerations. All the casuistical questions are concerned with competing ends, and the choice of competing ends is now a central function of practical reason. This was inconceivable under the formal conception of practical reason.

The rigor of formalism is not much present even in Kant's discussion of the duty to oneself as a moral being (*MM* 429–37). He says that this duty is opposed to the vices of lying, avarice, and false humility (servility). He condemns lying as a vice not because of any maxims, but because it obliterates the dignity of a liar as a human being and because it goes against the natural purpose of communication. By *avarice*, Kant means stinginess. It is a vice that makes it impossible to provide adequately for one's true needs in life. Servility is a vice by which one denies oneself dignity as a human being. It goes against the virtue of self-esteem. Kant handles all of these virtues and vices on substantive grounds and never tries to back up his views with formal considerations.

Kant divides duties to others into duties of love and duties of respect. Only in his discussion of the duties of love does he make use of the formula of universal law. He proposes to consider why the maxim of benevolence should be accepted as a universal law. Since I want every other man to be benevolent to me, he says, I should also be benevolent to every other man (*MM* 451). This sounds like the repetition of his argument in the *Groundwork* but takes an unexpected direction. Because "all other men" with the exception of myself would not be "all men," Kant says, the law prescribing the duty of benevolence should include myself because it is a universal law. Thus he links the universality of the law to the universal idea of humanity (*MM* 451).

In this argument, Kant derives the universality of the maxim of benevolence from the universality of humanity. The selfish maxim of getting help from others but giving none to others is rejected because it is inconsistent with the universality of this law. Kant never says that such a maxim cannot be univer-

21. Sullivan, *Immanuel Kant's Moral Theory*, 202.

salized. But he points out that it is incompatible with the idea of needy rational beings, united by nature in one dwelling place for mutual aid (*MM* 453). This argument is clearly based on natural teleology.

Kant uses even the formula of universal law just to ensure the principle of equality in the duty of mutual benevolence; "it permits me to be benevolent to myself under the condition that I also am benevolent to everyone else" (*MM* 451, trans. James Ellington). As far as the original maxim of benevolence is concerned, it is based on the duty of all men toward one another, that is, the duty of promoting the happiness of others (*MM* 450). Again Kant makes no use of maxims in his discussion of the duty of respect for others. The duty of respect is securely based on the dignity of human beings. They should never be used as a mere means, because of their dignity. We should never despise or mock other people, nor should we ever slander or abuse them. Pride is also a vice; it goes against one's proper esteem of others. Pride amounts to the demand for special esteem from other people, which goes against the equal dignity of all human beings. The duty of respect is far more important than the duty of love. The omission of the latter is only lack of virtue, but the omission of the former is a vice.

Let us consider the relation of the concept of dignity to moral law. In the second *Critique*, Kant asserted the primacy of moral law over the dignity of human beings: human beings have dignity because they obey moral law. This has led to the troublesome question of whether immoral people have any dignity. Many Kant scholars have found it quite difficult to give a satisfactory answer to this question. But this question is forestalled by the position Kant takes in the *Metaphysics of Morals:* human dignity is now assumed to be prior to moral law. The concept of human dignity now stands as one of the substantive ideas for the formulation of moral maxims.

Kant's theory of justice is not any less material or substantive than his theory of virtue. While the principle of virtue is concerned with the order of ends, the principle of justice is concerned with the order of freedom. The concepts of these two orders are equally material. One of the lessons he learned from Rousseau was the importance of freedom and the difficulty of coordinating individual liberties. Without law, Kant says, our external freedom can lead only to an anarchy of terror and savagery.[22] There are many different kinds of law for establishing a social order, and most of them result in orders of injustice. A just social order can be established by regulating the external freedom of everyone concerned by a set of rules that can be accepted as universal laws. By their universality, these laws secure the equality of everyone's freedom, and this equality is the justice of social order.

22. Kant, *Lectures on Ethics,* trans. Louis Infield (London, 1979), 17.

Equality of freedom means equality of rights; the concept of external freedom is interchangeable with the concept of rights. Kant says that the principle of innate freedom is the source of all rights (*MM* 237). The principle of innate freedom is the innate right to external freedom under universal laws. It contains the right to innate equality, independence from others, sovereignty over oneself, and liberty to do anything to others that does not by itself detract from what is theirs. The innate right eventually expands to the property right of acquisition and disposition.

All these rights belong to private law, insofar as they do not interfere with one another. Kant believes that they can be known a priori by every human being (*MM* 297). Hence they require no legislation. In this regard, public law is different from private law; it is an expression of the collective will (*MM* 311). Such a collective will belongs to a civil society, which is constituted by the collective action of a community. Kant accepts the theory of social contract as an idea of reason (*MM* 315). He identifies the state as the general united will (*MM* 313), thereby formally installing Rousseau's theory of general will at the center of his theory of public law.

The ultimate end of a civil society is to secure equality and justice for all citizens. Kant says that the well-being of a state should not be confused with the well-being or happiness of its citizens, which can sometimes be better attained in the state of nature or under a despotic government. The well-being of a state consists only in the constitution that conforms most closely to the principles of justice (*MM* 318). The well-being of a state is the central concern for Kant's theory of justice. Hence his conception of justice is as substantive as his conception of virtue.

In both parts 1 and 2 of the *Metaphysics of Morals,* Kant uses the three concepts perfection, happiness (or well-being), and human dignity for defining our duties. The duties of justice are motivated by the concept of human dignity and freedom. The duties of virtue to others are motivated by the concepts of happiness and dignity. The duties to oneself are motivated by the concepts of perfection and dignity. All these concepts are material, and the maxims of justice and virtue alike are based on these material concepts. The formal principle of universalization is used only to secure the mutual harmony and consistency of these material concepts and their maxims. Kant clearly abandons the formal concept of practical reason in favor of the material concept and thus reverses his Copernican revolution in ethics.

This reversal has gone unnoticed in Kant scholarship. Most Kant scholars have assumed that the *Metaphysics of Morals* is only the application of a moral theory laid out in the *Groundwork for the Metaphysics of Morals.* That was in fact Kant's own claim: the *Groundwork* was meant to lay the foundation for the *Metaphysics of Morals.* Taking his words at face value, some Kant scholars have tried to interpret the *Metaphysics of Morals* as a systematic application of the categorical imperative. Mary Gregor regards it as "a procedure which implies a patient search for criteria through which duties can be derived, step by step, from the categorical imperative." [23]

Instead of studying Kant's own application of the categorical imperative, Gregor says, most students of Kant's ethics disregard the *Metaphysics of Morals* and construct their own versions of a metaphysics of morals. As far as they are concerned, Kant might as well not have written the *Metaphysics of Morals*. But the neglect of this important work, Gregor maintains, has led to a gross distortion and misunderstanding of Kant's "formalism." If this work had been studied carefully, the prevalent views that the consequences, ends, and circumstances of our actions are morally irrelevant and that freedom from logical contradiction is a sufficient test of a moral maxim could never have taken root. [24]

Most Kant scholars have not paid serious attention to the *Metaphysics of Morals* not because they love to spin out their own metaphysics of morals, but because the *Metaphysics of Morals* does not cohere with the *Groundwork*. What Kant really offers in the later work is not a fulfillment, but an abandonment of the earlier work. Even in the earlier work, as I noted, he had to go through an endless series of tortuous maneuvers to produce substantive results from his empty formal program. He may have seen the futility of those maneuvers and decided to accept the necessity of material concepts for practical philosophy. This reversal appears to mark the end of his Critical Philosophy.

The Fusion of Two Worlds

Do we have any reason to think that Kant really made a decision to reverse his position? If he did, when did he make it? I propose that the momentous decision was made in the *Critique of Judgment*. The third *Critique* is usually assumed to be the last member of the trilogy in Kant's Critical Philosophy, but it was never in his original design. In support of this view, I shall advance the following evidence. In the winter of 1770–71, Kant became disappointed with his *Inaugural Dissertation* and decided to abandon his original plan of improving and refining it. Instead he started a new project called *Die Grenzen der Sinnlichkeit und der Vernunft* (The boundaries of sensibility and reason), which eventually materialized as his Critical Philosophy.

In a letter of June 1771 to Marcus Herz, Kant describes his new project as an investigation of the basic concepts and laws of the sensible world together with a sketch of the essential aspects of the theory of taste, metaphysics, and morality (*KGS* 10:121–24). This description of the new project appears to fore-

---

23. Gregor, *Laws of Freedom,* xii. Aune follows a similar method in *Kant's Theory of Morals,* 131–201.

24. Gregor, *Laws of Freedom,* xi.

tell the three parts of Critical Philosophy; taste, metaphysics, and morality appear to be the three respective topics for three critiques. In a letter of February 1772 to Herz, however, Kant describes his projected work as having two parts: theoretical and practical.

Each of these two parts will consist of two sections. The theoretical part will contain general phenomenology and metaphysics, and the practical part will treat general principles of the feeling of taste and sensuous desire and the first foundations of morality (*KGS* 10:129). The feeling of taste does not yet constitute an independent department, as Kant will claim later in the last *Critique*. He recognizes no distinction between the pleasure of aesthetic experience and the pleasures of inclination. In the same letter to Herz, he also describes his forthcoming book as "'Critique of Pure Reason' that will deal with the nature of theoretical as well as practical knowledge—insofar as the latter is purely intellectual. Of this, I will first work out the first part, which will deal with the sources of metaphysics, its method and limits. After that I will work out the pure principles of morality" (*KGS* 10:132, trans. Arnulf Zweig).[25]

Kant's habit of dividing philosophy into two basic divisions of theory and practice antedates his Critical period. In the *Prize Essay*, he recognizes two types of first principles in philosophy: the first principles of metaphysics and the first principle of ethics (*KGS* 2:273–301). In the *Dreams of a Spirit-Seer*, Kant recognizes two orders of creation: the order of physical objects and the order of spiritual beings. One is governed by Newton's law of nature, the other by the moral law of general will (*KGS* 2:315–83). In the *Inaugural Dissertation*, he reaffirms his notion of two orders in his distinction of the phenomenal and the noumenal world. The latter is a spiritual order governed by moral principles; the former is a natural order governed by physical principles.

In its format, the *Observations of the Feeling of the Beautiful and the Sublime* of 1764 is quite different from the other pre-Critical treatises. Not a systematic treatise, it is rather meant to be a collection of informal "observations." Moreover, it is devoted to the practical branch of philosophy in exclusion of its theoretical branch. Although the aesthetic concepts of the beautiful and the sublime are the central categories in this treatise, Kant never demarcates them from ethical categories. On the contrary, he maintains the unity of ethics and aesthetics by employing the same concepts of the beautiful and the sublime in his discussion of aesthetic and ethical properties.

In the *Observations*, Kant recognizes no important distinction between taste and desire. He lumps them together in the domain of feeling, which is supposed to belong to practical or moral philosophy. He is operating under the influence of Shaftesbury and Hutcheson, who had advocated the unity of all feelings and

25. Arnulf Zweig, ed. and trans., *Kant: Philosophical Correspondence 1759–99* (Chicago, 1967).

desires. In the second *Critique,* Kant goes beyond Shaftesbury and Hutcheson and recognizes two sources of feeling, the phenomenal and the noumenal. The phenomenal source is our desires and inclinations, which produce pleasure and pain. The noumenal source is the moral law and human dignity, which provoke the feeling of awe and the sublime. He does not yet see the need to make a special place for aesthetic feeling.

In his architectonic review of the first *Critique,* Kant reaffirms his two-part program: "Metaphysics is divided into that of the *speculative* and that of the *practical* employment of pure reason, and is therefore either *metaphysics* of nature *or* metaphysics of morals" (A841/B869). In the preface to the second edition of the first *Critique,* he reaffirms this binary demarcation of theoretical and practical philosophy (Bx). In the preface to the second *Critique,* he recognizes two faculties of the mind and two sets of a priori principles: theoretical and practical. This dyadic division is said to be the systematic basis for his Critical Philosophy (*CPrR* 12; *KGS* 5:12).

Kant announces the completion of his Critical program in the conclusion of the second *Critique,* in which he makes his moving observation about two wonders: "The starry heavens above me and the moral law within me" (*CPrR* 166; *KGS* 5:161–62). The first is located in the external world; the second in the inner self. The heavens and moral law represent Kant's two worlds, phenomena and noumena, the domain of natural necessity and the domain of moral freedom, which are, respectively, the objects of his inquiry in the *Critique of Pure Reason* and the *Critique of Practical Reason.* In the conclusion of the second *Critique,* Kant is summing up his accomplishments not only in that volume, but in his entire Critical Philosophy. Hence it reads like the coda for his Critical program in its entirety.

The first two *Critiques* have recurrent references to each other. The aim of the first *Critique* is to limit the domain of knowledge so as to secure the possibility of belief, the domain of the second *Critique.* The theory of moral law and freedom in the second *Critique* is formulated in the ontological framework of the first *Critique.* The dialectical chapters of the two *Critiques* in particular read like a well-orchestrated antiphony. In contrast to this inseparable mutual reference, the first two *Critiques* make absolutely no reference to the third. It is simply left out of this antiphony.

Kant begins the last *Critique* by reaffirming his binary division of philosophy: "Our entire faculty of cognition has two realms, that of natural concepts and that of the concept of freedom, for through both it prescribes laws *a priori.* In accordance with this distinction, then, philosophy is divisible into theoretical and practical" (*CJ* 12; *KGS* 5:174).[26] If this division of philosophy is correct,

26. *CJ* stands for Kant, *The Critique of Judgment,* trans. James Creed Meredith (Oxford, 1952).

the first two *Critiques* cover the entire domain of philosophy, leaving no room for another *Critique*. So Kant feels the need to make a special plea for his writing of the third *Critique*. He now claims to see an enormous chasm between the phenomenal and the noumenal worlds. This so-called chasm was never regarded as a problem in the first two *Critiques*; in fact, it was the ontological foundation for the Critical program. He now looks upon it as the most serious problem in his philosophy because the chasm makes it impossible for practical reason to translate its ends from the domain of freedom to the domain of nature (*CJ* 14; *KGS* 5:176).

Neither in the *Groundwork* nor in the second *Critique* had Kant ever regarded the chasm as an obstacle for practical reason. Why does it suddenly appear as an obstacle? As long as practical reason operates only with formal concepts and principles, it does not have to cross the chasm between the phenomenal and the noumenal worlds. Formal concepts and principles are not derived from the noumenal world; they are contained in formal practical reason itself. But the chasm is a serious obstacle for the material (substantive) conception of practical reason. Material concepts and principles are located in the noumenal world and have to be brought down to the phenomenal world for their realization. Kant's recognition of the chasm between the two worlds becomes inevitable with his reversion from formal to material practical reason.

In the last *Critique,* Kant proposes to use the faculty of judgment for bridging the chasm between phenomena and noumena. This faculty can establish the ground of unity and mediation of the two worlds, he says, because it lies between understanding and reason. How does the faculty of judgment mediate between the two worlds? This is the big mystery. In the last *Critique,* Kant makes no effort whatsoever to answer this question. It is the most baffling feature of the third *Critique*. After mentioning the problem of mediation at the beginning of the work, he seems to forget it completely from there on.

Instead of mediating the two worlds, the faculty of judgment fuses them into one. This is not to close our eyes to the textual fact that in the last *Critique* Kant does talk about the demarcation of phenomena and noumena and appeals to the supersensible in his account of aesthetic and teleological judgments. For Kant, however, the concept of the supersensible has two meanings: the existence of God and the Ideas of pure reason.[27] Though the existence of God is still beyond the domain of sense and phenomena in the last *Critique,* the transcendent Ideas become accessible even to imagination and sensibility in aesthetic experience. In our experience of the beautiful and the sublime, we cannot see the demarcation of the two worlds. The transcendent ideals are immanently real. Even the

---

27. Kant attaches special significance to the word *Idea* (*Idee*), which means a transcendent standard. He distinguishes it from the general notion of an idea (*Vorstellung*). I will capitalize the first letter of *Idea* to indicate this distinction.

faculty of judgment is not the third rational faculty, but an intimate joint operation of sense and intellect, imagination and understanding, ideas and feelings.
Because the third *Critique* fuses the two worlds into one, there is no longer any
need for them to be mediated.

The separation of the two worlds is the central theme of Kant's Critical Philosophy. Since the last *Critique* fuses the two worlds, it terminates the Critical
period and begins a new one, which I propose to call the post-Critical period.
In the first two *Critiques,* sensibility was restricted to the world of phenomena, the objects of sense and desire. The world of noumena, the transcendent
ideals and principles, was postulated only by the intellect. This created a serious gap and a severe strain between intellect and sensibility, between what can
be thought and what can be felt. This gap is a typical syndrome of scientific
consciousness, and Kant's formalism was its inevitable outcome. Once the gap
is eliminated, sensibility becomes coextensive with the domain of intellect, and
practical reason can leave behind the barren world of formal imperatives and
enter the rich world of substantive values.

Platonic Ideas

In the last *Critique,* reason regains its substantive function in its recognition
and appreciation of finality and teleology. The presence of substantive reason
is evident in Kant's technical use of Ideas in the last *Critique.* The concept of
beauty is an Idea of pure reason (*CJ* 76; *KGS* 5:232–33). It is an Idea of perfection, and it cannot be derived from experience. Kant insists that an Idea of
perfection is always prior to any actual instances or their average. He illustrates
this point by the relation of a *normal idea* (*Normalidee*) to the idea of an average. The normal idea of a horse is not the idea of an average horse. The latter
is an empirical concept, but the former is an Idea of reason. The finality and
beauty of nature concern the Ideas of reason.

Because Kant accepts the substantive view of reason in the third *Critique,* he
is finally released from the conflicting demands of formal and material reason.
He seems to forget the demarcation between form and content, the ultimate
basis for his architectonic for the first two *Critiques.* In the first *Critique,* he
maintained the rigid distinction between form and content not only for thought,
but even for sensibility. In the second *Critique,* he again adhered to the same
demarcation: the formal and material concepts of the good and the formal and
the material principles of practical reason. In the last *Critique,* however, Kant
abandons all dualistic demarcations: form and content, phenomena and noumena, sensibility and intellect, reason and inclination. He tries to establish a
truly unified world.

The *Metaphysics of Morals,* which was published seven years later than the
last *Critique,* fully substantiates the spirit of Kant's post-Critical philosophy.

As I have shown, the substantive Ideas of reason become central to Kant's exposition. In his theory of virtue, he appeals to the Ideas of not only moral, but natural perfection. Even the idea of happiness is an Idea of reason because it is a natural end of all human beings. This is a big turnabout. In the *Groundwork* (*KGS* 4:418), he had labeled the concept of happiness as an ideal of imagination; in the second *Critique,* he had stressed its empirical character. But the concept of happiness can be taken in two ways: as an empirical or a normative concept. On empirical grounds, the question whether someone is happy or unhappy can be determined by his or her subjective feelings. Happiness is a psychological state. When the concept of happiness is taken normatively, the distinction between happiness and unhappiness can be made only by normative criteria for assessing human excellence. A satisfied fool is happy by the empirical criteria, but not by the normative criteria.[28]

In his theory of justice, Kant again appeals to the Idea of reason, that is, the Idea of a just order for the exercise of external freedom. The original community of possession is an Idea; so is the concept of private possession in distinction from the empirical concept of physical possession (*MM* 250–55). The concept of civil society that limits individual wills in accordance with general will is also an Idea of reason because the concept of general will is an Idea (*MM* 306). The concept of a civil state is the state in the Idea (*der Staat in der Idee*) as it ought to be according to pure principles of justice, which serves as an internal standard (*norma*) for every actual union of men in a commonwealth (*MM* 313). The original contract, by which individuals can get out of the state of nature, is not a historical or empirical concept, but an Idea of reason (*MM* 315). So is the concept of an ideal state, which Kant identifies with a republican constitution (*MM* 341). The rational ideal of human community takes its final form in the Idea of a peaceful universal community of all nations (*MM* 352).

Where do all of these Ideas come from? In the *Inaugural Dissertation,* as we have seen, Kant locates those Ideas in the world of noumena and identifies them with Platonic Ideas. In the first *Critique,* he calls them the Ideas of pure reason and sharply demarcates them from the categories, the pure concepts of understanding. Though he repudiates the possibility of knowing the world of noumena, he retains the Ideas of pure reason as the foundation of his practical philosophy. In the Dialectic of the first *Critique,* he repeatedly claims that the Ideas of pure reason, if taken as a source of knowledge, lead only to dialectical illusions. But he is equally emphatic in asserting the necessity of those Ideas for practical philosophy.

Kant says that our knowledge of phenomenal objects can dispense with the

---

28. The distinction between the two conceptions of happiness is also important in Aristotle's ethics. For a good discussion of this point, see Richard Kraut, "Two Conceptions of Happiness," *The Philosophical Review* 88 (1979): 167–97.

aid of Platonic Ideas because the pure concepts of understanding are sufficient for their cognition. In the domain of practice, however, the Ideas of pure reason are absolutely necessary. For example, the concepts of virtue are Ideas of pure reason that cannot be derived from the world of experience (A3125/B373). The world of phenomena offers no objects that correspond to those Ideas; at best, it can offer some instances or exemplifications. The Ideas of pure reason are the archetypes that set standards for our conduct. Archetypes and standards belong to the world of noumena; the rules and laws of experience belong to the world of phenomena. The world of phenomena is the domain of what is done; the world of noumena is the domain of what ought to be done. Kant says, "Nothing is more reprehensible than to derive the laws prescribing what *ought to be done* from what *is done*" (A319/B375). Just as the pure concepts of understanding make possible the world of experience, so the Ideas of pure reason make possible the world of practice. This is Kant's transcendental argument for the Ideas of practical reason.

Kant's distinction between the domain of knowledge (or theory) and the domain of faith (or practice) is meant to be a rebuke to both rationalists and empiricists. Rationalists make immodest and illegitimate claims in extending the domain of human knowledge beyond the world of sensibility. Although empiricists are right in limiting knowledge to the domain of sense experience, he says, they are equally dogmatic in their denial of supersensible ideals. They do irreparable injury to the practical interests of reason (A471/B499). The contrast of these two dogmatic positions is represented by Epicurus and Plato. Though the philosophy of Epicurus encourages and furthers knowledge, it does so at the expense of practical philosophy. Though Plato supplies excellent practical principles, he needlessly permits reason to indulge in metaphysical speculation. Kant's world of faith is the world of Platonic Ideas. This world cannot be known because we have no intellectual intuition. But we have to believe in it for the sake of morality and religion, the two domains of practical reason.

The Platonic Ideas he enumerates are the Ideas of divine and human perfection: the most perfect being (*ens realissimum*) and human virtues (A313–19/B370–75; A571–78/B599–606). They are exactly the same Ideas of perfection and reality he had designated as exemplars of perfection in the *Inaugural Dissertation*. In the Dialectic of the first *Critique*, his discussion of Platonic Ideas is much richer than in the *Dissertation*. He even expands the domain of those Ideas by extending human perfection from individual virtues to social order. He describes a republican constitution as an Idea that allows "*the greatest possible human freedom* in accordance with laws by which *the freedom of each is made to be consistent with that of all others*" (A316/B373). At this point, Kant plans to use Platonic Ideas for all practical sciences of morality, legislation, and religion (A318/B375). His conception of ethics is basically the same as the one he had in the *Dissertation*.

At this point, Kant gives no indication that his conception of practical principles is formal. The Ideas of pure reason are material practical principles. Kant regards those Ideas as the source of all moral laws; they determine what *ought to be* and what *ought to happen* (A548–50/B576–78). When he divides the practical law into pragmatic law and moral law, he again appeals to the Ideas of pure reason. Pragmatic law is concerned with happiness; it is based on such empirical principles as our desires and the natural causes that satisfy them. Moral law governs the worthiness to be happy; it is based on a priori Ideas of pure reason (A806/B834). Even the notion of moral maxims that is to play a critical role in his formalistic ethics is stated in reference to Platonic Ideas. He says that practical laws are called maxims insofar as they are the subjective grounds of action, and that the function of maxims is to facilitate the observance of moral laws, which are based on Platonic Ideas (A812/B840).

Kant defines the function of practical reason in terms of Platonic Ideas. *Practice* means the practical employment of reason, which in turn means to realize the Ideas of pure reason in the world of phenomena (A328/B385). Practical reason reshapes the phenomenal world in accordance with noumenal ideals. This power is the causal power of practical reason: "Reason is here, indeed, exercising causality, as actually bringing about that which its concept contains; and of such wisdom we cannot, therefore, say disparagingly *it is only an idea*. On the contrary, just because it is the idea of the necessary unity of all possible ends, it must as an original, and at least restrictive condition, serve as standard in all that bears on the practical" (A328/B385).

Pure reason with practical causal efficacy is moral freedom. Kant says that freedom stands between an Idea and its realization (A317/B374). Free will is free of sensuous impulses but is bound by moral laws (A802=B830; A810=B838). Since moral laws are derived from the Ideas of pure reason, those Ideas are the foundation for the freedom of practical reason. This view of freedom is diametrically opposed to Kant's concept of autonomy in the second *Critique*. There he says that autonomy of the will is incompatible with any material concept of the good, and that even the ideals of perfection inevitably dictate heteronomy of the will. In the first *Critique*, Kant never recognizes the threat that the Ideas of pure reason pose for the autonomy of the will. Although those Ideas are material concepts, they cannot pose such a threat because reason is "the sole begetter of these ideas" (A763/B791).

By the time he writes the *Groundwork*, he wants to extend his Copernican revolution of theoretical reason to practical reason. In the first *Critique*, he had advocated that theoretical reason prescribes, through its categories, basic laws to nature, instead of discovering them. This is the ground for the conformity of objects to concepts. The Copernican revolution is due to the legislative function of theoretical reason. If practical reason is to be legislative in the same manner as theoretical reason, it should prescribe moral laws instead of finding them in

Platonic Ideas. Since it has to operate without any dependence on material concepts, it is purely formal, and its formal principle is the categorical imperative, a formal procedure for instituting all moral laws.

In the second *Critique*, Kant makes even a more systematic attempt to execute the Copernican revolution than in the *Groundwork*. He gives only the formula of universal law for the categorical imperative in place of the three formulas of the *Groundwork*. But the Copernican revolution in practical philosophy is quite a different proposition from the Copernican revolution in theoretical philosophy. As I noted earlier, pure practical reason does not have the rich conceptual resource that pure theoretical reason has. Just imagine what kind of legislative function pure theoretical reason could perform if it were not equipped with the categories. It would have to devise all a priori laws of nature from the meager resource of its logical principles. That sort of horrendous task is imposed on practical reason in the name of self-legislation or autonomy by the Copernican revolution.

Though the Analytic of the second *Critique* is Kant's best effort to live up to his notion of formal practical reason, it is spoiled by the Dialectic. The transcendental dialectic of practical reason cannot begin without the concept of the highest good, which is an Idea of pure reason. The dialectic also presupposes the idea of justice, though it is not even mentioned. The concept of the highest good involves the idea of exact proportion between virtue and happiness, and this idea is none other than the idea of justice. Kant's repeated claim that moral goodness is the ground for being worthy of happiness makes sense only on the presupposition of justice. Hence his arguments for the existence of God and the immortality of the soul ultimately hinge on the idea of justice. The transcendental dialectic of practical reason is the interplay of the Ideas of pure reason, and these Ideas are not formal but substantive. There is no room for formal reason in the Dialectic of the second *Critique*.

In Kant's philosophy, however, the dialectical level is far removed from the level of practical life. In the *Critique of Practical Reason*, he manages to keep the Ideas of practical reason in this remote region. In the *Critique of Judgment*, he decides to bring those ideas down from the dialectical to the practical level. In the *Metaphysics of Morals*, he brings down two Platonic Ideas to the two practical domains of justice and virtue. These are the same Platonic Ideas he had singled out as the basic Ideas of practical philosophy in the Dialectic of the first *Critique*. These two Ideas can be traced back to Plato's *Republic*, whose central topic is justice in the soul and in the state. But these two Ideas make different appearances in the two books. In the first *Critique*, they remain transcendent Ideas. In the *Metaphysics of Morals*, they are articulated into immanent Ideas such as the Ideas of self-perfection or individual rights in the two domains of virtue and justice.

The sustained development of Kant's practical philosophy falls into four important periods: the pre-Platonic period before the *Inaugural Dissertation*, the first Platonic period from the *Dissertation* to the first *Critique*, the formal period from the *Groundwork* to the second *Critique*, and the second Platonic period from the last *Critique* and thereafter. There is an important difference between the first and the second Platonic periods. Platonic Ideas are transcendent in the first Platonic period but become immanent in the second Platonic period.

The conventional binary demarcation of Kant's career into the pre-Critical and the Critical periods gravely distorts the complexity of his checkered career. It gives the misleading impression that the idea of formal practical reason began in the first *Critique* and stayed with him for the rest of his life. But this idea occupies Kant's attention only for a few years in his long career. The *Groundwork* was published in 1785 and the second *Critique* in 1788. Before the *Groundwork*, he had embraced Platonic Ideas for more than ten years; after the second *Critique*, he returned to Platonic Ideas for good. He tried to work out the idea of formal practical reason only for a short interval between these two long Platonic periods.

CHAPTER EIGHT

Platonic Retrieval

Kant calls a Platonic Idea an archetype; it sets the standard for measuring what takes place in the world of phenomena. The idea of a perfect state is such an archetype. Kant writes, "This perfect state may never, indeed, come into being; none the less this does not affect the rightfulness of the idea, which, in order to bring the legal organization of mankind ever nearer to its greatest possible perfection, advances this maximum as an archetype" (A317/B373–374; trans. Norman Kemp Smith). Platonic Ideas cannot belong to the world of phenomena because they are the criteria for evaluating what goes on in the world of phenomena. So Kant locates them in the world of noumena. The world of noumena is also called the supersensible world because it transcends the domain of sensibility.

The idea of a supersensible world does not begin with Kant or even Plato. Many religions affirm the world of such supernatural entities as gods and goddesses, spirits and demons, angels and devils. But such a supernatural world is radically different from the world of Platonic Ideas. The former is a world of objects; the latter is a world of ideas. One is composed of concrete entities; the other consists in abstract entities. Further, the two perform different functions. The religiously conceived supernatural world provides the power of salvation and edification, whereas the world of Platonic Ideas presents norms and standards of behavior.

The normative conception of supersensible entities is the unique and striking feature of Platonism. Platonic Forms function as norms and standards not only for ethics and politics, but for logic, mathematics, and aesthetics. We cannot settle the question of whether a mathematical computation is correct or incorrect by an empirical investigation of how people make computations or by taking a poll. We have to appeal to the normative standards of computation. Likewise, the question of whether an inference is valid or invalid cannot be determined without appealing to the normative standards of logical inference. How can we account for the existence of normative standards? Platonism offers a unique answer to this question.

The Sophistic Crisis

The crisis that the Sophists brought on ancient Greece was very much like the normative crisis of the modern West. The Sophists were highly critical of traditional beliefs. They discarded the traditional view of law, which held that it is a divine gift, and advocated that it is only a human contrivance. For this purpose, they stressed the distinction between nature (*physis*) and law (*nomos*). In the *Gorgias*, Callicles condemns law because it goes against nature. It is the justice of nature that the superior should rule the inferior and that the weak should serve the interests of the strong (*Gorgias* 483d). But the weak try to tame the strong for their own safety and security: "We mold the best and the most powerful among us, taking them while they're still young, like lion cubs, and with charms and incantations we subdue them into slavery, telling them that one is supposed to get no more than his fair share, and that that's what's admirable and just" (*Gorgias* 483e–484a, trans. Donald Zeyl). The majority of the weak institute laws to control the minority of the strong; this is the origin of social contract theory.

In Callicles' account of law and nature, the most important element of human nature is its obsession with self-interest. It is human nature to promote self-interest at the expense of others. It goes against human nature to be constrained by the force of law. In the *Republic*, Thrasymachus advocates this egoistic view of human nature in his outburst against Socrates. He calls justice another's good and the advantage of the stronger (*Republic* 343c). The ruling class makes laws to suit their interests, and justice lies in the obedience to those exploitive laws. This account of law is different from that of Callicles, who condemns laws for going against the interest of the strong. In Thrasymachus's view, the strong would not suffer from the constraint of law but exploit it in their domination of the weak.

If law and justice are mere instruments of self-interest, their legitimacy becomes questionable. Whether law and justice serve the interests of a few strong people or the great multitude of the weak, they are always instruments of coercion. Might makes right. This is the essence of legal positivism; there are no standards of right and wrong other than those set by positive law. For many Sophists, the idea of legal positivism was linked to the relativity of truth and value. Sophistic relativism was perhaps best stated in Protagoras's thesis of *homomensura:* "Man is the measure (*metron*) of all things."

The Protagorean thesis appears to endorse the extreme form of normative relativism. But Protagoras the Sophist is a baffling figure; he does not subscribe to the prevailing Sophistic view of law as an instrument of exploitation. He regards law as an instrument of rationality; by the institution of law, mankind moves out of a state of brute nature and builds civilized societies. Law is the mother of human progress beyond the natural state of savagery (*Protagoras*

320c–322d). If he believes in human progress, he should also believe in objective standards. The idea of progress makes sense only by presupposing some notion of standards. He also professes to teach virtues for expensive fees, an enterprise that would also be senseless without presupposing some objective standards. Hence the question of objective norms and standards is an overriding issue for Protagoras, and this appears to go against his relativist thesis of homomensura.

If there are no objective standards of right and wrong, we have to accept positive laws as the ultimate criteria of justice. Normative positivism offers a clear decision procedure, namely, the appeal to fact. But such a decision procedure is unacceptable for settling normative questions. In the *Euthyphro*, Socrates says that it is much more difficult to settle normative questions than questions of fact. When we disagree about the relative size of two things, we can settle our disagreement by measuring them. Likewise, we can settle a disagreement about the relative weight of two things. But we have no reliable procedure for settling disagreements about questions of what is just and unjust, honorable and dishonorable, good and bad (*Euthyphro* 7cd; also *Phaedrus* 263a).

Because Protagorean relativism presents the most serious normative problem, Plato subjects it to a most careful Socratic scrutiny in two of his dialogues, the *Protagoras* and the *Theaetetus*. Plato opens the *Protagoras* by portraying Protagoras as a Sophist who is in great demand as a teacher of virtue. In the dialogue, the question of virtue naturally leads to the question of measure (norms and standards). Accepting Protagoras's hypothesis that pleasure and pain are the ultimate good and evil, Socrates and Protagoras agree on a method of making a decision. People make mistakes in their choices because they are misled by appearances. What appears to be pleasant turns out to be painful, and vice versa, in the same way the perceptual properties of size and thickness turn out to be different from what they really are. When one is overcome by present pleasure and overlooks future pain, one is making a computational error. Hence the art of measuring is the right procedure for making decisions (*Protagoras* 356e). It is the art of hedonistic calculus.

The Socrates–Protagoras agreement is remarkable. In the *Euthyphro*, as we have seen, Socrates had admitted the important difference between factual and normative disputes. There is a decision procedure for settling factual questions about the relative size or weight of things, and the procedure is the art of measurement. But, he had said, there is no such art of measurement for settling normative questions. In agreeing with Protagoras, Socrates is now accepting an art of measurement for normative questions.[1] But we should not

---

1. It has been a matter of serious dispute whether Socrates accepts the hedonistic measure sincerely or only for the sake of debate with Protagoras. Because Socrates is consistently against hedonism in Plato's other dialogues, it is hard to believe that his acceptance is

forget that theirs is a hypothetical agreement; it is based on the hypothesis that pleasure and pain are the ultimate good and evil. In fact, Plato concludes the dialogue with Socrates' admission that both the protagonist and the antagonist have contradicted themselves and completely reversed and exchanged their respective positions.

In the *Theaetetus*, Socrates again takes up the question of normative standards. He does not debate with Protagoras as he did in the *Protagoras;* neither does he simply criticize Protagoras's doctrine. Instead he takes on the singular role of being a spokesman for Protagoras. He presents and articulates Protagoras's thesis and even defends it against objections. As Paul Woodruff points out, this is unprecedented in Plato's works. Why does Plato use this special dramatic device for the exposition of Protagoras's thesis. Woodruff writes, "Perhaps Plato valued him as the source of many doctrines closely related to his own." [2]

One overriding concern that Plato shared with Protagoras is the question of measure or standard. After explicating the Protagorean thesis of homomensura in the context of the perceptual world ("What appears cold to you is cold for you"), Socrates points out that the Protagorean thesis eliminates the distinction between wisdom and ignorance. If knowledge and truth are totally relative to each person, there can be no objective standard for the distinction between the wise and the ignorant. This is embarrassing to Protagoras as a professional teacher. If he is not wiser than others, he has nothing to teach his students and surely no reason for getting paid (*Theaetetus* 161de).

Socrates tries to save Protagoras from this embarrassment by proposing a distinction between the world of perceptual objects and the world of practical wisdom. Although we are all equal in the world of perceptual truth, Protagoras should say, we are not equal in the world of practical wisdom. When the same food tastes sour to a sick person and good to a healthy person, Protagoras would hold, both perceptions are equally true (*Theaetetus* 166e–167a). But the conditions of the two persons are not equal; one of them is in better condition than the other. Wisdom is the power of changing the condition from worse to better. A physician does it by drugs, and a sophist by discourse. Husbandmen do the same thing with plants because plants can be changed from unhealthy to healthy conditions.

The distinction between wisdom and ignorance is based on the distinction between a wholesome (*kresta*) and an unwholesome (*ponera*) condition (*Theaetetus* 167b). Although thoughts in both conditions are equally true, thoughts in

---

sincere. This standard view is stated by Gregory Vlastos in his review of Terence Irwin's book *Plato's Moral Theory*, "The Virtuous and the Happy," *Times Literary Supplement*, February 24, 1978, 230–31.

2. Paul Woodruff, "Plato and Protagoras" (manuscript).

one condition are better than thoughts in the other condition. In Socrates' interpretation, Protagoras would have demarcated truth from wisdom, fact from value (*Theaetetus* 171e). Although subjectivism rules in the domain of fact and truth, he would hold, objectivism prevails in the domain of value and wisdom. His position is the exact reverse of today's positivism, which accepts subjectivism in the domain of value and objectivism in the domain of fact.

The distinction between the domain of truth and the domain of wisdom requires two different interpretations of homomensura. In the domain of truth, every human being is as good a measure as every other human being. In the domain of wisdom, however, some human beings are better measures than others (*Theaetetus* 171e).[3] One is a positivistic measure, the other a normative measure. The latter requires discrimination between normal and abnormal conditions, while the former does not. The measure of hedonistic calculus is positivistic; all pleasures and pains count equally, whether they belong to sick or healthy people. On the other hand, the measure of practical wisdom in medicine, rhetoric, and husbandry is normative. Protagoras is caught between the two conceptions of measure. In the *Theaetetus*, Socrates as Protagoras's spokesman states both of them in one breath: "For I hold that whatever practices seem right and laudable to any particular State are so, for that State, so long as it holds by them. Only, when the practices are, in any particular case, unsound for them, the wise man substitutes others that are and appear sound" (*Theaetetus* 167c, trans. F. M. Cornford; the point is repeated in 171e–172b).

The first of these two sentences recommends the positivistic measure of right and wrong, but the second endorses the normative measure.[4] As if to highlight the difference between the two measures, Socrates attributes them to Protagoras twice in the *Theaetetus*. Plato is using Protagoras to demonstrate the important difference between the two types of measure or criterion. He also shows the disastrous consequence of rejecting normative criteria; it obliterates the distinction between good and evil and wisdom and ignorance. He evidently regards

3. This may appear to contradict the parable of Zeus as given in the *Protagoras,* which says that political virtues are distributed equally to all mankind. But equal distribution does not necessarily mean the distribution of equal amounts.

4. A. T. Cole says that Protagoras offers two different measures of good and evil for the art of medicine and the art of oratory. For the art of medicine, the measure is the feeling of patients: what seems to be good to them is good. There is no difference between what is really good and what seems to be good. If so, the measure of good and evil for the art of medicine is clearly positivistic. For the art of oratory, Cole says, Protagoras maintains the distinction between what is good and what appears to be good, what is really good for a city and what seems to be good to its citizens. The function of an orator is to recognize what is good for the city and what is harmful for it, even when they are not recognized by the citizens. In that case, the measure is not positivistic but normative. But it is highly unlikely that Protagoras offers two different measures for two different arts. For details, see Cole, "The Apology of Protagoras," *Yale Classical Studies* 19 (1966): 109–18.

Protagoras as an ideal figure for demonstrating the gravity of these problems concerning criteria because of his well-known formula of homomensura and relativism.

Protagoras's idea of normative measure is not restricted to the practical wisdom of medicine and rhetoric. He is portrayed as a teacher of the correctness of words and of diction. There are two ways of deciding questions concerning the correctness of words and diction: positivistic and nonpositivistic. The positivistic method is to appeal to popular usage; this is an appeal to linguistic social facts. The nonpositivistic method is to appeal to some normative criteria. In Plato's dialogues, Protagoras uses nonpositivistic criteria for settling the questions of correctness. In the *Cratylus* (391c), Protagoras is said to have taught the fitness of names. In the *Phaedrus* (267c), he is said to have taught rules of correct diction and many other fine precepts. In the *Protagoras* (339d), Protagoras faults a poem by Simonides for making inconsistent statements. Consistency is a logical, not a positivistic, criterion.

These questions of correctness and consistency clearly transcend the positivistic world of facts. They are questions of rationality par excellence; they concern speech, the first manifestation of human rationality. Protagoras was as much a rationalist in this regard as he was in his evolutionary account of nomos and physis. If he can admit the normative distinction between correct and incorrect names and consistent and inconsistent meanings, Plato may have thought, he should equally accept the normative distinction between the wholesome and the unwholesome, the just and the unjust. Plato pictures Protagoras as a rationalist caught between positivism and idealism and presents his predicament with unmistakable sympathy and understanding. Plato may sympathize with him because he himself has had to work his way out of the same problem.

Woodruff's conjecture that Protagoras was a source of Plato's ideas may now be substantiated. To this end, what is noteworthy is the affinity of Protagoras to Socrates. Like Protagoras, Socrates accepts the conventionalist view of nomos. In the *Crito* (51e), he says that he entered into an agreement with Athens to abide by its laws. But the acceptance of conventionalism by itself was nothing remarkable in those days because it was becoming a popular view. It was accepted by many others, including Antiphon, Lycophron, and Hippias. What connects Socrates and Protagoras closely is the question of normative standard or measure. Most conventionalists still tried to find norms and standards in nature, this tendency being best exemplified by Antiphon. By his standard of nature, laws are bad if they go against nature; they are good if they are in accord with nature.

Socrates and Protagoras agree in rejecting naturalistic standards for settling normative issues. Socrates makes this rejection in his distinction between factual and moral disagreements in the *Euthyphro*. He recognizes the art of measurement for settling factual disputes, but not for settling normative disputes. Yet he does not become a relativist or a skeptic. Instead he firmly upholds the distinction between wisdom and ignorance. This distinction can be vindicated, however, only by finding a suitable notion of measure for the domain of value or wisdom. On these essential points, he is in total agreement with Protagoras.

Let us assume that Protagoras was faced with the same problem: finding a right standard for normative decisions. Then his formula of homomensura can be taken as his solution of the problem. The baffling feature of this formula is that it can be taken either as a naturalistic or as a nonnaturalistic standard. In the world of perception, it functions as a naturalistic standard. In the *Theaetetus* (155d–157c), Socrates presents Protagoras's theory of perception as a theory of physicalistic interaction between the sense organs and their physical objects. Perception is always true because whatever a sense organ registers in its perception is a part of nature. The naturalistic or positivistic standard is infallible and egalitarian.

In the world of art, medicine, and rhetoric, Protagoras believes, nature cannot provide the standards of judgment. He knows that the acceptance of naturalistic standards would obliterate the distinction between good and evil, wisdom and ignorance. He claims to be a moral teacher. His function as a teacher depends on the existence of normative standards, which are clearly different from naturalistic standards. So his formula of homomensura has to be given a nonnaturalistic interpretation. To be sure, nonnaturalistic normative standards are perfectly compatible with conventionalism, insofar as convention (nomos) is understood to transcend nature (physis).

The art of measurement in the hedonistic calculus is only one special version of homomensura; man is now taken as the measure of pleasure and pain. Even this hedonistic measure can be taken in two ways: naturalisticaly and nonnaturalistically. The naturalistic measure can make no normative distinction between the good and the bad, the noble and the base, the higher and the lower, in the domain of pleasure and pain. All pleasures and pains are equal. But they are not equal for the nonnaturalistic measure. The two ways of understanding homomensura only reflect two ways of understanding the nature of man and his world: naturalistically and nonnaturalistically. By the institution of nomos, Protagoras has said, mankind has gone beyond the state of nature. He has two conceptions of mankind: one of nomos and one of physis, and these two conceptions underlie the two conceptions of homomensura. One of them can be accounted for in terms of physicalism, but the other cannot. How can the conception of nonnatural norms and standards be accounted for? This is the unresolved question for both Protagoras and Socrates.

The Socratic Resolution

In the *Theaetetus*, we have seen, Plato presents Protagoras in a quandary over normative criteria. He is depicted as a man who could not make up his mind between the two versions of his homomensura. One of them belongs to the world of body and the other to the world of mind. In the *Phaedo*, Plato presents Socrates' own struggle with these two worlds. As a young man, Socrates says, he became absorbed in physical science (*Phaedo* 96a). He was fascinated with the idea of explaining all things in terms of physical causes. But he soon realized that he was the most stupid creature in the world. The reason he cites for this realization is quite unusual. By the model of physical science, he says, it was impossible to explain why ten is greater than eight, or why the addition of one and one is two. What was the physical cause for generating the *two*? Was one of the ones becoming two with the addition of the other one or were two of them becoming two? He became disillusioned with physical science when he realized that these simple things could not be explained in terms of physical causes.

Through these unusual questions about numbers, Socrates is highlighting the difference between normative and physical sciences. The idea of causal explanation is central in physical sciences, but not in normative sciences. The idea of causation does not even enter logic and mathematics. A rational account in normative sciences requires norms, whereas a rational account in physical sciences is automatically assumed to be a causal account. Hence the physicalistic view of the world is irrevocably tied to the causal view, and Socrates is ridiculing it by extending it to the domain of mathematics.

Then Socrates heard of Anaxagoras's theory that mind was the ordering principle of all things (*Phaedo* 97c). This view of the universe appeared to make much better sense to Socrates than the idea of physicalistic explanation. But when he read the work of Anaxagoras, he became disappointed. Instead of using mind as his principle, Anaxagoras fell back on the same sort of mechanical explanation as the philosophers of physical science did. On Anaxagoras's theory, mind did not behave any differently from the way material elements do in the theories of materialist philosophers. In these theories of mechanical explanation, Socrates says, the common mistake is not to recognize the difference between causes and conditions. In talking, for example, one employs many material elements—muscles and bones, voice and air. But those material elements are only conditions, and the cause of talking belongs to the mind (*Phaedo* 98de). To find a cause is to give a rational account.

In his disappointment over Anaxagoras's philosophical practice, Socrates adapted the Anaxagorean theory of rational account and devised the method of definition (*Phaedo* 99e). It starts with a postulate (*hypotheseis*) and draws out its consequences. If the consequences harmonize, the postulate will be accepted as true. Hence he calls it an indirect method (*Phaedo* 99e). In this indirect method of hypothesis, he also appropriated Anaxagoras's theory of Forms and postulated the existence of Forms. These Forms are assumed to be absolute; for example, the Form of Beauty is absolutely beautiful. On the other hand, beautiful things are not absolutely beautiful; they are beautiful only to the extent that they participate in the Beautiful in the absolute (*Phaedo* 100b–e).

The Forms are ideals that can never be fully exemplified in any instances. With the postulation of Forms, Socrates establishes the world of mind, which is independent of the world of body. He says that Forms cannot belong to the body and its senses. They must belong to the soul; they are accessible only to intelligence. Because they are inaccessible to the senses, they are rejected by materialists and positivists. This leads to the demarcation between the two worlds of mind and body, the intelligible and the visible. While Socrates was engrossed in physical science, he recognized only the world of body. He became disillusioned with mechanical explanations because they were totally useless for understanding the life of the mind. As we have seen, he was distressed over the fact that the model of mechanical causation cannot account for such simple mathematical operations as the addition of one and one. At this point, Socrates seems to assume that the unique feature of mental life is its reliance on standards and ideals. If mind is the ordering principle, he says, it always aims at the best (*Phaedo* 97d–98b). If the mind has arranged the positions of the sun and the stars, it must have so arranged them because that arrangement is the best one. It is simply against the nature of mind not to seek what is best. The principle of optimality is innate to the nature of the soul. Hence he repeatedly denies that anyone can do wrong willingly and knowingly. Now the principle of optimality must presuppose the standards of good and evil and the ideals of perfection. Without them, it is impossible to say what is good and what is bad or what is best and what is worst. On the other hand, the world of body knows no difference between good and evil or best and worst.

Socrates' two models of explanation correspond to Protagoras's two types of measure. When Socrates explains Protagoras's idea of perceptual truth, he gives a mechanistic account of perception. Sensations are produced by the mechanical operation of physical objects on sense organs (*Theaetetus* 156a–157a). The mechanical theory of sensation dictates the relativity of sensation. Every sense organ is different from every other sense organ, and the mechanical impact on different sense organs can never be the same. Hence every sensation is different from every other sensation. Paradoxically, the relativity of sensation assures the equality of all human beings as the measure of all things because the physical world recognizes no objective standards. The conception of man as the normative measure belongs to the world of mind. It is concerned with the distinction of good and bad, better and worse, which cannot be found in the physical world.

If Socrates' two models of explanation correspond to Protagoras's two notions of measure, they must have gone through the same experience and wrestled with the same problems. In their youth, both of them had embraced physicalism only to recognize its inadequacy for the world of soul. Both of them played critical roles in redirecting the attention of philosophy from the world of nature to the world of human value. Both of them tried to find objective standards that can account for the normative dimension of human life. It is this bond of common concern and experience that entitles Socrates to assume for himself in the *Theaetetus* the role of spokesman for Protagoras's ideas.

Socrates differs with Protagoras on one important point. Protagoras never thinks of any world other than the world of body, and this unitary view makes it difficult for him to render the two different accounts of homomensura. Since he recognizes only the physical world, there appears to be no place for the normative distinction between wisdom and folly. The two conceptions of homomensura are incompatible with his conception of one world. Socrates overcomes this problem by claiming that the world of soul is independent from the world of body.

In the *Republic,* the separation of the two worlds is complete. But the separation gets modified and restated in the *Sophist*. The Eleatic Stranger describes the problem of two worlds as the battle of gods and giants (*Sophist* 246a). The giants, who recognize only the reality of physical objects, are materialists. For them, the mark of being real is to be tangible and visible; they refuse to recognize intelligible and immaterial Forms (*Sophist* 246ab). The gods are idealists, who insist on the reality of changeless Forms (*Sophist* 248a). They demarcate the world of Being from the world of Becoming and claim the former as the true reality. The eternal Forms belong to the world of Being, they say; mutable physical objects belong to the world Becoming, half real and half unreal.

The Eleatic Stranger tries to reconcile these two camps by demanding that both concede something. He asks the materialists to revise their criterion of reality; they should concede that visibility and tangibility are not the true marks of reality. Instead, they should claim the power (*dynamis*) of acting and being acted upon as the true mark of reality (*Sophist* 247e). Of the idealists he asks that they not see immutability as the only mark of reality. If reality is immutable, it can have no life and no intelligence (*Sophist* 248e). The idealists must admit the reality of changing and moving; they have to expand their notion of reality so as to accommodate both the changing and the changeless things. The reconciliation of materialists and idealists gives Plato's new picture of reality; the permanent and the changeable are the two elements of one world.

In the *Laws* (889a–890a), Plato again confronts the challenge of materialism, the view that all things are ultimately derived from nature and chance. According to materialists, the Athenian says, the original elements of the universe are fire and water and earth and air, which exist by nature and chance. Then come such physical objects as the earth, sun, moon, and stars; they are created by the chance combination of inanimate elements. Then follows the creation of heaven and earth, all animals and plants; again their creation is governed by blind nature and chance. The mind or god has nothing to do with it. Finally art springs up as a product of nature and chance. Some arts imitate truth, as in the case of music and painting. In the case of medicine and husbandry, some arts cooperate with nature. The art of politics also cooperates with nature, but to a smaller degree; the art of legislation has no natural basis.

According to materialists, the Athenian continues, the gods exist not by nature, but by art and by the laws of states, which are different in different places because they are made by agreement. The principles of justice have no existence at all in nature; mankind are always debating about them and altering them. Since art and law have no basis in nature, they have no authority except for the moment and at the time they are made. In the absence of a normative basis for art and law, might alone makes right. This materialist view of art and law leads young people into impieties; they are led to believe that the gods do not govern the universe. The materialist philosophers persuade them that a true life according to nature is to live in domination of others rather than in subjection to them.

In the *Statesman* (283c–285e), Plato again brings up the problem of measurement. The Eleatic Stranger says that there are two types of measurement. One of them compares two objects directly to each other and determines their relative length or weight, and the other compares the two objects in reference to a measure (*metron, metrion*) or standard (*Sophist* 284d). The second method is the method of normative measure. It requires Platonic Forms. The first one is the positivistic measure and requires no standard. Through normative measure, the Eleatic Stranger says, arts become possible. He is only giving here a fuller account of the Protagorean notion of normative distinctions in arts and practical sciences. Because arts are based on normative measures, they can take mankind beyond the state of nature, which knows only positivistic measures. Normative measures take mankind from the world of body to the world of soul.

Definition and Intuition

In his early dialogues, Plato tries to delineate the ideals of perfection for the domain of virtue. What is piety? What is temperance? What is courage? These Socratic questions set the stage for the definition of virtues but usually lead to no satisfactory result. Socrates and his interlocutors do agree on examples of a virtue but cannot find a suitable definition of it. There have been many attempts to explain this negative outcome, and two of them are noteworthy. One of them refuses to accept the standard view that the Socratic definitions fail, and the other stands on the Wittgensteinian view that such definitions are by nature impossible.

Gerasimos Santas is a fervent spokesman for the view that Socratic definitions produce positive results.[5] He lays out the Socratic conception of definition. Socrates is dissatisfied with a definition by examples; a definition should give the *eidos,* or Form, that is exemplified by those examples. The definition of bees should spell out the essential properties of all bees. The definition of courage should give the property that is shared by all instances of courage; the definition of virtue should give the eidos shared by all virtues (*Meno* 72bc). The Socratic definition is an eidetic, or essential, definition; it is meant to spell out an eidos, or essence, of a whole class. Santas holds that Plato's early dialogues produce forty-one such definitions. He lists three definitions of courage: a certain endurance of the soul, wise endurance, and the knowledge of what is to be dreaded or dared in war or in anything else. He gives seven definitions of temperance: the doing of everything orderly and quietly, a kind of quietness, modesty, the doing of one's own business, the doing of good things, the knowing of oneself, and the science of the other sciences and itself.[6]

This list of Socratic definitions cannot satisfy the requirement for an essential definition. The Socratic idea of an essential definition does not permit more than one definition for one virtue, whether it is courage or temperance. But Santas lists three for courage and seven for temperance. In fact, many of these definitions are rejected in the course of Socratic scrutiny in the dialogues. Santas's list of forty-one Socratic definitions does not contain even one that can meet the Socratic requirement of eidetic definition. That may prove the truth of Wittgenstein's thesis that examples share no eidos, but only a family resemblance. If there is no eidos, then it is impossible to give Socratic definitions. This is the Wittgensteinian account of Plato's early dialogues.

The negative account of Socratic definitions appears to be sounder than the positive one. But what does the negative account reveal about Platonic Forms? As Peter Geach asks, does it indicate that they do not exist and that the Socratic idea of definition only reveals a Socratic fallacy, namely, that of assuming that one cannot correctly predicate a term without being able to give a general criterion for its use in a definition?[7] Against this negative conclusion, I would like to propose the following account. Let us make use of the legal distinction between formal rules and informal standards. Traffic rules that require motorists to stop at red lights and stay under a specified speed limit are examples

5. Gerasimos Santas, *Socrates: Philosophy in Plato's Early Dialogues* (London, 1979), 98–100, 106–08.

6. Santas, *Socrates,* 99

7. This view is represented by Peter Geach, *Logic Matters* (Berkeley, 1972), 33–34.

of a formal rule. The standards of due care in parking a car and in driving through a crowded area are examples of an informal standard. The standards of a reasonable person in American tort and contract law are other examples. Unlike formal rules, informal standards cannot be stated in formal propositions. Formal rules are determinate; informal standards are indeterminate.

Our understanding of informal standards is different from our understanding of formal rules. We can have a propositional knowledge of formal rules, but not of informal standards because they cannot be stated in propositions. Even when we know what is required of a motorist by the standard of due care, we cannot fully state our knowledge in the form of a definition. The standard of due care dictates different requirements under different circumstances, and those different requirements cannot be captured in a single formula. This is the same problem Socrates repeatedly runs up against in his search for a definition. In the *Laches,* for example, he realizes that the essence of courage cannot be described in a single formal rule of behavior. In the *Charmides,* he recognizes the same problem for the essence of temperance.

What Socrates is seeking in his definitional search is a propositional understanding, which is quite different from our intuitive understanding of informal standards. By *intuitive understanding* I mean our understanding of standards and criteria that cannot be expressed in propositional forms. I want to distinguish between knowledge by intuition and knowledge by definition. One is given by definition, the other by intuition. In his early dialogues, Plato never fully recognizes the importance of knowledge by intuition. He takes for granted that knowledge proper should be knowledge by definition. Anything we know is not worthy of being called knowledge unless it can be stated in a proposition or definition.

In the *Meno* (80e), Meno points out the paradox of Socratic definition. We cannot seek to define something unless we already have some idea of it. If we already have such an idea, there is no need for seeking a definition. He recognizes a form of knowledge that precedes propositional knowledge but does not call it intuitive knowledge. Intuitive knowledge is indispensable to the Socratic definition from beginning to end. The Socratic definition usually begins with some examples and instances of what is to be defined. It is impossible to recognize and agree upon those examples and instances as being the right ones without having some intuitive knowledge of what is to be defined. It is equally impossible to recognize the deficiency of any proposed definition without checking its adequacy against our intuitive knowledge. Even when we reach the right definition, we can recognize its rightness only by comparing it with our intuitive knowledge.

Plato tries to account for intuitive knowledge through his doctrine of recollection (*Meno* 85d). By interrogating a slave boy, Socrates elicits some basic propositions about squares and their diagonals. Since the boy had never been taught geometry in this life, Socrates holds, he must have known it in his previous life. He is now only recollecting what he has known all along. But the doctrine of recollection entails the doctrine of reincarnation, which holds that the soul existed before the birth of its present body and will survive its death. Although the doctrine of reincarnation, if true, proves the immortality of the soul, it is not a good account of the slave boy's knowledge. It may be easier and simpler to explain his recognition of simple geometrical truths by the modern doctrine of innate ideas, that is, the slave boy has been born with elementary mathematical ideas. This is the reason for the modern tendency to discount the doctrine of recollection. For example, as Myles Burnyeat points out, it is played down by J. N. Findlay and ignored altogether by Terence Irwin.[8]

The theory of innate ideas, however, cannot deliver what Plato wants for his theory of Forms, their independent existence. Although the doctrine of innatism assures that innate ideas are independent of sense perceptions, it cannot guarantee that those ideas are objectively real. As Burnyeat states, innatism does not support "Plato's deeply realist conviction that knowledge is *of* something which exists independently of the knowing mind."[9] The doctrine of innatism would make the existence of Platonic Forms dependent on the empirical existence of human minds. The realism of Platonic Forms would be replaced by the subjective idealism of human minds.

The ills of both innatism and recollectionism can be avoided through the doctrine of intellectual intuition. Socrates could have accounted for the geometrical understanding of the slave boy by saying that he was helped to intuit elementary geometrical truths. When the slave boy recognizes those elementary truths, it is in fact impossible to tell whether he is recollecting what he has seen before or recognizing what he has never seen before. The slave boy himself is not aware of his previous understanding.

Socrates argues for the doctrine of recollection on the ground that the slave boy has never been given any geometry lessons. But the fact that he has never been trained in geometry is equally compatible with the doctrine of intellectual intuition. If true, this doctrine assures the realism of Platonic Forms, and the doctrine of Forms need not depend on the doctrine of reincarnation. On the other hand, the doctrine of recollection cannot dispense with the doctrine of intuition. Even if the soul recollects what it has seen in its previous life, it could not have seen the Forms without intellectual intuition. In Plato's theory of Forms, the doctrine of recollection can be no more than a bridge to the doctrine of intuition.

8. Burnyeat makes this observation in his review of Findlay's and Irwin's books on Plato, "The Virtues of Plato," *New York Review of Books* 26 (September 27, 1979): 56–60.
9. Burnyeat, "The Virtues of Plato," 59.

Although Plato never explicitly recognizes the importance of intuitive knowledge in his early dialogues, he states its importance emphatically in the later ones. In the *Theaetetus,* Socrates examines the view that knowledge is true belief plus a rational account (*logos*). He tests three ideas of logos, and one of them concerns the relation of simples and complexes. To give an account of a complex is to enumerate the simple elements that make up the complex; to know a complex is to know its parts. According to this view, simple elements can never be known because they are not composed of parts. In that case, the knowledge of a complex is paradoxical; it is obtained by enumerating its elements, which cannot be known. Even more paradoxically, the complex is knowable, but its elements are unknowable. As Socrates says, this is an absurd view (*Theaetetus* 206b). It can be avoided only by affirming that simple elements can be known without logos, without enumerating its parts.

With the admission of simple elements, Plato's doctrine of Forms gets complicated. There should be two kinds of Form: simple and complex. Aristotle notes that Plato postulated Forms as the objects of Socratic definitions (*Metaphysics* 987b1–8). This is clearly true of his early dialogues. The Form of a triangle is the essence to be captured by its definition as a figure bound by three straight lines. If a Form is understood as the object of a definition, it is bound to be complex. A definition dissects a *definiendum* into *definiens*. In his early dialogues, Plato shows no awareness of simple Forms, but in the middle dialogues he begins to talk about them. In the *Phaedo* (74abc, 78cd), he mentions the Forms of Unity and Equality and even informally talks about the incompositeness of Forms such as Equality and Beauty. In the *Republic,* he stresses the indefinability of the Form of Good. It is indefinable because it is simple.

In the early dialogues, Plato is preoccupied with the problem of Socratic definition; he regards it as the only way to get to know Forms. With the distinction of simple and complex Forms, however, he begins to take a different attitude toward complex Forms. He no longers regards complex Forms as primitive, as he did in the early dialogues; they can be constructed by the combination of simple Forms. This is the art of blending or weaving simple Forms to produce complex Forms. In the *Sophist* (253a), the Eleatic Stranger explains the nature of this art by the example of combining the letters of the alphabet to make words. This is the same example that Socrates used in explaining the relation of simples and complexes in the *Theaetetus* (203a–205e). Now the Eleatic Stranger calls the art of combination the science of dialectic (*Sophist* 253d).

Platonic Intuitionism

Some Plato scholars have thought that the very idea of simple elements in the *Theaetetus* is incompatible with Plato's theory of Forms. Gilbert Ryle makes

use of Wittgenstein's logical atomism to make this point.[10] Simple objects cannot be described; they can only be named. If Forms are simple, they cannot
be objects of logos. They cannot be explained or accounted for because they
cannot be objects of propositions. As objects of logos, Ryle claims, complex
Forms do not fare any better than simple Forms. Since a complex Form is a
conjunction of simple Forms, it is impossible to give an account of the former
as long as the latter remain unaccounted for. Because Forms, simple or complex, cannot be objects of logos they cannot be objects of knowledge in the
Platonic sense.

The central point of Ryle's claim is that the doctrine of simple elements is
incompatible with Plato's theory of Forms. This highlights how closely Plato's
theory of Forms has been associated with the idea of Socratic definition. Socrates regarded his definition as logos. Since a definition is a complex entity,
some Plato scholars have assumed that it is impossible to give logos for simple
elements. If Forms are simple, they cannot be known. This view has been
countered by a theory of intuitive knowledge; simple elements can be known
by direct acquaintance.[11] Knowledge by direct acquaintance is intuition. The
view that Platonic Forms can be known by intuition is Platonic intuitionism.

I have tried to show that Platonic intuitionism has been lurking all along be-
neath Socratic definitionism, although it comes to be officially recognized only
in the *Theaetetus* and the *Sophist*. Let me recapitulate its development in Plato's
thought. Plato began with the idea that Socratic definition is the only way to
know Forms. But Socratic definition can neither begin nor end without presupposing some intuitive knowledge of Forms. Intuitive knowledge is only a
background knowledge until Plato brings out into the open the distinction between simples and complexes. Simple Forms cannot be defined; they must be
intuited. Moreover, intuition need not be limited to simple Forms; even complex Forms must be intuited before they can be analyzed into simple Forms.
Intuition must be presupposed by the art of definition.

I propose that the distinction between definition and intuition marks the difference between the early and the later Plato. This is not to say that the early Plato
was not aware of the problem of intuition. In the *Meno,* as we have seen, the
paradox of Socratic inquiry clearly indicates the role of intuitive understanding
as background knowledge. But Plato never officially accepts it as a form of
knowledge. In the *Symposium* (211a), Diotima describes the direct vision of
Beauty absolute, simple, and everlasting. But Plato places this vision beyond
logos and knowledge; it is like a mystical experience. In the early dialogues,

10. Ryle's view is related and discussed in R. C. Cross, "Logos and Forms in Plato," in R. E.
    Allen, ed., *Studies in Plato's Metaphysics* (London, 1965), 13–32.
11. The intuitionists are David Ross, H. F. Cherniss, A. E. Taylor, F. M. Cornford, and
    R. S. Bluck.

intuition is never fully accepted as a form of knowledge because it is devoid of logos. In the later dialogues, Plato seems to feel he can no longer ignore the role of intuition as the initial and basic access to the world of Forms. So I propose that whereas Plato inherits the method of definition from Socrates, that of intuition is uniquely his own.

In the transition from Socratic definitionism to Platonic intuitionism, the *Republic* is a critical landmark. It is in effect caught between the two methods. Book 1 of the *Republic* reads like a typical Socratic dialogue; Socrates engages his interlocutors in the definition of justice and discredits the proposed definitions one after another. In book 2, the Socratic inquiry takes an unexpected turn: Socrates and his company begin to construct a state. Only after constructing an ideal state do they name the four virtues: wisdom, courage, temperance, and justice. What is the relation between the Form of Justice and the virtue of justice? Socrates says, "Further, we have heard many people say, and have often said ourselves, that justice is to perform one's own task and not to meddle with that of others" (*Republic* 433a, trans. G. M. A. Grube).

Gregory Vlastos takes this statement as the definition of justice and therefore as a representation of the Form of Justice.[12] In the *Republic,* Vlastos points out, justice arises in the context of cooperation and reciprocity. By division of labor and by exchange of goods and services, all the participants benefit reciprocally. This is the basic or original idea of justice (*Republic* 443c), and it dictates that everyone should do his or her own share and should not meddle with anyone else's. This notion governs the construction of the ideal state.

What is remarkable about this basic idea of justice is that it is not presented as a result of a laborious attempt at definition. One of the comical touches in the *Republic* is the way Socrates and his interlocutors locate the virtue of justice. After identifying the three virtues of wisdom, courage, temperance, Socrates assumes the air of a hunter about to set out in search of the final virtue, justice, and builds up the expectations of Glaucon and Adeimantus. He says, "So now we must concentrate our attention like hunters surrounding a coppice, lest justice escape us and vanish without our seeing it, for obviously it is somewhere around here. Look eagerly, now, in case you see it before I do, and tell me" (*Republic* 432bc, trans. Grube).

This is a familiar ploy in the Socratic game of searching for a definition. But for all the aroused expectations, the episode ends in an anticlimax. Socrates says, "My good friend, [justice] seems to me to have been rolling about right in front of our feet for some time, in fact from the beginning, and we did not see it. This was quite ridiculous of us. As people sometimes look for the very thing

12. Gregory Vlastos, *Platonic Studies* (Princeton, 1973), 117–23; "The Theory of Social Justice in the *Polis* in Plato's *Republic,*" in Helen F. North, ed., *Interpretations of Plato* (E. J. Brill, 1977), 6–11.

they are holding in their hands, so we paid no attention to it, but were looking away in the distance, which accounts for our not seeing it" (*Republic* 432de, trans. Grube). When Glaucon confesses not to know what he is talking about, Socrates says they have been using the idea of justice all along in constructing the ideal city. If they have had it all along without the benefit of special instruction, they must have got it by their commonsense intuition. Moreover, Socrates recognizes that this conception of justice lies within the common understanding of many people (*Republic* 433b). All these phenomena indicate that the idea of justice belongs to the intuitive understanding of normal people, though they may not be aware of having it.

If the Form of Justice is the original model, the virtue of justice in an ideal state is its articulation. The ideal state shows how the Form of Justice can be realized under a set of concrete circumstances. Insofar as the Form of Justice is concerned, it stands without reference to any particular circumstances. It is the Form prior to its articulation, and its articulation in the *Republic* is only an outline or sketch (*Republic* 504d). Since the outline or sketch is also called a model, we have to distinguish two types of model: the original and the articulated. The original model is the Form, and the articulated model is the ideal city that has been constructed by the articulation of the Form.

Socrates recognizes justice on three levels: the Form of Justice, justice in an ideal state constructed in discourse, and justice in a real state realized in the world (*Republic* 472e–473a). He warns that a complete picture of justice is quite different from the sketch and that it can be gained only by a longer and a harder way (*Republic* 435d, 504b–e). When Glaucon asks what is this longer and harder way, he replies that it is the greatest study, the study of the Form of the Good (*Republic* 505a).The study of the Good belongs to the science of dialectic. In the *Republic*, Plato introduces dialectic after mathematics. Mathematics is an incomplete science on two counts. First, it uses physical objects as images and, second, it stands on a set of hypotheses that it cannot account for (*Republic* 511a). Socrates says that the science of dialectic goes beyond the hypotheses of mathematical sciences and comes to know the first principles (*Republic* 533c).

How does the science of dialectic go beyond hypotheses? As Julia Annas remarks, there are two ways of understanding the dialectical method because the word *hypothesis* can be given two different meanings.[13] It may mean a hypothetical proposition (postulate) or a hypothetical concept. If the word *hypothesis* is taken to mean a hypothetical proposition, a hypothesis can be accounted for by deducing it from a higher proposition. This is the deductive method. But the deductive method can lead to an infinite regress. The higher

---

13. Julia Annas, *An Introduction to Plato's Republic* (Oxford, 1981), 287–89.

proposition may turn out to be another hypothesis that needs a still higher proposition for its justification. On the other hand, if the word *hypothesis* means a hypothetical concept, it can dictate a different method for dialectic. A hypothetical concept means a concept whose meaning is hypothetically assumed. Its meaning can be accounted for by clarifying its relation to other concepts. For example, the Form of Justice can be fully accounted for by clarifying its relation with such other Forms as Unity, Plurality, the Good, Whole and Parts. Annas likens this dialectical method to the method of conceptual analysis.[14] In the *Sophist* (253d), Plato clearly favors this view of dialectic.

These two methods are equally compatible with the claim that the science of dialectic is synoptic (*Republic* 537c). The deductive method can produce the highest proposition from which all hypothetical propositions can be derived, and the highest proposition can give a synoptic view of all lower propositions. The method of conceptual analysis can lay out the systematic interrelation of all basic Forms, and the understanding of such a systematic interrelation can give a synoptic view of all special sciences. Of these two methods, the deductive method appears to be much less plausble than the other. It is highly unlikely that one can find one proposition from which all other propositions can be derived. No wonder Plato settles for the other method in his later dialogues. In the *Republic*, however, Plato is still torn between the two conceptions of his highest science.

These two conceptions of dialectic are closely affiliated with Socratic definitionism and Platonic intuitionism. Socratic definitionism is the method of hypothesis; it proposes a hypothetical proposition that can explain the phenomena under investigation. It naturally leads to higher and higher hypotheses. It establishes a chain of hypotheses, and its method is deductive. On the other hand, Platonic intuitionism ultimately appeals to the intuition of simple elements, which cannot be accounted for by propositions. The logos of simple elements can be known by explicating their interrelation. When they are taken singly without their systematic relations, they are known only provisionally or hypothetically. This is our intuitive understanding of those elements, which becomes true scientific knowledge only when it is dialectically examined and clarified. The science of dialectic explicates our intuitive understanding of Platonic Forms.

The science of dialectic is ultimately concerned with the Form of the Good because it is the highest Form. In some passages, Socrates describes dialectic as the art of attaining the intuitive vision of the Good. But he also stresses that it is a journey from Form to Form to the highest (*Republic* 532de). These two descriptions indicate two features of Forms. Every one of them is an object of

---

14. Charles Kahn takes a similar view of the dialectical method in "The Meaning of 'Justice' and the Theory of Forms," *The Journal of Philosophy* 69 (1972): 567–79.

intuition insofar as it is simple; every one of them is an object of explication insofar as it is related to other Forms. All of them are related to the Form of the Good because all of them are the ideals of perfection and the standards of valuation. The Form of the Good is the fountain of all perfection and valuation. Like any other Forms, the Good can also be known in two ways: intuitively and dialectically.

Two Views of Platonic Forms

There have been two versions of Platonism, and these may be called the concrete and the abstract versions. The concrete version understands Platonic Forms as concretely real as anything can be. For example, the Form of Beauty is as concrete as any beautiful object on earth. Likewise, the Form of Justice is absolutely full and real. The abstract version takes the Forms as abstract entities. As an abstract entity, the Form of Beauty can never be beautiful in the same way as beautiful flowers are. The concrete version takes Platonic Heaven as a world of plenitude; this was the favored version among medieval Christians. This version of Platonic Heaven was in full accord with their religious faith that the kingdom of heaven was much fuller and richer than this paltry world. The abstract version of Platonism is well known among mathematicians; Platonic Forms are only abstract norms. Platonic Heaven is a world of skeletal objects.

The difference between these two versions can be explained in terms of mathematical Platonism. Plato says that there are mathematical Forms and that they are the objects of mathematical propositions. How much of mathematics is really contained in Platonic Heaven? The two versions of Platonism will give different answers to this question. According to the concrete version, Platonic Heaven contains the complete edifice of mathematics, from arithmetic and geometry to calculus and topology. According to the abstract version, it contains only the most abstract mathematical ideas—for example, the basic ideas of set theory—and that mathematical systems have to be constructed from those basic ideas. This version is the bedrock view of Platonism (Platonic Heaven provides only the bedrock for the construction of mathematics); the other is the skyscraper view.

These two versions of mathematical Platonism give different accounts of mathematical knowledge. According to the skyscraper version, mathematical understanding is just to comprehend mathematical Forms and their relations by scanning Platonic Heaven. Nothing more than this Platonic vision is required to achieve complete mathematical knowledge. According to the bedrock version, however, Platonic vision is not sufficient for complete mathematical knowledge because it can give only the basic mathematical Forms. The recognition of these Forms is mathematical intuition, which is only the beginning of mathematical understanding. Further and higher mathematical knowledge can be gained only by constructing mathematical propositions on the basis of mathematical intuitions. Construction and intuition are two essential features of mathematics for the bedrock version of Platonism, whereas construction is gratuitous for the skyscraper version.

These two versions of Platonism also obtain for ethical and political Forms. According to the skyscraper version, the Form of Justice provides a complete normative standard for all occasions and societies; it is permanently fixed for all eternity. Karl Popper echoes this rigid version of Platonism when he stresses that the Form of the ideal state is permanently fixed and all we have to do is to make an exact copy of this original.[15] Some Plato scholars have thought that this determinate version of Platonism captures Plato's claim that Forms are absolute and immutable standards of perfection. If they are absolutely concrete, they must be determinate. Plato's writings offer plenty of textual support for this view of Forms, but also plenty against it.

In the *Republic,* as we have seen, Socrates and his interlocutors do not really copy the Form of Justice, but rather construct an ideal state in accordance with their understanding of justice as the idea of all doing their respective parts in a scheme of cooperation and reciprocity. If this abstract idea of justice is the Form of Justice, it cannot function as a determinate standard of justice for all occasions and societies. It is too indeterminate. Platonic Forms are essentially indeterminate, according to the bedrock version of Platonism. The Form of Justice is only the normative foundation for constructing determinate social orders. On this foundation, Socrates and his interlocutors construct a series of states, beginning with a tiny city of a few farmers and artisans, expanding it to a city of pigs, and ending with the ideal city. Even after constructing an ideal state, Socrates says that an ideal state can take the form of a monarchy or an aristocracy. This shows that Platonic Forms are abstract and general ideals that can be realized in many different ways. For they are indeterminate.

We have also seen the indeterminacy of Platonic Forms in Socratic definitions. There is no determinate formula or proposition for capturing the essence of a virtue because it is an indeterminate standard. The indeterminacy of Platonic Forms comes up again in the comparison of government by a good ruler and government by good laws in the *Statesman* (294ab). A good and wise ruler can govern a state by directly consulting the Forms, and such a direct vision of Forms cannot be correctly codified into a system of laws. No legal rule can ever perfectly fit all relevant cases; at best, it can aim at the problems under average circumstances. The difference between these two systems of government is like the difference between the treatment of a patient under the direct care of a physician and his treatment under a system of prescriptions. The latter can

15. Karl Popper, *The Open Society and its Enemies* (London, 1945), 1:86.

never be as good as the former. Likewise, the rule of law is only second best. Platonic Forms are too indeterminate to be formalized in a set of rules.

If Platonic Forms are indeterminate, they cannot offer rigid standards of perfection for all eternity. In fact, if they were to offer rigid standards of perfection, they would be invalidated almost at every moment of application. For this reason, the skyscraper version of Platonism has often been subject to ridicule. The bedrock view of Platonic Forms is much more viable and sensible than the skyscraper view. The indeterminacy of Platonic Forms makes them flexible standards, and their flexibility assures their eternal durability.

If Platonic Forms are abstract and indeterminate, they cannot directly serve as normative standards. They have to be translated into concrete models for particular contexts. This process of translation is Platonic construction. Plato constructs an ideal state not only in the *Republic,* but also in the *Laws.* He refers to his construction as a process of building models or sketches (*Republic* 472c). This process has two points of reference. On one hand, it looks at the Forms; on the other hand, it looks at the world of nature (*Republic* 501b). If Platonic construction spans these two points of reference, it can produce different results under different circumstances. Although the Forms remain the same, the natural conditions may change. Even if the natural conditions remain unchanged, our understanding of the Forms may change. In fact, Plato himself produces two different constitutions in the *Republic* and the *Laws.* And we should consider the basic difference between these two models of construction as a way of understanding his constructivism.

John Rawls says that the conception of human beings as being free and equal is the basis of his constructivism. In Plato's constructivism, the conception of human beings is equally important. In the *Republic,* he assumes a drastic inequality of human beings; there is a glaring difference especially between the few who are fit to become Guardians and Auxiliaries and the many who are destined to be only Artisans. The former are wise and rational enough to be compared to the immortals; the latter are deficient enough in wisdom and intelligence to be ranked close to beasts. This is what Gregory Vlastos calls Plato's bifurcation of the human race, which goes together with his bifurcation of the world into the sensible and the intelligible realms.[16] The ignorant mass are trapped in the cave, while only a few philosophers can get out of the cave and see the sun in the world of divinity. The blessed few have divine vision; the mass in the cave are blind (*Republic* 484cd). Only a few can have true knowledge, and the many can at best have correct belief or opinion.

Since the multitude cannot manage their own affairs, it is in their best interest to be placed under the governance of the Guardians. The dictatorship of a philosopher-king logically follows from the bifurcation of the human race. This

16. Vlastos, "The Theory of Social Justice in the *Polis* in Plato's *Republic,*" 31.

is dictated by the idea of justice, which governs the differentiation of social functions in accordance with natural talents. The caste system proposed in the *Republic* follows from the differentiation of talents and their development, as Plato understands them. It is an idealized slavery, as Vlastos calls it. But the slavery is for the benefit of the slaves rather than their masters. As Vlastos observes, the masters do not get very much in return for their enormous burden of taking on boring administrative duties. On the contrary, they keep on making sacrifices for the state. Therefore, the union of masters and slaves is supposed to be a bond of love (*Republic* 590d).

Plato's view of human inequality, however, is incompatible with some of his other beliefs. If Platonic intuitionism is correct, all human beings have direct access to Platonic Forms. Even the exalted dialectic of the wise only explicates the same intuitive understanding that they share with the common people. Such a shared understanding is impossible in the bifurcated world of the *Republic*. In the *Sophist,* Plato conflates the world of body and the world of mind by reconciling materialists and idealists. In such a unified world, Platonic intuitionism constitutes a strong basis for human equality.

Plato's demarcation between knowledge and belief takes on different meanings for the bifurcated and the unified worlds. After eliciting geometrical knowledge from the slave boy, Socrates calls the boy's intuitive ideas true beliefs (*Meno* 86a). He says that those ideas will stay with the boy's soul forever. Toward the end of the dialogue, he gives a different picture of true beliefs. Although they are as good as knowledge, they can fly away at any time unless they are fastened by a chain (*Meno* 97e–98a). In a unified world, the intuitive understanding of Platonic Forms can serve as a source of belief or opinion. It is the sort of belief the slave boy has about geometry; it can never be lost because it is innate to us. In the bifurcated world, belief cannot be the intuitive understanding of Platonic Forms. Those trapped in the cave have no access to the sun and the stars. They can acquire belief only by indoctrination; belief is not an innate possession, but an acquisition, and hence can easily be lost.

In the *Republic,* Plato believes that people in the artisan class are not truly capable of virtue. In his discussion of the four virtues, Socrates first assigns wisdom to the ruling class and courage to the auxiliary class. One would expect him to assign the third virtue to the artisan class—but he does not. Instead he distributes the virtue of temperance to all three classes. Though artisans participate in productive activities, they are not worthy of having their own virtue. This is the apex of their degradation in Plato's ideal city. Evidently Plato regards them as not fully rational enough to have their own virtue. But this view is incompatible with their role as artisans. Art is an activity of rationality and intelligence. If they are capable of art, they can surely participate in the life of intelligence and virtue.

In the *Statesman,* Plato is no longer sure of finding godlike rulers. This point is conveyed in the myth of two ages (*Statesman* 269c–274e). The history of the universe repeats the cycle of two ages, the age of Kronos and the age of Zeus. During the age of Kronos, the universe rotates in one direction with divine assistance. At the end of this age, the god relinquishes his control, and the universe reverses the direction of its motion and begins to move with its own force. This new cycle is the age of Zeus. In the age of Kronos, Kronos personally governs mankind and all other animals by appointing divine demons as their shepherds. It is the age of peace and prosperity. There is no personal possession of wives and children and no need for political constitutions because political decisions are made by the divine ruler. His rule is direct and personal, like that of a philosopher-king.

During the age of Zeus, Zeus terminates divine government and leaves the universe to run by its own force. After the initial shock, the universe gains some control and tries to run itself in accordance with the instructions it had received from the god. But its adherence to the instructions deteriorates as time goes on, and an age of strife and chaos sets in. Human beings especially were in the direst straits at the beginning of the age of Zeus, being weak and defenseless and ravaged by wild beasts. They were eventually helped by divine gifts. Prometheus brought fire, and Hephaestus introduced crafts. With the aid of these crafts, mankind has been managing its affairs.

The Eleatic Stranger says that he is telling this story as an aid to clarify the nature of the royal art (*Statesman* 269c). What then is the relevance of this myth to the kingly art of government? After finishing the myth, the Eleatic Stranger tells the young Socrates that they have been making a mistake on a grand scale in their definition of a true statesman (*Statesman* 274e). Whereas they were supposed to define the king and statesman for the present cycle of history, they were giving a definition suitable for the other cycle. The king who can govern without a constitution belongs to the age of Kronos. There is no point in having a constitution if there is a wise ruler who can personally administer the state. In the age of Zeus, when the wise ruler departs from the scene, the world has to run in accordance with the instructions it has received from him. The constitutions are the instructions, and they are only substitutes for his practical wisdom. But these substitutes become a necessity in the age of Zeus because there are no longer any divine rulers.

The philosopher-king clearly belongs to the age of Kronos; such a true statesman is "a god, not a mortal" (*Statesman* 275a). Nor can the glaring difference between the ruler and the ruled obtain in the age of Zeus. The Eleatic Stranger concludes, "The divine shepherd is so exalted that no earthly king can ever attain to his eminence. Those who rule these states of ours in this present era are much more like their subjects in nature, and far closer to them in training and in nurture than ever a shepherd could be so to his flock" (*Statesman* 275bc, trans. J. B. Kemp).

Plato is now repudiating the glaring difference in wisdom between the ruler and the ruled and asserting their basic similarity and equality. The Eleatic Stranger reinforces this point by making a further observation. Although the royal art belongs to the art of herding animals, it is radically different from the art of herding animals other than human beings. In the art of herding human animals, the herder and the herded belong to the same species; in the art of herding other animals, they belong to different species.

Since the Eleatic Stranger accepts the basic equality of the ruler and the ruled, he stresses the importance of consent of the ruled for a legitimate government. The presence and absence of consent mark the difference between the royal art and the art of tyranny. The Eleatic Stranger says, "Tendance of human herds by enforced control is the tyrant's art; tendance freely accepted by herds of free bipeds we call statesmanship" (*Statesman* 276c; trans. Skemp). This definition of tyranny is quite different from the one given in the *Republic,* in which tyranny is defined mainly in terms of interest. Tyranny is understood as government in the interest of the ruler rather than of the ruled, and the question of consent is not important in this earlier conception of tyranny. The consent of the governed becomes important only when they have their own wisdom, whereas interests are always important whether they are wise or ignorant.

Contextual Relativity

The myth of two ages illustrates Platonic relativism. The same Form of Justice cannot be realized in the same way for the two cycles of history because the two cycles present different conditions. A form of government suitable for the age of Kronos is not suitable for the age of Zeus. The realization of Forms should be situation-relative. In the *Cratylus* (389cde), Socrates makes the same point by using the analogy of shuttle-making. When a carpenter makes shuttles, Socrates says, he has to look at the Form of Shuttle, the material for making a shuttle, and the future use of the shuttle. The first of them is invariant, but the second and third are variable. The realization of a Form must be sensitive and relative to the second and the third conditions. Relativity in the realization of Forms derives from their indeterminacy. Indeterminacy and relativity are inseparable in the domain of realization.

In the *Laws* (713), Plato is prepared to accept the reality of our world as it is. He reaffirms the impossibility of true statesmanship and the necessity for rule of law in the age of Zeus. He rejects the bifurcation of humanity and no longer believes in the capacity of a mortal to wield autocratic power without corruption (*Laws* 713c). Further, he no longer believes in the bond of love between slaves and masters; he declares that they can never be friends (*Laws* 767a). He again says that true statesmanship belonged to the god and his demons in the age of Kronos. Since such an ideal is impossible for us, he has to meet the necessity of devising a rule of law. So he has the Athenian propose a constitution suitable for the present cycle of history.

The constitutional state restores the democratic rights of citizens suspended in the *Republic*. Even when the wise rule the ignorant, the Athenian says that the consent of the ruled is important for good government. He also stresses the importance of persuading the common people to accept the law. The legislator should attach a proper preface or preamble to every piece of legislation so that the common people can understand the reasons for the law (*Laws* 722e–723a). Citizens should not only obey laws but understand them, and their obedience should be based on their understanding. This is the basic cognitive requirement for the governed in the proposed constitutional state. In the *Republic*, Socrates sets a high cognitive standard for the rulers, but none whatsoever for the governed. He expects only blind trust and obedience from them. In the *Laws*, the Athenian recognizes the basic difference between dealing with free people and handling slaves. You can expect blind obedience from slaves but only "reasoned" compliance from free human beings. He explains this point by an analogy.

According to the Athenian, there are two types of physicians. In their training and treatment of patients, one group of physicians follows the "empirical" method and the other group follows the "scientific" method. The empirical physician learns the trade by simply observing his master and obeying his directions in empirical fashion. He never gives his patient a rational account of his disease and only gives him some empirical injunction in an autocratic manner. His dictatorial method is suitable only for treating slaves. The scientific physician learns his art in a scientific manner and tries to gain a scientific understanding of the patient's illness. For this purpose, he freely communicates with the patient and his family, thereby learning something from them and instructing them about the nature of his illness. Above all, he does not impose his prescription on his patient in an autocratic manner but persuades him to accept it freely. His rational method is suitable for treating free persons (*Laws* 720a-d).

There are two types of lawmakers, the Athenian says, just as there are two types of physicians. The lawmakers for a city of free people should behave like scientific physicians. They should treat citizens as free persons rather than as slaves. Slaves can be given unexplained commands, but free human beings are entitled to explained commands. Slaves are objects of compulsion, whereas free human beings are objects of persuasion. In the *Laws*, all citizens receive the sort of rational, respectful treatment that only Auxiliaries are entitled to in the *Republic*. Although Plato has not become a liberal egalitarian in the *Statesman* and the *Laws*, he has advanced a strong egalitarian view of humanity and politics.

Plato's understanding of practical rationality is another important element in his constructivism and relativism. In his early dialogues, he appears to recognize no important distinction between theoretical and practical reason. In the *Meno* (87e–89a), Socrates stresses the importance of practical wisdom for the right use of good things such as health and wealth, courage and temperance. In the absence of good sense, he says, these so-called good things can lead to harm and misery. He appears to assume that the good sense required for practical wisdom is propositional knowledge. In the Socratic dialogues, he stresses the importance of finding right definitions; in the *Republic,* he never questions the necessity of theoretical knowledge in the making of a philosopher-king.

To be sure, Plato never says that theoretical wisdom alone is sufficient for running a state. After many years of dialectical training, a prospective ruler is required to go through an even longer period of practical training. But Plato seems to assume that practical training is nothing more than the application of theoretical knowledge to concrete situations. If one has a correct theory or definition of a virtue, he believes, one can gain the right application of it. Conversely, one can never have a truly correct practice of virtue without a correct theoretical understanding of it. Practical wisdom is handmaid to theoretical wisdom. This thesis of theoretical primacy over practice is maintained in Plato's early dialogues and in the *Republic*.

The thesis of theoretical primacy seems to run counter to some important features of human life. There are people who are proficient in theoretical understanding but deficient in practical affairs. Conversely, there are people whose practical undertakings are excellent, though they are not well equipped with theoretical understanding. If practical wisdom always has to be derived from propositional or theoretical knowledge, practice as a whole will be in a sorry state. One can never be truly virtuous until one can give a Socratic definition of virtue. Even Plato's idea of a true statesman appears to go against the primacy of propositional knowledge. A truly wise statesman knows what to do on each particular occasion but cannot state his wisdom in a series of propositions. This is why Plato regards constitutions as mere imitations or approximations of true statesmanship. The wisdom of a statesman appears to vindicate the independence of practical wisdom from theoretical knowledge.

In the *Statesman,* Plato acknowledges the independence of practical wisdom. The Eleatic Stranger begins his definition of political science by establishing the distinction between pure and applied sciences, a difference that corresponds to the distinction between theoretical and practical sciences (*Statesman* 258e). The statesman is not required to go through rigorous training in dialectic. We no longer have to wonder what the statesman is going to do with his immense knowledge of mathematical and philosophical sciences. The royal art is called the art of weaving (*Statesman* 305e), the same metaphorical label used to describe the science of dialectic in the *Sophist*. But the political art of weaving does not consist in the application of what is achieved by the dialectical art of weaving. The dialectical art weaves ideas or Forms in order to reach definitions and classifications; the political art weaves the subordinate arts for the constitution and maintenance of a state. These two arts of weaving are the arts of Platonic construction. One is the art of theoretical construction; the other is the art of practical construction. One belongs to theoretical science and the other to practical science. They are both synoptic or royal arts, and they preside over all other arts, but their synoptic roles are different and independent of one another.

The independence of practical wisdom from theoretical knowledge accentuates situation-relativity. As long as practical wisdom is no more than a copy of theoretical knowledge, it does not have the freedom to respond to each particular situation. The independence of practical wisdom also undermines Plato's strong conception of human inequality. Whereas theoretical wisdom is a privilege of the few, practical wisdom is widely shared. In the *Statesman* (267e–268c), the Eleatic Stranger observes that a unique feature of the kingly art consists in being challenged by many other arts. The kingly art can have so many challengers and competitors because practical wisdom cannot be the privilege of a few.

Plato's new conception of practical wisdom leads him in the *Laws* (756b) to propose a council of elders as the preferred governing body. The legislator has to be assisted by this council, whose membership is large (360). Moreover, the elders should be elected by the people. This highly democratic system of government clearly reflects Plato's egalitarian view of practical wisdom; it is incompatible with the idea of a philosopher-king in the *Republic*. The relation between the legislator and the council of elders roughly corresponds to the relation of Forms and the circumstances of their realization. What the elders can offer to help the legislator is their experience and their understanding of circumstances. Though they may not be able to help the legislator better understand Forms, they can surely facilitate his understanding of the reality of their world.

Another important change in Plato's philosophy concerns his conception of values. In his early dialogues, he was obsessed with the unity of all virtues, which amounts to the unity of all values. In the *Republic*, Plato tries to fulfill the unity of all values in his ideal state. He stresses the unity of all classes; happiness should belong not to individuals or classes, but to the state as a whole. The ideal of unity also dictates the community of wives and children for the ruling class. They should not be allowed to know their biological parents or children so that they can treat each other as members of one family (*Republic* 463bc). There should be no distinction between mine and thine (*Republic* 462c). The observation of such conditions is intended to make the state truly "one" so that all its members live and feel like a single individual or family.

In the unity of the state, the analogy of the state to the soul goes too far. John Rawls has said that the principle of utility overlooks the distinction of persons in the summation of happiness and misery. Surely the Platonic unity of state obliterates the distinction of individuals in the experience of happiness and misery. If there are no individuals, there is no social basis for justice. As Socrates says in the *Republic,* the question of justice arises in the context of social cooperation for mutual benefit. The idea of cooperation and mutual benefit makes no sense in a world in which the distinction of persons is obliterated. The Platonic unity of state does not solve the problem of justice but dissolves it by fusing individuals into an organic social unit.

The Platonic unity of values is finally exemplified in the Form of the Good. This Form unifies all values into one, whether they belong to individuals or community. To be sure, Plato is keenly aware of the ever-present conflict of values but attributes all such conflicts to the failure of this world in living up to the ideals. But the Form of the Good seems to disappear in the later dialogues except in the *Philebus.* In the *Statesman,* Plato is more concerned with the plurality of values than with their unity. Toward the end of the dialogue (306b), the Eleatic Stranger proposes to make a startling statement about the virtues of courage and temperance: they are in a certain sense enemies, opposed to each other in many areas of life. Whereas the virtue of courage demands intensity and aggressiveness, the virtue of temperance demands control and gentleness. The Eleatic Stranger adds that his observation goes counter to the conventional view that all virtues are in harmony.

The conventional view is exactly the Socratic doctrine that all virtues are one. It is the same doctrine that had preoccupied Plato in his early and middle dialogues.[17] The Eleatic Stranger is saying that the conflict of values and virtues is inevitable. He is advocating the plurality of values in place of their unity and gives a new meaning to the idea of statesmanship as an art of weaving: it weaves conflicting values into one web of state. The art of statesmanship in the *Republic* could have been described as the art of fusing different elements into an organic unity. Unlike a product of fusion, a woven fabric allows its constituents to retain their individuality and plurality.

In the *Sophist* (244b–245e), Plato rejects the excessive demand of Parmenides for the unity of Being and is willing to accept its plurality. So he encourages the reconciliation of materialism and idealism. The plurality of Being goes hand in hand with the plurality of values. The Parmenidean unity of Being is the logical consequence of stressing the abstract at the expense of the concrete. The more faithful and sensitive we become to the concrete, the more we gain awareness of plurality and relativity. Different situations demand different treatments; plurality and relativity are inseparable twins in the world of concrete reality.

In the *Laws,* Plato no longer insists on the organic unity of the state. And

17. For a good discussion of this point, see Paul Woodruff, "Socrates on the Parts of Virtue," *Canadian Journal of Philosophy,* Supplementary Volume (1976): 101–16.

he does not demand the community of wives and children. Although the land remains the common property of the whole city, it is divided into allotments for individual use. He extends the idea of weaving opposites to the form of government. The Athenian states that a good government is a mixed one (*Laws* 693de). Monarchy is the government of wisdom; democracy is the government of freedom. By mixing these two forms, it is possible to have both wisdom and freedom and friendship between the ruler and the ruled. This is a surprising development in Plato's thought in light of his ridicule of democratic freedom in the *Republic* (562b–564b). The mixture of wisdom and freedom, monarchy and democracy, is supposed to be achieved in the council of elders (*Laws* 756e).

Three vital points have critically transformed Plato's philosophy. He has rejected the notion of glaring human inequality in favor of basic equality, the dependence of practical wisdom on theoretical knowledge in favor of its independence, and the unity of all values in favor of their irreducible plurality. All three of these revisions involve what Alfred North Whitehead has called the fallacy of misplaced concreteness.[18] The skyscraper view of Platonic Forms misplaces the concreteness from the immanent to the transcendent world. The early Plato commits this mistake, and the later Plato tries to correct it by adopting the bedrock view.

Plato's move from the skyscraper to the bedrock view of Forms is reflected in his theory of knowledge. In the *Republic,* Socrates repeatedly stresses the determinacy of Forms and the indeterminacy of visible (empirical) objects (*Republic* 479a-e, 509d-511c, 517b-c). Because the Forms are determinate, they are truly intelligible. Because empirical objects are indeterminate, they are not truly intelligible. To put it another way, the Forms are much more intelligible than empirical objects. This account of human knowledge belongs to the skyscraper version of Platonism. In the *Statesman,* Plate gives quite a different account. The Eleatic Stranger notes the difference in giving rational accounts of empirical and nonempirical objects. There is no trouble in giving a rational account of empirical objects; one has only to point to them. But a rational account of nonempirical objects cannot be so readily given; it requires a special art of dialectical weaving (*Statesman* 285e-286a). According to this view, the Forms appear to be much more indeterminate and much more difficult to comprehend than empirical objects. It belongs to the bedrock version of Platonism.

Kant accepts the bedrock view of Platonic Forms in his *Inaugural Dissertation* (2.7). Because Platonic Forms are so indeterminate, he writes, our metaphysical knowledge can never be as clear and as distinct as our geometrical knowledge. Our knowledge of geometry is clear and distinct because it is supported by sensibility. On the other hand, he says, metaphysical propositions are always vague and confused because they concern abstract entities that transcend the

18. Alfred North Whitehead, *Science and Modern World* (New York, 1960), 75.

concrete domain of sensibility. Kant is reversing Plato's characterization of the two domains of cognition. Plato had indeed claimed that we can have absolute knowledge of the intelligible world and only a reliable opinion about the visible world. This claim surely presupposes the skyscraper view of Platonic Forms.

When the critics of Platonism say that the theory of Forms is utterly incredible and fantastic,[19] they usually have in mind the skyscraper version. But they seldom realize that the skyscraper version is only one of two versions Plato has given us. Neither do they realize how difficult it is to do away with the bedrock version. As Socrates says in the *Phaedo*, we cannot have even our elementary notions of unity and equality without Forms. Elementary logic and mathematics would be impossible without Platonic Forms. Many eminent logicians and mathematicians of our age—Bertrand Russell and Alfred North Whitehead, for example—concur with Socrates on this point. The construction of a logical or mathematical system presupposes Platonic Forms.

Platonic Transcendence

Plato's construction of an ideal state goes through a series of modifications after his initial attempt in the *Republic*, largely because he keeps revising his views about human nature and the nature of value. His enterprise of continuous revision, however, is guided by his adherence to the ideal of justice. In the *Republic*, the *Statesman*, and the *Laws*, he operates with the same Form of Justice. In the later dialogues, he may not use the expression "the Form of Justice," but he refers nevertheless to transcendental normative standards as "justice and injustice" (*Laws* 714b), "a measure or standard of comparison" (*Statesman* 283e-284d), and "not a copy, but the absolutely real" (*Statesman* 300e). And yet Plato has been condemned by Karl Popper as being the father of totalitarianism. I would like to take a close look at this condemnation.

Popper's central charges against Plato are, first, that he exalts the dictatorship of a philosopher-king, second, that he rejects the equality of human beings, and, third, that he sacrifices the happiness of individuals for the totalitarian unity of the state (*OS&E* 86–117).[20] All of these charges against the *Republic* are justifiable, notwithstanding Gregory Vlastos's valiant attempt to defend the immortal classic.[21] But we have seen that Plato came to see the falsity of his basic assumptions about the inequality of human beings and the unity of values, both of which were essential to his constructivism in the *Republic*. Popper's critique freezes Plato's thought in the *Republic*, and that is surely an unfair way of responding to a great philosopher.

19. For example, Leo Strauss, *An Introduction to Political Philosophy* (Detroit, 1989), 196.
20. *OS&E* refers to Karl Popper, *The Open Society and its Enemies* (London, 1945).
21. Gregory Vlastos, "The Theory of Social Justice in the *Polis* in Plato's *Republic*."

Popper's substantive criticism of Plato is easily disposed of, but his criticism is not limited to Plato's substantive ideas. Popper maintains that Plato's method is fundamentally misguided because it overlooks the basic difference between natural and normative laws (*OS&E* 57–73). Whereas natural laws cannot be altered because they are based on nature, normative laws can be altered because they are independent of nature. The distinction between natural and normative laws is the distinction between nature (physis) and convention (nomos). Convention does not depend on nature. Going against this conventionalist view of normative laws, Popper maintains, Plato tried to understand normative laws as the expression of spiritual nature. This is Plato's methodological mistake.

The right way of understanding the relation of nature and convention, according to Popper, is through critical dualism or critical conventionalism (*OS&E* 60). Unlike natural laws, normative laws are neither true nor false because they have nothing to do with nature. They can be good or bad; they introduce standards. Because they cannot be found in nature, they can be called artificial. They are products of our decisions. The distinction between nature and convention is the distinction between facts and decisions. Decisions can also be called attitudes. Popper's critical conventionalism turns out to be a restatement of emotivism and noncognitivism. Instead of the familiar distinction between fact and value, he uses the distinction between facts and decisions.

On Popper's theory, critical conventionalism is the final product of human evolution, and it ushers in the open society. This evolution originates in naive naturalism or naive conventionalism, which belongs to tribal consciousness in a closed society and which does not know the distinction between nature and convention. But such naive consciousness breaks down when people begin to notice that different societies have different conventions and that conventions can be altered. Thus begins critical consciousness and its awareness of the distinction between nature and convention. It has to travel through three stages before reaching the final stage of critical conventionalism. The first is called biological naturalism, which explains normative laws as the expression of human biological nature. The second is ethical positivism, which accepts might as the source of right. The third is spiritual naturalism, which explains normative laws as the expression of human spiritual nature. The last, Popper says, is Plato's position (*OS&E* 73).

How does Plato explain normative standards as the expression of human spiritual nature? According to Popper, Plato holds that spiritual human nature far exceeds biological human nature. The soul is prior to the body. Human beings cannot be made happy by the satisfaction only of biological needs, and they cannot fulfill their spiritual needs without forming a society. This supposedly leads to Plato's conventionalist view of society; a state is an artificial arrangement arrived at for mutual benefit (*OS&E* 77). Popper says that Plato tries to justify the state in terms of human spiritual nature. But nothing can be deduced from human spiritual nature except the bald assertion that normative laws are born of reason and true thought. Popper concludes, "From all this it can be seen that arguments derived from Plato's spiritual naturalism are quite incapable of helping to answer any question which may arise concerning the 'just' or 'natural' character of any particular law. Spiritual naturalism is much too vague to be applied to any practical problem" (*OS&E* 78).

Since spiritual naturalism is a vacuous criterion, Popper says, Plato indiscriminately uses it to support whatever view he wants to advocate. He endorses conservatism on the ground that laws should not be changed once they are well formulated. When he advocates the unity of his ideal state, he is only expressing his nostalgia for a closed tribal society. He is a reactionary who cannot withstand the pressure of an open society. He is incredibly more backward than Protagoras, who was the first critical conventionalist to teach that institutions and conventions had raised mankind above the level of brutes (*OS&E* 66, 77). Plato's appeal to human spiritual nature is motivated by two concerns: the positivistic tendency to reduce norms to facts (Plato reduces norms to the fact of human spiritual nature) and the fear of making ethical decisions on our own instead of shifting the responsibility to something other than ourselves, such as God, nature, or society (*OS&E* 73). In short, Plato is an escapist and a victim of nostalgia, pining over the lost paradise of a closed tribal society.

What is strange and remarkable about Popper's account of Plato's escapism is that he never takes Plato's theory of Forms seriously. He mentions it only once: "It [the soul] is the divine principle by which he participates in the Form or Idea, in the divine primogenitor of his race" (*OS&E* 75). But he never associates Platonic Forms with Plato's theory of normative standards. Such an omission is largely owing to the fact that he never takes Plato's idea of transcendent norms seriously. For the same reason, he never notices the connection between Plato's claim for the primacy of the soul over the body and his theory of Forms. Plato was convinced that transcendent norms cannot be located in the physical world. If the physical world is the only reality (the only domain of facts), as Popper claims, our normative ideas and judgments can never be anything more than by-products of nature. There is no ontological ground for demarcating decisions from facts, as he does, because our decisions belong to the physical world as much as any other events and occurrences.

All honor and glory to Protagoras as the first critical conventionalist. But greater honor and glory to Plato for recognizing the most critical questions facing any critical conventionalist. If normative laws are artificial, how can they be used as normative standards? If they are artificial, are they not arbitrary? Popper wants to deny the arbitrariness of artificial conventions. Though mathematics, music, and literature are artificial products, he holds, they are not arbitrary (*OS&E* 65). Surely he does not want to maintain that all artificial products are equally valuable and acceptable. How then can we tell the difference between good and bad music, good and bad artificial products? As far as the products of nature are concerned, nature itself usually provides the standards for evaluating them. In the world of human conventions and artifacts, we can appeal to the positive norms of our society. But what can we appeal to in criticizing those positive norms, if not to transcendent norms? This is the role of Forms in Platonic criticism, and their role here is as important as their role in Platonic constructivism.

What norms does Popper appeal to in his criticism of Plato? What is his standard of judgment in condemning Plato for his inegalitarianism and authoritarianism? He may say that he relies on his personal decision. If it is only his personal decision or attitude, it may carry no significance whatsoever for anyone else and in fact may not have much significance even for him. The glory of personal values and decisions has been celebrated by existentialists. They have told us that we have the right to assign to everything whatever value we want and that we should never be troubled by other people's values. But Kierkegaard, the father of existentialism, long ago saw how hollow was the victory of this subjectivism. He called it the despair of defiance, the highest form of despair. In a defiant assertion of subjectivity, he says, "the self is its own master, absolutely its own master, so-called; precisely this is the despair, but also what it regards as its pleasure and delight. On closer examination, however, it is easy to see that this absolute ruler is a king without a country, actually ruling over nothing." [22]

Such a defiantly autonomous self is always "building only castles in the air, is only shadowboxing." Kierkegaard says that its despair lies in its inability to find earnestness: "It recognize no power over itself; therefore it basically lacks earnestness and can conjure forth only an appearance of earnestness, even when it gives its utmost attention to its imaginary constructions. This is a simulated earnestness. Like Prometheus stealing fire from the gods, this is stealing from God the thought—which is earnestness." [23]

Even in this age of individual freedom and autonomy, Stephen Darwall writes, our self-respect or the sense of our own worth can never be solidified by personal values alone. He says that one solution for this problem is to find intersubjective values.[24] We can exchange mutual assurances for our shared values. This exchange can take place in many different forms, ranging from a small support group to a grand religious establishment. Our mutual assurance need not be voluntary; it can be imposed on us by a totalitarian regime. In fact, the main cause of modern totalitarianism has been not the idea of transcendental

22. Kierkegaard, *The Sickness unto Death* (Princeton, 1980), 69. Translated by Howard Hong and Edna Hong.
23. Ibid., 68–69.
24. Stephen Darwall, *Impartial Reason* (Ithaca, 1983), 146–67.

norms, but its rejection. Since the French Thermidor, totalitarianism has been the most effective way of filling the normative vacuum that results from the denial of objective values. It is the collective counterpart of the absolute form of individual autonomy.

What reasons and arguments can Karl Popper use in defending liberty and equality against irresponsible existentialists and ruthless totalitarians? All he can say is that he has made the decision to value liberty and equality. But they can counter his decision with theirs, their decision not to be deterred by his decision. In the world of normative discourse, whether ethics or mathematics, decisions made without the support of normative standards will bring nothing but normative chaos. This has been the common problem with emotivism, prescriptivism, and existentialism. They have been proposed as extraordinary ways of getting somewhere without the aid of transcendent norms. Without the authority of those norms, one emotive assertion can be countered by another; one proposed prescription can be matched by another. One existential decision cannot be any more or less legitimate than another. Eventually we come to feel that there is no objective ground for any normative distinctions.

Beyond existentialism and totalitarianism, there is another way of having intersubjective assurance for our values: by appealing to prevailing positive norms. Such an appeal is perhaps the most reliable method not only in daily life, but even in theoretical inquiry. In his theory of justice, as we have seen, John Rawls appeals to the social ideals embedded in our culture. Such a positivistic appeal is perfectly fine, but only insofar as we have sound positive norms. Yet how can we tell whether our positive norms are sound or unsound? Normative positivism cannot answer this question.

Let us return to the original question: On what normative standards does Karl Popper stand in his critique of Plato? He cannot say he is expressing only his personal decision or attitude. He has no ground to claim that his personal decision or attitude is any better than Plato's. Neither can he say that he stands on the prevailing norms of our society. He has no right to hold that those positive norms are any better than the norms of Plato's Athens. In Kierkegaard's words, Popper can give his critique of Plato earnestness only by assuming the transcendent validity of his own criteria. This is to accept Platonism in his critique of Plato.

The transcendental function of Platonic Forms is the heart of Platonism, and this point is completely missed by Popper's critique of Platonism. By the power of Platonic Forms, we can take a critical stance toward the prevailing norms. By virtue of their transcendent standards, we can feel even the injustice inflicted on strangers on the other side of the globe. By virtue of those standards, we can feel indignation at the oppression of the weak, not only in our age but even in antiquity. Platonic Forms enable us to have a sense of justice that cuts across national boundaries and cultural barriers. They give us a transcendental intersubjectivity of values that is neither propped up by our voluntary mutual assurance nor imposed on us by external coercion. There is no way of accounting for this dimension of our intersubjective experience without accepting Platonic Forms.

Without Platonic Forms, we would be prisoners of our positive norms and share with the denizens of the Platonic Cave a fate of benighted existence. The syndrome of the Platonic Cave need not be limited to the tribal consciousness of a primitive society; it is equally present in the positivistic consciousness of our scientific world. For the positivistic consciousness is governed as much as the tribal consciousness by its own provincial norms and standards. Positivism has its own cave, the cave of an exclusively materialistic universe, and this cave is so deep and dark that it allows no view of any other dimensions of reality.

The transcendent function of Platonic Forms can lift us above our provincial norms and standards. This is the power of Platonic *anagogia*, or ascent, which can liberate mankind from tribal consciousness and open up the possibility of critical consciousness. Surely it is unfair for Karl Popper to label Plato as a reactionary who is scared of the challenge of an open society and who is bent on restoring the closed society of tribal consciousness. Plato does not shy away from the challenge of an open society; on the contrary, he rejoices over freedom of thought and flight of imagination. But he is indeed worried about the normative chaos that is sure to eventuate if the institutional authority of tribal consciousness cannot be replaced by the normative authority of critical reason. Far from being a reactionary caught between the closed and the open society, he is a revolutionary in the battle for a new order of reason.

Our ideal is not an open society, pure and simple; an open society can be an open anarchy. Our society should be not only open but just; even its openness should be subject to the constraint of justice. Hence the Form of Justice should be the ultimate standard and principle for the constitution of our society, as Plato has instructed us. Popper was so obsessed with the fear of totalitarianism that he never recognized that an open society too has its dangers. It never occurred to him that an open society could, without the constraint of justice, be a normative anarchy. And he did not perceive the fatal link between normative anarchy and modern totalitarianism. His timidity and shrillness are thus misplaced and misdirected. Instead of denouncing Platonism as the foe of an open society, he should have welcomed it as the only hope and resource for overcoming our normative crisis.

Throughout his life, Plato took upon himself the mission of reorienting the life of reason from theoretical speculation to practical problems. In the pre-Socratic world, the function of reason had been restricted to achieving theoretical understanding of the physical universe. Then Protagoras and Socrates appeared as the new prophets of reason and proposed using reason to understand the nature of human existence, to examine our value schemes, and to reform our social institutions. This was a daunting idea for their age, and Plato dedicated his entire life to its fulfillment. Hence his special feeling of indebtedness to Protagoras and Socrates.

But what is the life of reason? This is Plato's central question. From Socrates, Plato learned that the life of reason can be understood in two contexts, materialism and spiritualism. If materialism is true, human reason is only an appendage to the physical world and can never have norms and standards other than those produced by the working of the physical universe. Materialism dictates the life of reason in accordance with positive norms, which emerge as products of nature. But Plato believed that materialism is proven false by our capacity for critical reflection, which attests to our power of transcendence. Such power of transcendence is the foundation of the open society. Yet the open society leads only to normative anarchy, and the transcendence of reason, unless guided by the light of transcendent Forms, is but an uncharted flight into the darkness of nihilism. This is the essence of Plato's teaching, and it is his everlasting legacy to the life of reason.

CHAPTER NINE

Normative *Anagogia*

I have extensively examined here the roles of intuition and construction in normative theory. I have demonstrated that there are no independent or self-contained procedures of construction and that our normative intuitions constitute the indispensable foundation of all forms of constructivism. These intuitions concern the deepest problems in moral theory. What is the ultimate ground of moral and social norms? Are they rooted in human nature or are they products of convention?

These metaphysical questions do not arise in the commonsense morality of precritical consciousness, which accepts moral and social norms as solid, secure fixtures of the world. For the precritical consciousness, moral facts and moral properties are on a par with physical facts and physical properties. But such a naive consciousness cannot withstand the critical scrutiny of skeptical consciousness. As we have seen, the skeptical consciousness can emerge either with a physicalistic understanding of the universe, which recognizes only the reality of physical objects, or with a recognition of cultural relativity, which questions the validity of all normative standards. In either case, it forces the distinction between nature (physis) and convention (nomos).

Nature and Culture

As I indicated in the last chapter, the physicalistic view of the universe allows no room for norms and values. In that regard, there is no difference between Democritus and Galileo, Newton and Einstein, or Einstein and Heisenberg. For them, the reality of physical objects and their properties and relations is the only reality. Whatever does not belong to the world of physical reality is a matter of convention, which can have no objective existence. Hence physicalism or materialism naturally leads to normative skepticism: moral and social norms are most likely to be subjective creations rather than objective realities.

The relativity of convention is its variability; moral and social conventions vary from culture to culture. This is the fundamental difference of culture from nature. Nature cannot be other than what it is; it is more or less fixed for our whole species. But convention is more or less variable. By nature, a human being is a featherless biped. Under normal circumstances, we are born with two legs and no feathers. But our institution of marriage can be either monogamy or polygamy; it is a matter of convention.

Matters of convention can vary not only from society to society, but even within one and the same society. The variability of convention means the variability of moral and social norms, and the recognition of their variability has forced the distinction between nature and convention. Whatever is variable cannot be objective, and whatever is not objective cannot be truly real. For this reason, the relativity of culture and the variability of convention have also been the ground for normative skepticism.

If human culture is a human invention, how can we justify the moral and social norms that are embedded in any given culture? One easy answer to this question has been through normative positivism. The positive norms and rules of any given society are the social facts that constitute its normative world, and they are as factual or natural as the physical facts that constitute its physical world. The distinction between social and physical facts should not be understood as the demarcation of two entirely different ontological domains. It only divides two regions within one world of facts. Social facts are regarded as a special class of natural facts because they belong to our own species. Though our own species is special to us, it is only one of countless species of plants and animals. And the facts of this species are as physical or natural as the facts of any other species of plants and animals.

Once the question of normative standards is accepted as a question of fact, the problem of their justification becomes much easier to handle. In general, facts do not require justification; at best, they may be explained. Within a positive normative order, however, it is possible to talk of justifying lower norms in terms of higher ones. But the highest or ultimate norm cannot be justified. On the contrary, it is the ultimate source of all normative justification. It is called the basic norm (*Grundnorm*) by Hans Kelsen.[1] It is the bedrock of all positive norms. In justification, it functions like an axiom in an axiomatic system. Axioms do not require justification. On the contrary, they are the ultimate grounds for justifying or validating whatever can be derived within an axiomatic system.

According to normative positivism, every normative judgment presupposes some positive norms of some culture. Since positive norms vary from culture to culture, a normative judgment that is true in one culture may be false in

1. Kelsen, *The Pure Theory of Law* (Berkeley, 1970), 195; trans. Max Wright.

another. Normative positivism leads to cultural or moral relativism. Such relativism gives no ground for criticizing the positive norms of any society. It can allow the critique of prevailing practices and institutions only in reference to the positive norms that are supposed to inform those practices and institutions. That is, it permits only internal criticism. This limitation is the most serious defect of normative positivism and cultural relativism. We cannot be content with an internal critique of Nazi Germany or of our own culture. Our moral sense seems to demand an external critique and an external perspective. How can we take an external perspective of the moral and social norms of any culture? Plato offered his theory of Forms in answer to this question.

Plato offers many arguments for the existence of transcendent Forms, the normative standards that transcend the positive norms of any culture or society. The theory of Forms is not Plato's invention; what is new in his theory is the separation of Forms from the phenomenal world. Democritus had a theory of Forms: the nature of atoms is determined by their Forms. The concept of Forms (*eidos* or *idea*) was not limited to the concept of physical shapes, although it was etymologically connected with the idea of form or shape. The concept of Forms was broad enough to be interchangeable with the concept of properties or universals. In this extended sense, the concept of Forms was also important in the philosophy of Anaxagoras.

For Anaxagoras, Forms are not transcendent, but immanent; they are parts or ingredients of physical objects. In some of his early dialogues, as John Brentlinger points out, Plato accepts a theory of properties similar to Anaxagoras's theory.[2] In the *Lysis* (217d–e), Socrates says that hair becomes, in old age, white through the presence of whiteness. The presence of whiteness in white hair makes the property of whiteness an immanent Form, which is a part or an ingredient of the hair. The idea of immanent Forms is restated in the *Meno* (73a–74d). In the *Phaedo,* however, Plato advocates the separation of Forms and particulars and makes the Forms transcendent.

Aristotle too accepts a theory of immanent Forms; his substantial forms are in the world of substances, such as a tree or a horse. Because the Form of Horse is in particular horses, it can be known only by an empirical investigation of those actual entities. There is no need to postulate supersensible normative entities. The Form of Horse is not only actual but also normative. It is the essence of a horse; it is what a horse should be. This theory of immanent Forms amounts to the unity of facts and norms insofar as the Forms are understood as normative ideals; it also means the unity of physis (nature) and nomos (law and convention). This idea underlies Aristotle's normative conception of nature in

2. John Brentlinger, "Incomplete Predicates and the Two-World Theory of the Phaedo," *Phronesis* 17 (1972):61–79.

opposition to the Democritean nonnormative and purely mechanical conception. It also eventually leads to the Stoic theory of natural law, which resolves
the physis/nomos dispute by advocating their unity.

Aristotle's theory of immanent Forms and the unity of physis and nomos may
indeed be plausible in the world of trees and horses. In most cases, healthy trees
and horses do exemplify common characteristics by the sheer force of nature,
and those common characteristics may be regarded as their immanent Forms.
But this is not the case with human beings because they are creatures of culture. In the domain of culture, we cannot find normative standards by simply
investigating nature because culture transcends nature. Even in the world of
animals, the simple natural method of determining normative standards does
not always work, when those animals are subject to human culture. The behavior of domesticated horses is different from that of wild horses. What is natural
to wild gorillas (for example, nursing a baby gorilla) is not natural to captive
gorillas. Although the theory of Forms is a fixture in ancient Greek philosophy,
Plato alone insists on the separation of Forms from the phenomenal world.

Why does he insist on their separation? What is his motive in separating them?
These have been difficult questions for Plato scholars; they have proposed many
theories to explain Plato's motive.[3] In my view, his ultimate motive was to give
a normative account of the wide variation in human culture. He could not take
the naturalistic view that culture is only an extension of nature. He firmly endorsed the Protagorean-Socratic view that culture transcends nature, as I noted
in chapter 8. In that case, it is impossible to find normative standards for human
culture in the world of nature. Neither could he take the positivistic view that
one culture is as good as any other or that there are no transcultural normative
standards. He must have transcendental normative standards for comparing and
evaluating different cultures. Such transcultural normative standards are the
Platonic Forms. They alone make possible Platonic *anagogia,* which can take
us out of our normative cave and give us a transcendental perspective.

We can subject the positive norms of any given society to a critical evaluation
only in reference to normative standards that transcend all particular societies.
To look at positive norms from the perspective of transcendent norms is to
take a transcendent perspective. If there were no transcendent Forms, it would
be impossible to take a transcendent perspective. Without transcendent norms,
we would be imprisoned in normative positivism and cultural relativism. For
this reason, Kant endorses Plato's theory of transcendent Forms, "especially
in the field of the practical" (A314/B371). In the normative world, he insists,
empiricism is absolutely useless: "For whereas, so far as nature is concerned,

3. John Brentlinger gives a good survey of these theories in his "Incomplete Predicates and
the Two-World Theory of the Phaedo."

experience supplies the rules and is the source of truth, in respect of the moral laws it is, alas, the mother of illusion!" (A318/B375).

Skepticism and Constructivism

During his Critical period, Kant developed a strong skepticism of our intellectual power to apprehend Platonic Forms and decided to formulate a theory of practical reason that does not depend on the existence of those Forms. In making this Critical move, he abandons the old conception of material reason and adopts a new conception of formal reason. Totally disengaged from all material concepts and principles, formal reason is capable only of logical functions. This conception of rationality was not known in the ancient or medieval world; it appeared on the modern scene as a product of modern science and its empiricism.

The theory of formal reason is a skeptical view of practical reason; it denies the power of rational intuition. This denial of cognitive power goes hand in hand with the denial of transcendent norms. If there are no independently existing norms, they must be created. This is the rationale for constructivism. When constructivism replaces intuitionism, the procedure of construction becomes the central issue for normative discourse. Thus constructivism has eclipsed the long tradition of intuitionism in our age of normative skepticism. But constructivism can take various forms, and Kant's categorical imperative has been foremost among them all.

The categorical imperative is meant to be a formal procedure for constructing moral maxims and standards. But his formal constructivism is limited to the first formulation of the categorical imperative; it alone is consistent with his formal conception of pure reason. The other formulations state material principles, although they are claimed to be only alternative expressions of the same formula of universal law. But this austere formula has no way of producing substantive results, and Kant has disguised its vacuity by smuggling in substantive considerations under the guise of formal considerations.

Constructivism need not be confined within the narrow boundaries of formal rationality. It can be extended to the domain of instrumental rationality. Though reason has no power of intuiting independently existing norms and standards, it can serve an instrumental function. The instrumental view of reason has been advocated by Hobbes and Hume. Though the ultimate ends and values are set by desires and passions, reason can be used in the fulfillment of those ends and values. Hume says that reason is the slave of passions.

In the normative world, instrumental reason can propose its own procedure for constructing norms and standards. It can begin with individual desires and preferences that are normatively neutral and then devise a set of norms and precepts best suited for the satisfaction of those desires and preferences. These instrumental norms and precepts should be accepted as moral norms and precepts. Such instrumental constructivism stands on the thesis of equivalence between the precepts of instrumental rationality and the precepts of morality. In chapter 5, I showed that this thesis is far from true.

These two forms of constructivism, formal and instrumental, are claimed to be morally neutral procedures. They are meant to construct moral norms and precepts on the basis of morally neutral formal reason or desires and passions. In this regard, John Rawls's constructivism is different from both of them; it begins with the moral conception of persons as being free and equal. This Kantian ideal is the bedrock for his constructivism; it is the ultimate source for the constitutive constraints to be placed on the original position. On what ground can he say that this Kantian bedrock is the right or the best foundation for constructing the principles of justice? Utilitarians have claimed that the principle of utility is a better foundation for constructing a normative system. The Kantian and the utilitarian bedrocks give different moral criteria and perspectives, and there is no morally neutral perspective to compare them and adjudicate their competing claims, as I showed in chapter 2. This is the problem of justification for Rawls's original position.

Rawls can resolve his problem of justification only by showing that his Kantian perspective is morally superior to any other moral perspective. He cannot do this without taking a transcendental perspective. But he has tried to justify the original position on the ground that the Kantian conception of moral persons as being free and equal is a social ideal embedded in our political culture. Insofar as this social fact is the basis for his justification, his theory of justice is a special form of normative positivism. As a social fact, the Kantian ideal functions like Kelson's basic norm (*Grundnorm*). But this positivistic approach is equally compatible with liberalism and Nazism. Even Nazi institutions can be justified by the ideals embedded in Nazi culture. Positivistic justification is always internal; it can condemn only internal inconsistencies of normative ideals. It can never make pronouncements on the objective merit or demerit of those ideals because it can offer no external or transcendental perspective.

Rawls is not oblivious to the transcendental perspective. But he feels uneasy about its metaphysical implication: it presupposes the acceptance of transcendent norms, Platonic Forms. For the same reason, as we have seen, Kant too wavered in his allegiance to Platonism. In its skyscraper version, Platonism has indeed been an object of distrust and derision. But its bedrock version is an altogether different story. It appears to be not only much more plausible and sensible, but unavoidable and ineliminable, if we want to avoid positivism and relativism. As I noted in chapter 8, Plato himself came to favor this view of the transcendental normative standards in his later dialogues. Kant also accepts the bedrock version of Platonism in his description of an ideal constitution as "a necessary Idea": that which allows "the greatest possible human freedom in accordance with laws by which the freedom of each is made to be consistent with that of all others" (A316/B373). In the *Metaphysics of Morals,* he restates this skeletal or minimal idea of the state as the principle of justice, which he then employs as the ultimate premise for constructing all private and public laws.

The bedrock view of Platonic Forms presents the problem of indeterminacy. The idea of liberty or equality is indeterminate; it can be given variant determinate contents under different circumstances. In a farming country that can provide enough land to all farmers, equality may mean an equal division of available land. In a hunting community, which requires the close cooperation of hunters, an equal division of hunting grounds for individual hunting is unlikely to be the best way of realizing the principle of equality. It can be better realized in an equal distribution of mutual benefits and burdens in the cooperative enterprise of hunting. Platonic Idealism requires not only fidelity to transcendent norms, but also sensitivity to concrete situations in the articulation of those norms. Transcendent norms and the concrete situations in which they are to be realized are the two poles of Platonic normative discourse.

The two poles of Platonic normative discourse require two motions: the ascent to transcendent norms and the descent to concrete situations. If we begin with transcendent norms, we move from the top down to concrete situations; if we begin with concrete situations, we move from the bottom up to transcendent norms. It has often been said that Kant's method moves from the top down, while Hegel's moves from the bottom up. It is further assumed that the two methods are in competition against each other and that we have to choose one over the other. But that is a mistaken assumption. The two methods are like two hands, both of which are needed for clapping; they require each other in Platonic normative discourse.

Even John Rawls's theory of justice can be restated in the Platonic language of ascent and descent. We ascend to the highest ideals of liberty and equality and construct the original position for translating those highly indeterminate ideals into concrete principles. The original position is a procedure or device for descending to a concrete level. No doubt the descent is not going to stop at the two principles of justice but will continue even to more concrete levels as the veil of ignorance is gradually lifted, step by step. We can reverse the process. We can begin with particular considered judgments about concrete issues and uncover rules and precepts underlying those judgments. We can extend this ascent by examining those rules and precepts and then explicating the principles that inform them. The two movements of ascent and descent need not be separate; they can be simultaneous.

Indeterminacy and Relativity

The acceptance of Platonic Forms, however, does not resolve the problem of normative indeterminacy, which has preoccupied John Rawls and many other liberals. Plato thought that the world of Forms is clear and determinate, whereas the world of phenomena is vague and indeterminate. There are two different contexts for understanding the determinacy and indeterminacy of Platonic Forms. Though they are determinate in the transcendent realm, they can still be indeterminate in the phenomenal world. For example, the concept of a triangle may be determinate insofar as it can be given in a clear definition. But its realization in the phenomenal world can nevertheless be indeterminate; it can take many different concrete shapes. Likewise, the concept of equality is determinate in its transcendent realm, but its realization is indeterminate.

The indeterminacy of realization is especially true of the bedrock view of Platonic Forms. According to this view, transcendent norms are only general concepts that serve as an outline or a limit of our ideals, and their realizations are invariably indeterminate. The indeterminacy of transcendent norms is at the same time their relativity. If the same transcendent norms can be realized in different ways, normative standards appear to be infected by cultural relativism. If moral and political norms vary from culture to culture, they are unlikely to have independent existence. Hence the relativity of norms is a reasonable ground for normative skepticism. But there are many forms and degrees of relativity, and they have different implications for skepticism.

We may distinguish between total and partial relativity. When two systems of norms are so different that there is no common ground for a meaningful comparison, they are totally relative. If two normative systems have some common ground, they can be compared in reference to a common standard even though they are not identical in every respect. This is a case of partial relativity, which is compatible with the acceptance of transcendent norms. Partial relativity requires the acceptance of a common standard for the comparison of different normative systems, and the required common standard can be linked to transcendent norms.

Total relativity allows no common ground between different normative systems. They are so different that there is no common standard for comparing them. I am not even sure that such a relation of total difference ever obtains between different cultures or societies. Surely, the difference between liberals and conservatives is not that sort of relation. Even the difference between communists and capitalists does not approach such a level of total relativity. In spite of their grave differences, they share enough important grounds for a meaningful debate.

The distinction between partial and total relativity is equivalent to the distinction between total and partial indeterminacy. If the ideal of justice is totally indeterminate, then it is compatible with any social system. Though the ideal of justice cannot always give a determinate answer to every question of justice, it is only partially indeterminate if it is still useful for branding certain social systems as unjust. Partial indeterminacy is constrained; its indeterminacy is permitted under a set of constraints. Total indeterminacy is unconstrained; it obtains without constraints.

As John Rawls says, there is no way to eliminate the indeterminacy of our intuitions, whether our intuitions are transcendent or immanent. We may not find even effective ways of reducing their indeterminacy. At most, we can hope to find suitable constraints on our intuitions. Normative discourse is bound to be a discourse of constrained indeterminacy. We can never find conclusive solutions to difficult normative issues. And we should have no reason to assume that there is a right answer to every hard question. But we should not resign ourselves to having to live in the land of total indeterminacy.

Let us imagine that we do have to live in the land of total indeterminacy, as some deconstructionists have claimed. Then our problem is how to cope with total relativity and total skepticism. We can no longer say that liberal democracies are better than Nazi Germany or Stalin's Russia. Total relativity does not give us a vantage point for comparing them, and it does not offer a common standard for comparison. All our normative discourse shall come to a dead end, and we can no longer retain the power of making even elementary moral judgments. Bertrand Russell describes such an experience of normative skepticism: "When I am compelled, as happens frequently in the modern world, to contemplate acts of cruelty which make me shudder with horror, I find myself constantly impelled towards an ethical outlook which I cannot justify intellectually. I find myself thinking, 'These men are wicked and what they do is bad in some absolute sense for which my theory has not provided.' "[4]

Russell shudders with horror because his moral intuitions are still alive, but his ethical theory denies him the right to say even the obvious: concentration camps are wicked. This is the height of normative skepticism, and it blatantly goes against our basic intuition. There is a glaring gap between our intuition and our theory. Richard Rorty seems to refer to this normative gap by his well-known label "liberal irony."[5] The irony of skeptical liberals lies in the fact that they cannot say even that their ideals are right because they also have to say that their ideals are only products of historical contingency. Rorty's theory of normative ideals is a historicist version of normative positivism. Every system of positive norms is a chance product of historical development. There is no vantage point for comparing different normative systems. Liberals have no more

4. Russell, *Human Society in Ethics and Politics* (London, 1954), 128.
5. Richard Rorty, *Contingency, Irony, and Solidarity* (Cambridge, 1989).

right to pronounce their normative judgments on Nazi Germany than do Nazis have the right to subject liberal democracy to their critique.

Liberalism and Skepticism

Many liberals have taken it for granted that one cannot be a true liberal without a heavy dose of skepticism. In our age, skepticism has been mistakenly regarded as an essential ingredient of liberalism. What can a skeptical liberal do without acknowledging transcendent norms? She fully affirms her liberal ideals as the basic norms of her society but feels unsure of their validity in other societies. When she witnesses those ideals being trampled in other cultures, she has no right to say that there is anything wrong with them. At best, she can say that they are wrong by her liberal criteria, but she has to add that she has no right to apply her criteria to other cultures.

It has often been said that skepticism is the foundation of liberalism and its spirit of tolerance. Because no one has objective knowledge of normative truths, we ought to be tolerant of each other. But total skepticism is no special friend of liberalism. It can equally condone Nazism and Stalinism, slavery and robbery. If I am totally uncertain that slavery is wrong, I have no reason to condemn it. Neither has skepticism any special connection with toleration. Total skepticism can equally endorse persecution and repression. Perhaps the liberals need to distinguish between total and partial skepticism or between constrained and unconstrained skepticism. Partial skepticism does not suffer from Cartesian doubt. Instead of doubting everything, partial skepticism recognizes the epistemic basis for any meaningful doubt. In the normative world, the epistemic basis can be secured only in the acceptance of some basic norms or values that transcend different cultures.

Some skeptical liberals, Richard Rorty among them, have advocated radical or total skepticism. Rorty has said that the ideals of liberal democracy are only products of historical contingency. He sees no reason to assume that they have any objective validity or truth. In fact, there is no right or final language for asserting normative truths, including the rightness of liberal tradition.[6] But he still wants to uphold liberal values. In his view, the reality of pain is at the center of liberal politics, and the elimination of cruelty is its ultimate goal. He proposes solidarity as the best way to achieve this end and equates liberal politics with the politics of solidarity.

But solidarity is not a monopoly of the liberals. In fact, it is one of the universal social goods that can be claimed by any political group. Democrats and Republicans each have their own solidarity. Nazis had their solidarity against

6. Ibid.

the solidarity of the Jews; Christians claim their solidarity against that of the heathens. We may need some criteria for discriminating good from bad solidarity. Rorty offers one: a greater human solidarity is better than a smaller one.[7] By this criterion, German solidarity was better than Jewish solidarity because it commanded a greater number of people.

Rorty may have meant to say that a greater solidarity is better than a smaller one because the former can be more effective in preventing and eliminating the evil of pain than the latter. In that case, he does not care about solidarity for its own sake; he recognizes only its instrumental value in eliminating pain. This brings us back to his professedly liberal thesis that pain is the ultimate evil and that the elimination of cruelty is the ultimate aim of liberal politics. But we are still left with some questions, and they transcend liberal societies. Is pain the ultimate evil only in liberal societies? Or is it the ultimate evil in other societies, too? Is the elimination of cruelty the ultimate political end only for liberal democracies or for other political orders, too? Are there not even more important political goals than the elimination of pain?

By appealing to the existence of pain and its elimination, Rorty may be trying to locate the minimal political ideal that transcends all cultures. He may be proposing a thin theory of evil, which can be pitched against John Rawls's thin theory of the good. A thin theory of evil may sound even better and more plausible to normative skeptics than a thin theory of good. The former requires a much thinner normative commitment than the latter. For this reason, some normative theorists have favored negative over positive utilitarianism in the belief that it is much easier to agree upon the negative principle of minimizing pains than the positive principle of maximizing pleasures.

A thin normative theory may indeed be easy to justify, but it delivers precious little. Not all pains are alike; not all of them are evil. Some pains are even worth having. A thin theory of pain offers no criteria for discriminating worthy from unworthy pain. Neither does it offer criteria for discriminating the right ways of eliminating pain from the wrong ways. The single criterion of pain can assign no special value even to pleasure. Pleasure can be counted only as one of the countless items that do not belong to the domain of pain. Recognizing the unique value of pleasure requires an altogether different criterion from the criterion of pain.

If our only end is to minimize pain, we can completely ignore all questions of pleasure, leaving them out of our hedonistic calculus. And the best way to realize the principle of minimizing negative utility is to eliminate all living things because every living creature is susceptible to pain. The total destruction of life is the most perfect fulfillment of negative utilitarianism. It is much more effective than Rorty's idea of solidarity. The principle of solidarity is as liable

7. Ibid., 192.

to produce pain as it is to eliminate it. Hence if the elimination of pain is our only ultimate value, the principle of solidarity is not any easier to justify than the principle of mutual destruction. The negative principle of minimizing pain has these embarrassing implications because it is so thin or porous as to permit almost anything. This is a common problem with all thin normative theories. Though they appear to gain much in their initial simplicity, they turn out to be too indeterminate and too indiscriminate in spinning out their networks of normative rules and standards.

In the end, thin normative theories are not much easier to justify than thick ones. Thin or thick, all normative theories have to be justified on two phases: their initial acceptance and their final implications. And there are two perspectives for the normative deliberation in these two phases. We can take an external perspective by appealing to transcendental normative standards or an internal perspective by relying on the positive values of our culture. When Rorty proposes a thin theory of evil as the common basis for his ethics of universal solidarity, he does not merely want to impose the provincial perspective of his own political culture on the whole world. He is aspiring to a transcendental perspective. Even his thin normative theory cannot be formulated without appealing to some transcendental normative standards, if it is meant to have any transcendental significance.

It is impossible to avoid positivism, relativism, and provincialism in the normative world without taking a transcendental perspective. And it is equally impossible to take such a perspective without ascending to transcendental normative standards. This normative ascent is Platonic *anagogia,* or transcendence; this is what it means to climb out of the cave of a provincial culture and survey the whole world from Platonic Heaven. Without such a flight of transcendence, we would not even be able to recognize the provinciality and relativity of our uncritical perspectives. Moreover, we would have no reason to be dissatisfied with our provincial or positivistic perspectives. These two—the recognition of normative relativity and the dissatisfaction with a provincial perspective—are the essential features of normative skepticism. But neither of them is possible without some awareness of transcendental normative standards. On the surface, normative skepticism appears to be an outright objection of Platonism, but it gives perhaps the most convincing testimony possible to our awareness of Platonic Forms. This is a transcendental proof for the existence of transcendental normative standards: the existence of Platonic Forms is a necessary condition for the possibility of normative skepticism.

Index